RUNNING DIALOGUE

HOW TO TRAIN...

FOR 5 k TO THE MARATHON

FROM BEGINNER TO EXPERT

By DAVID HOLT

Registered Nurse

NOTICE
The information in this book is not intended to be a substitute for professional fitness or medical advice. As with all exercise programs, seek medical approval before you begin.

Library of Congress Catalog Card Number 97-093823
Holt, David
  Running Dialogue: how to train 5K to the marathon...beginner to expert, by David Holt.
  Includes index, cartoons and photos.
  1. Running-Training 2. Running-Humor 3. Self-help running
  796.42-dc20
ISBN 0-9658897-4-2

To Gerry North, English National cross-country champion, who taught me all I ever needed to know about running. Watching his perfect form when he was fifty and sixty years old was a joy. Hearing his advice was a privilege.

Book editor and consultant about English versus American use Andora Hodgin. Remaining wackiness or errors are the authors.
Cartoons Hilde Keldermans.
Photos...no one person should take the blame.
The photographed...you have my thanks.

Printed on recycled paper

My thanks to the runners of Portsmouth AC and our rivals and friends who made the early 80s so much fun. Gerry, Gus, Martin and Keith. To the Steves and David's.
To the Yeovil Olympiads for the late 80s; Alan, John and the Marks. To Yanos and crowd for 1989--ten times one mile--you wicked people.
Tim, Jim, Brad, Steve, Dorothy and Maria for Ventura.
The constantly changing members of my current running group at the track and on long runs.
To those who read and contributed to the book. Greg Horner, Robert Hollister, Kevin Young, Bill Rupp and the others who have put up with my ear bending about the book for the past 12 months. To Dr. Pruit DPM and Doug Simms, Physical Therapist for their comments on the injury sections. To Sharon K. Smith M.S., R.D. for her comments on nutrition.
To Dr. Cobble of Los Angeles, Professor George Brooks of Berkley and Dr. Benjamin Levine of the University of Texas, for interviews and input.

Special thanks to John Babington, Roy Benson, Scott Douglas, David Costell, Ph.D. Jack Daniels Ph.D,. Frank Horwill, John Pagliano, DPM, Bruce Tulloh, Gary Tuttle, and Harry Wilson.

CONTENTS page

INTRODUCTION

A SCHEDULE FOR THE MILLIONS

RACING ON 15 MILES A WEEK

This section is for the 5 million people who run currently 250-999 miles per year. Beginners should start with Chapter One. Refer to the rest of the book as needed to help you prepare for those two or three races a year, and to get even more fun from your running.

I've assumed a four or five mile run is done during the week-end--this schedule has it on Saturday--the same day most races occur. Which leaves you three to four miles for each midweek run. It doesn't matter which days you run, but Monday lunch time, Tuesday evening, and Thursday pre-work will allow you to spread the load while experiencing a variety of run locations. You can exercise close to work, on the way home from work and close to home--avoiding the "same old, same old" routes which many people do.

You've already laid the foundations to your running with perhaps years of 10 to 20 miles per week. Our simple aim is to do a mile of quality per mid-week run. You will replace one mile of steady running with a mile of faster running every four months. You will end the year doing three miles fast each week and 12 at your regular pace.

As a fifteen mile a week runner, you've attained most of part one's health goals. While you may complete the health benefits by running for 40 minutes each day, it is not the main concern of this schedule.

The thrust of this section is to get you closer to your racing potential.

Your first goal is to add a Part Two session. On a set Monday, four months before a 5 k race, and after an easy mile warmup, stride eight times 100 meters with easy running of 100 meters rest between each effort. That's it...it's that simple--but do not sprint. The exact distance does not matter. Do eight times 20-25 seconds if you prefer; or lamppost to lamppost alternating fast with slow. Note the form guide in chapter four. These strides will improve your running economy.

On the second Monday, do four times 200 meters; or about 45 seconds; or two-three lampposts; run the same distance recovery.

The third Monday, do three times 300 meters, or 75 seconds--whichever is shorter.

On the forth week, do a 300, a 200 and three at 100.

The second month do: 10 x 100; 5 x 200; 4 x 300; A 300, 2 x 200 & 3 x 100.

Third month: 12 x 100; 6 x 200; 4 x 300; A 300, 2 x 200 & 4 x 100.

Month four do 16 x 100; 8 x 200; 5 x 300; and 2 x 300, 3 x 200, 4 x 100.

You now have your first mile of speedwork. Do that 5 k race. Beware of starting out too fast. Your relearned speed will need to be kept in check for the first mile; think about your style.

For the next 9 months, as you add other sessions, retain the Monday session. Rotate the sessions from month four--the order is not important.

After the first race, it will be time to add a second mile of quality. We'll recruit this from Part Three.

On a Thursday, do a half mile fast effort (or four minutes--whichever is longest). This should be at the pace at which you would race a 5 k.

The second week, do 2 x two-and-a-half minutes, or 400 meters.

The third week, do two times 600 meters.

The forth, try a 1200 meter or three quarter mile effort...but not more than 8 minutes at speed.

These must not be time-trials.

Take the same amount of time for rest between efforts as the efforts themselves.

INTRODUCTION for the SIX MILLION

Month six, you can increase the pace by 10 seconds per mile, or 2-3 seconds for each 400 meter section. This is two mile pace, the pace at which your VO2 maximum is improved. Do:
A half mile with three minutes rest, followed by a quarter mile.
3 x 400 meters or 2½ minutes
2 x 600 meters
1200 meters or go up to 10 minutes.
The seventh and subsequent months progress to:
2 x 800; 4 x 400; 3 x 600; Mile or 12 minutes at good pace.

Seven months in, and you already have two miles at fast pace. It will take several months for your body to adapt to these changes...that is, before it shows up in those occasional race times.

Now is the time to reduce recoveries to 100 after a 200 effort, and 90 seconds after a 400. Continue to enjoy the sensations of fast running as we move on to making 20 percent of your mileage quality, by adding a Part Four session.

Ignoring the mileage aspect of Part Four, let's look at resistance training.

Soft dirt, mud, grassy areas, sand or shingles and snow offer the opportunity to make the legs work harder. Seek these surfaces out and do fartlek as described in Part Two...or do timed efforts of 30-120 seconds.

Just as you did with the Monday and Thursday session, start this Tuesday session with half a mile, or up to five minutes at speed. Do this session every other week, adding a minute, or about 200 meters, until you reach one mile--it will take eight weeks.

On the non-fartlek weeks do hill repeats.

Start with two minutes worth, and build a minute at a time on the alternate weeks that you will be doing them--after 16 weeks you will reach eight minutes of hill reps. Use a mixture of short and long efforts; 45 to 90 seconds; use several hills by rotation.

Once you're used to the resistance training, try a three week rotation. Every third week, skip the resistance session--do quality on two days only. But add part of the resistance mile to your other sessions. Do 5 or 6 times 400, or 3 x 800. Or try one and a half miles at good pace instead of the mile. The second session can be 12 times 200 or four each at 300, 200 and 100. Monday and Thursday would be ideal for the speedwork; Tuesday would be a very easy run.

After a few more months, (12-15 months into speed running), you might find you want to do the resistance session AND one and a half miles of speedwork on the other two days. This would give you four miles of hard running those weeks.

Take care that the fast running does not comprise more than 20 percent of your miles. Adding a fifth run of four miles or increasing the length of the weekend run from five to eight miles would keep the proportion about right! The longer run would do wonders for your endurance too.

You can take an entire week off from quality training every 6 to 8 weeks when the mood strikes you. Try not to take more than two consecutive weeks off though.

Rather than taking a prolonged break, maintain one speed session...alternate resistance, short and long reps.

Keep the sessions easy to manage. You don't need to visit a track. Watch beepers, counting lampposts, striding between stop signs, or counting the number of times your left foot touches the ground--all have their uses. Indoors, you can simply raise the treadmill by two percent for 60-90 seconds a few times to get a great session. No downhills to worry about either.

There's no need to do more than the three or four miles mid-week to get in this quality stuff. Because you only do a mile of speed each time, it should not make you feel stuffed either.

If you feel completely pooped after an easy mile and a shower, you probably ran the session too fast. A pleasant, satisfying tired feeling is what you're after.

Keep the weekend five miler real easy...always. While it's no more difficult mentally to do a few changes of pace--running moderately hard for 3 or 4 lampposts and easy for two on those midweek runs--you need the weekend longer run at a sedate pace to look forward to.

Be warned though. Your 15 miles a week may soon approach 20, as it is natural for you to desire an increase in that weekend run. If you are tempted, don't add more than five minutes, or one mile at a time. Don't add distance on consecutive runs.

Don't be afraid of leaving those fine five million or so runners in the United States who enjoy 250-999 miles a year...to join the no more elite half a million who do 1,000 to 1,500 miles.

Finally, as homage to part six, in the week leading up to a race, cut back to half a mile at speed on Monday and Wednesday. Cut a mile off all your runs, and take a day off.

*   *   *

No time to run?

Early morning, lunch time or pre-dinner runs with quality, demand no more time than the easy four miles you've been used to. If you can get out the door to do a four miler...you can enjoy a mile of quality too.

High mileage AND low mileage runners need organization. The above schedule is a major chore if the person has to pick up progeny from daycare within 10 minutes of regular work finish time. Yet this may only need adjusting one day a week.

Monday can be the most fun. Whereas colleagues may have a miserable Monday back at work, the runner gleams because he or she spends the morning looking forward to the lunch hour run.

Thirty minutes of the hour are spent running--fifteen in the park which is half a mile from work. On return to the building, the small towel and favorite brand of periwash from the supermarket make rapid work of the perspiration. Though it'll be another 12 hours before bacteria would give a hint of body odor, a little antiperspirant is applied.

The runner eats a sandwich in the remaining 15 minutes of the break, and is the sweetest smelling person in the afternoon conference. The only aura coming from this person is the satisfied post-run aura.

Tuesday evening...leave work early, or arrange to pick up the children later. Do the run in an area on the way home, even if it requires a short detour.

Thursday...it's pre-work. This should help you through that often most difficult day of the week. If the early rising knocks you out, find a quiet spot for a third of your lunch break, and take a healthy nap.

Maybe all three runs done at the same time of day suit you best. Be adaptable. Getting dropped off five miles from the Sunday brunch spot can give the other spouse quality time with his or her parents. Dare to be different. Each problem is an opportunity to adapt.

Don't live vicariously. If explained right, a child will understand why you are running for half of the baseball game--rather than putting on weight sitting in the bleachers. Encourage their exercise with self exercise.

Now spoil yourself, read the rest of the book.

Heart Disease

Men who run greater than 40 miles per week have less coronary heart disease than those who do less than 10 per week. Most of the benefit is from the increased stimulation to the heart, but part of the gain is from:

The fact that the person found the time to run more;

reducing overall stress levels;

therefore more relaxed than the 10 mile a week runner.

Because he exercises more, he's less likely to be overweight.

Quick Fix

Think you'll be able to lose five pounds in five days on the new three shakes a day diet--you can--provided you burn 4,250 calories every day.

Most people who need to lose weight burn about 2,000 per day; that is part of the reason they are overweight--the second reason is over-consumption of food.

To lose a pound of fat you need to burn 3,500 calories. Add in the 750 or so from those three shakes, and you see where the 4,250 came from. Yet the advertisers keep a straight face when they make their claim. Actual weight lose is mostly from the shunting of fluid which occurs when you suddenly deny yourself food. You will use up some of your glycogen stores, which contains lots of water.

The day you re-commence normal eating, the stores, and the water, is replaced. Follow the advice in Chapter 22--make subtle changes in your eating habits.

PART ONE--THE FOUNDATIONS

During the first few weeks' training, you will progress to run for 40 minutes, without stopping, several times a week. Those who can do so already, stride through to Part Two.

"Exercise is based on the overload principle. You exercise to a modest level of fatigue--after a recovery phase, you exercise again, gradually increasing the amount of exercise or resistance. With appropriate rest, the body adapts."

CHAPTER ONE

GETTING STARTED

Friday at last. Happy hour--which for me, means a stroll in the hills. Huffing a bit, about halfway round my favorite loop I saw the light. It--or I should say, he--was hovering by the side of a sycamore.

"It wasn't that tough a week," I whispered to myself.

He came alongside me, wavering somewhat as he kept pace.

"I do exist," he said, reading my thoughts. "You haven't lost your...how do you say...marbles."

"Mind," I said. "I haven't lost my mind."

"That's right. You're not talking to yourself--you're talking to an alien."

I looked him square in the face--it would be a few visits before I figured out where the human equivalents for sight and the like were--and said. "I talk to aliens and people who are alienated all day...that's one of the joys of a so-called civilized society. This is my downtime. I'm not amenable to an alien dialogue."

"I'm an individual...not a dialogue."

"So am I. Now leave this individual alone."

"What are you looking at?" I said on his second visit.

"I'm not sure, I think its label must have fallen off."

"Charmed I'm sure," I thought, as he asked.

"What are you?"

"Just a guy. Homo Sapien...top of the food chain."

"Strange," he said, "I talked to a group of coyotes a few days ago--seemed to think they were the top of this planet's hierarchy. No work; leisurely life; run whenever they like. In fact, you look like a runner."

"Despite this desk job flab," I said lifting my shirt.

"That will fall away as you take up more regular exercise."

He left me alone...eventually. But he saw me every Friday afterwards. And I'm pleased he did.

You may have read about him in our first book...*An Alien Visitation.* If you have, I apologize for any repetition of his activities in this second book. I felt the need to include some of the details from *Visitation* to negate the need for you to search out a copy of it...said copies becoming more and more difficult to locate, due, no doubt, to their unusual resale value. This book then, is self-contained.

The biggest problem my new running friends had when check reading the material was, "Why did you take advice from a legless person. How could he possibly know anything about running?"

Crustaceans have less consciousness about running than the Alien now has the ability to run. But the Alien knows more about running theory than any animal on this planet has the ability to run. Regretfully, the story of how he came upon most of this knowledge would make this volume too cumbersome.

With the Alien's agreement, as this training guide is being published, I am preparing a detailed book of his species history and physical development. Our work, the completion of the trilogy, will take many years. Please be patient with us. In the meantime, use and enjoy his simple running maxims.

"What's wrong with just walking?" I said on his sixth visit.

"Absolutely nothing. It's very commendable, worthwhile for relaxation and maintaining health. You shouldn't consider it 'just walking,' By walking, you're doing more than most of your brethren already.

"It's just that you have a body type, a presence, that screams out *runner.* I'd like to see you try."

"Yes. You said that I looked like a runner."

"You do."

We'd already gone over the basics of what will be in the third volume. Enough for me to believe his ideas.

"How should I start?"

"You have."

"What?"

"Started."

"Hey," I said. "Did horses push the carts on your planet?"

"What I mean is...walking has prepared you for running. Your muscles--including the heart--are in good shape. All you need do is run easily for a minute...then walk a minute...and alternate running and walking for the middle part of your loop.

"As you get used to running, do two minutes run, one walk. With practice you'll find the pace at which you can run easily. Increase the running part each week until the only walking sections are where you have a good view to enjoy."

Over the next few weeks we discussed how others could start a running program. Here is what he said.

"If you have any doubts about your health, I suggest you see a doctor type person. Although exercise is good for you, a twenty minute run is not the way to begin a fitness program...if it has been preceded by years of smoking, drinking, or eating to excess.

"Exercising, rather than diet alone is the best way to lose excess weight. Those who exercise, will maintain muscle mass better than those who lose weight with diet only. Plus it gets you started on your way to fitness. But please don't use exercise simply to lose weight. Exercise for fun--the bonus is that it makes weight control easier, and contributes to your health.

"A few weeks of walking, swimming and riding a bicycle, combined with weight loss if necessary and a cessation of smoking, should prepare the body for its first run.

Set short-term goals. For example:

Lose 10 pounds while walking a mile three times a week.

Reward yourself by adding a swim or two.

Lose another five pounds and the reward can be a cheap bicycle...

Which allows you to add two rides a week to lose the next few pounds:

When your reward is a bit more walking.

"Don't be concerned with how you look when exercising--no one else is. You might want to avoid flamboyant movements which bring attention to yourself, but there are millions out there who use exaggerated body actions to good effect--power walkers have minimal injury risk.

"Once you can walk 40 plus minutes without feeling tired, you can try running. If you get short of breath, dizzy, or have chest pains while walking, seek a medical opinion before proceeding.

"The first run should be at a gentle pace. Your breathing rate will go up a bit, but you must not be gasping for air.

"Choose an area devoid of hills and work out a route which takes half an hour to walk. Start running very slowly, if your breathing becomes labored...stop. Walk until it is back to normal, then resume running at slower pace. It may take many attempts before you find a pace your heart and lungs can handle.

"At this stage, all running should be at a pace which enables you to talk while running. If you cannot talk with reasonable ease, you are running too fast. The aim is to get around in comfort to give you the hunger for more. And more you can have--but not until you've recovered from the first run.

Want the newest machine to help you lose weight? Forget it. That's what most people do with the machines hiding under their beds, used once or twice before the people vegetate once more.

Think you'll get fit in 20 minutes a day, three times a week, or 15 minutes, or the way those ads are going, on five minutes a week? Dismiss that idea, too. Oh sure, you'll get stronger than on no exercise, but you will be eons away from true fitness.

Want a machine to lose weight from a specific part of your body...to sculpt yourself? Keep dreaming. Exercise will make you lose weight from the entire body, not from a spot which you'd like to designate. Toning the muscles underneath the fat can make you feel as if you're losing fat from a special area--indeed, you'll lose a bit from inside the muscle, but unless the muscle was riddled with fat, and until your entire fat shell decreases, you won't see a benefit. Regular, whole body exercise, burning calories, is what you need.

"In addition to avoiding heart attacks and loss of interest due to starting out with too fast a run, we must avoid over-training. Runners often suffer from overtraining--usually due to too much mileage or training too fast. If you ran too fast in your first run; if you have aching muscles for days afterwards; you're having your first experience of over-training.

"Pace yourself to enjoy the sensation of running without feeling exhausted during or after the run.

"To decrease the general aches from properly exercised muscles, get into the habit of stretching before and after running. This will maintain your flexibility--allowing a full range of movement--and thus reduce the risk of injury.

"Muscles are 10 percent shorter than normal when you wake up; 10 percent longer after warming up. Muscles work better when they are long--they exert the same force with less effort, so flexibility will aid your running."

He outlined the following exercises. We suggest you use them before or after running. One stretch for each group of muscles is sufficient--you can choose others from Chapter 18.

Calf Muscle
--stand 3-4 feet from a wall, put your outstretched hands on the wall, shoulder width apart. Keep the knee straight and the heels flat on the ground. Lean in towards the wall slowly, keeping the body and knee straight: Stop when you think the calf is at its limit...when it and the Achilles tendons feel stretched.

Next--as above but 2-3 feet away. Bend the knees until you feel the stretch--again, keep heels on the ground.

Quadriceps--front of the thigh--stand upright, hold one foot and pull it up towards your bottom while keeping the knee pointed downwards.

Hamstrings--back of the thigh--sit on a soft surface, keep the knees straight and bend forward at the waist. Move your head down towards the knees or beyond.

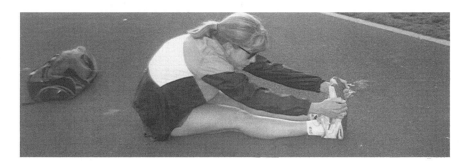

Hip muscles--stand upright, or lie on a comfortable surface. Grasp one leg at the shin; pull the knee up towards the chest.

I-T band--as above, but bring the left knee across the chest towards your right armpit; then re-stretch it towards the right side of pelvis. Do a similar technique for the other leg.

Trunk--stand with the feet apart, keep the hips facing front. Bend over to one side as far as possible...hold, then repeat to the other side.

--Rotate the top of the trunk to look behind. Keep the hips facing forward...hold, swing slowly around to the front...then to the other side.

Lower Back--feet together or apart, knees bent or straight...bend over and ease your hands towards your feet. Just hang loose; let the tension go; don't force it.

Be pedestrian with these exercises--do them slowly--no bouncing. When the limit of a muscle is reached...hold the position for 10 to 20 seconds before relaxing. Rapid movement induces a mechanism to resist stretching: this must be avoided. Repeat each stretch two or three times.

Stretching reflex.

Near the junction of tendon and muscle lie muscle spindles and Golgi tendon organs (also called proprioceptors) which initiate the tendon-muscle reflex to prevent a muscle from lengthening too far. If the muscle tension is too high, the muscle will not be allowed beyond a certain length. Hold a stretch for 20 or so seconds, and this deep myastatic reflex eases...your muscle is allowed to go a percent or two longer...which is why you should hold a stretch, then seek a little extra pain free elongation after 20-30 seconds.

After his basic stretching insights and warnings to start out sensibly, the alien said this.

"Subsequent runs should follow every other day until you can run easily, the distance you used to walk in 40 minutes. Use several routes to avoid the boredom of running in the same area. When you feel ready to increase your run, add a loop to your present course...or use an out and back system. Run for half your intended running time away from the start point, and aim to run back in the same time.

"Increase the time of the run by a few minutes at a time, but get used to it before moving on. When you can manage thirty minutes at a time we'll consider the number of runs each week. This means training on consecutive days...once and then twice a week. Your target is to run five times a week, but not for the same length of time. Shorter runs become the rest days between the long runs.

"As you get fitter you will begin to notice things in your area you hadn't looked at before--from the substandard road, to hidden paths and plants. Be kind to your strolling pedestrians; you will soon be moving three times faster than they do. Don't run on streets that require weaving in and out of people. Choose quiet streets, or the times of day when they are least used. Busy streets can upset your rhythm.

Variety

Run in areas that offer different terrain. In addition to several road and path circuits, find some grass. Grass should be short so you can see the holes. Use the middle of a fairway near dusk in the beginning, move to the semi-rough for a harder session later. The edge of a recreation ground or park will be fine provided it's over half a mile around the outside. Parks and woods are better for steady runs--you won't have to do several laps to complete the time of the run. Avoid ankle strains from holes by using wide dirt trails.

Use flat surfaces; not the sloped beach, banked indoor track, or cambered road. Slopes make your feet roll too much. But avoid concrete, too, and the jarring from going up and down sidewalks.

"Soon, to paraphrase your nursing friend, you will find running is more relaxing than a laxative...or did he say, sedative. And you'll be ahead of the 97 percent of the U.S. population who can't run three miles."

People won't see you. Make eye contact.

CHAPTER TWO

ANIMALS, WEATHER and HEARTRATEs

One day, as I was running through the park with the alien floating by my side, a medium sized dog showed far too much interest in me. Seeing the inept way in which I dealt with this and previous canines, he set himself up between the offending animal and myself. The dog immediately laid down, placed its head on its paws, and watched as I continued to run. The alien said the following:

"Although running on grass and paths is better for your legs, as you've found out, it brings you into frequent contact with man's best friend. When running on roads and sidewalks, you seldom come across dogs without their pets. Alas, when dogs enter a park, woods, or a recreation ground, they usually let their pets off the leash, to sit down for a rest, or amble around...perhaps throwing sticks or balls to assist the dog in its exercise session.

"Part of this session may involve chasing you. Few dogs will have a go at the runner, though at times it will seem as if each one you meet would like to take a bite out of your lean, muscular legs. Most dogs will either ignore you or look up from their ball chasing activities to wish you an enjoyable run. A few, however, will take chase, or run at full speed to meet a runner.

"What is the dog thinking, do you suppose?"

"I hadn't thought of dogs as being deep thinkers."

"I didn't mean to imply they're as cognizant as you; but they do possess cunning. Anyway...he's having the time of his life--then someone comes charging towards him. It's not surprising if some are unpleased by this intrusion.

"To decrease the dogs fear of attack, I suggest you give him a wide birth when possible. If the dog is ahead of you, veer off somewhat--no abrupt turns--just aim away from him at 45-60 degrees.

"Sit down there, boy, and read your paper while I get some exercise."

"Slowing down will reassure him also. If he still shows interest in you...stop. Say something reassuring to him. Talk as if to a friend, at a neutral volume. Don't smile...showing your teeth signals aggression to these animals.

"Only shout at him if he's about to attack you. Provided he is wagging his tail, and perhaps looking playful, you should be safe. If the hairs on the back of its neck are standing up, and talking has not calmed you (I mean him) down, a tactical withdrawal may be required. This will involve moving away while facing the dog--you don't want to give him a clear shot at your rear.

"Most runners believe in friendship. In this situation, a runner can simply get down on one knee and call the dog to them. This thwarts any cunning the dog might have used. Many dogs come quietly up to the kneeling runner. The dog no longer feels threatened; he therefore doesn't feel the need to threaten you. Some dogs will scamper back to their pets. A few will still give the impression they want to fight. One or two are very difficult to gauge."

The alien is right. The week that I wrote his dog advice down, I did a run in a different part of town. "Neighborhood Watch," read the sign...should be safe from burglary here I thought. Well, every house seemed to posses barking dogs--some behind fences, a couple chained at the front--and finally of course...loose dogs: Three of them.

I was unsure about the six month pup, it was barring its teeth a little too much. But the other two, though barking, seemed friendly enough. When I got down and called them to me, the aliens predictions were fulfilled. One just ran back to the house. A second came up to be stroked, then joined his companion. The pup slinked round at an angle, about 60 degrees from my front.

I faced him again, slapped my thigh, and held out my hand (palm downwards) for him to smell. I talked soothingly to him. "Come here, you great seething mass of over-aggressive, retarded piece of proto-plasm." Not being a linguist...he complied. It took several minutes for me to calm this skittish pup enough to be able to stand up and back away. I probably should have used this next approach.

Later in the run, I came to the back of a property from which three inviting trails led. Two dogs came at a modest tempo towards me. Their intent was clear. My reaction was swift. Outrunning never being an option with dogs, I turned and walked back from whence I came. Perhaps because I was moving away from "their" property, they slowed somewhat. When the lead dog was 45 feet away I used my firmest no-nonsense shout, "Stay." It had the desired effect. After I'd walked another 30 yards, I resumed running.

I've since found the one syllable approach to be the best. "No," works quite well. Now, back to what the alien said if the dog's servant is present.

"Request its owner to restrain it. Some dogs will chase runners all the time. If talking to its pet fails, consider the next step. Don't attempt violence towards the dog--your courts take a dim view of it. If you do more than defend yourself from attack, you could be in trouble. If possible, find out the owner's name--then walk away from the area. Having walked out of chasing range, resume your run.

"The dog clearly has a right to exercise, but by law it must be kept under control. If you have a problem about one or more dogs in an area, a word with the Police may help. They, or you, can get a court restraining order requiring the dog to be kept under control. If a dog

19

has bitten you, report this to the Police. Although a dog usually gets more than one bite before its life is in danger, the first report ought to remind the owner of his duty to keep it under control.

"Shouting at the dog is of use in an actual attack, as is your aptly named Halt spray, which has saved many lives. Mace and pepper sprays are also effective. Inexpensive, they are easily attached to shorts or carried in the hand--Halt should be a part of your running gear."

In due course, the training schedule might look like this.

Sat -- 30 minutes paths and grass
Sun -- 20 mins road
Mon -- 30 mins road & park
Tue -- rest
Wed -- 30 mins road
Th -- 20 mins grass
Fri -- rest

"Now you've got above the two hour threshold, let's consider other things. Many people think running is a cheap sport--until they find out how expensive shoes, weather suits and sundry equipment cost. But it needn't cost you your earth. All you need is a little protection from the ground (shoes) and the elements (clothing).

Snakes are not dangerous, unless you're allergic to their poison or you habitually play with them.

Most people bitten by snakes don't receive Venom; those who do receive it can usually get to an antivenin source before it will cause serious damage. If you're allergic to the Venom however, you could go into anaphylactic shock; unless you have expert assistance, you'll be one of the 20 or so in the U.S. who die from bites--out of 45,000 bitten.

Bees aren't dangerous either, though they may appear to be if you just found out they kill three to five times more people than snakes in the U.S....and you're being chased by a swarm because they happened to like your 10th mile of the run aroma.

Give beehives a wide birth. If you're the one in two hundred who is allergic to stings, always carry your epinephrine.

"At this stage, one pair of running shoes will be sufficient for all of your needs. However, they need several qualities. In addition to being comfortable, they require enough cushioning to protect you from the shock of landing on a hard surface thousands of times on each run. To help traction on wet grass and paths they will need a sole with waffles, ripples and or studs.

"Avoid the expensive shoes with special devices--a cheap, but robust shoe will do for starters. If it becomes apparent from the way your shoes wear down that you have a problem, we can consider other options.

"Your shoes may last 500 miles if you're lucky. When they are half-way to wearing out, you might consider specializing. A second pair for runs on asphalt would be useful. Then alternate the shoes as you do the terrain you run on. An assistant in a sports shop which has a good running equipment section will often give sound advice...most of them are runners themselves.

"What clothing you wear when running will depend on the time of year, the effort you put in, and your personal feelings. Runners who want to look good, will need a couple of multicolored track suits or sweats, and a goretex breathable waterproof--to put in their closet--because they won't be running in the rain.

"The main thing is to stay warm. Shorts; lightweight and normal thickness track bottoms, or tights--each have their uses depending on the conditions. A good supply of T-shirts and sweatshirts in various thickness' will take care of the trunk. For wet days, you will need a lightweight showerproof jacket and possibly trousers. Great care is needed when wearing these because you can easily overheat.

"When the temperature is low, do wrap up well. Gloves and hat are usually required at some stage of the winter. The outer garment should be almost windproof. If you are increasing the length of your run, use circuits close to a warm base. On windy days, a forest will give you shelter, but it will also stay frosty longer than areas where the sun has had a chance to work. Houses can give you good shelter too--choose a street that is at right angles to the wind's direction.

"When running an out and back route, always start into the wind; this will decrease the possibility of you feeling chilled on the way back. Running back into the wind with tired legs makes the session feel harder. If you overheat, take the top sweatshirt off and tie it

21

around the waist. If you feel warm early in the run, stop to adjust what you're wearing. Stash the extra gear to pick up on the way back. The hat is the easiest regulator though, take it off as required.

"Your people seem to think that to keep warm in winter, the clothing must wick the perspiration away from the skin, to the outer layer, so it can evaporate."

"Whereas your...species."

"You can call us a people if it would make you feel more comfortable."

"What are your people's views on winter running?"

"The reason you perspire is to lose heat. Sweating during a winter run would suggest you are wearing too much. Now, if the sweat evaporates at the surface of the clothing, it's not evaporating by conduction, which *would* cool your body. It's evaporating by other means."

"Radiation and convection...just like most of our heating systems you mean."

"Yes:

"Now, David. They also say that if sweat is allowed to stay trapped on the skin, the exerciser will get cold. In fact, he will only get cold from his own sweat if he stops exercising, or if he changes the rate at which he exercises. He won't get cold if he does it properly--he will remain cool enough to continue exercising in comfort with minimal sweating.

"But it is difficult to figure out how many layers to wear for certain conditions. A small, waterproof fanny pack, with a long sleeve T-shirt, is of immense use. If conditions worsen, you can use it as an extra layer. If you start too fast; if you've slowed down and begin to feel cold; you can exchange the dry one for the inner shirt you had on for the first part of the run. Then head back to your base at a pace which won't make you sweat up too much. The inner layer should be like a diaper lining, able to make you feel dry for hours.

"I agree with your people about the outer waterproof layer...it should be breathable. It should allow moisture to escape. Just make sure you don't put too much heavy stuff underneath--you shouldn't be sweating like you would in summer. Realistically speaking, you people don't have a product which allows that much moisture to get out. To paraphrase your peoples old expression...dress to lightly perspire, not to sweat. Regarding winter running, cold weather doesn't give you pneumonia, people do. But get some dry clothes on once you've finished the run.

"Muscles do produce large amounts of heat as a byproduct of repeated contractions--learn to dissipate the heat with minimal sweating--don't overdress.

"To complete your getup, you should buy a runner or cyclist bib to help motorists see you. This needs a bright eye-catching *fluorescent* part for daylight recognition, and a *reflective* part for night-times up to you to make yourself visible and therefore safer on the roads. When possible, use roads mainly as a way of getting to paths, tracks and grass where most of your running can takes place.

"This is too good to mess up."

"Roads are the domain of engined vehicles. Having dressed to be seen, remember to keep your eyes and ears open for them. Keep to the sidewalk if there are few cross streets; face oncoming traffic if there's no sidewalk. On country roads, it may be safer to switch sides when traffic is only coming from one direction. I'm thinking in particular of the left hand bend as you approach oncoming traffic (in countries driving on the left side of the road...a right hand bend).

23

They won't, until nearly upon you, see even a brightly clad runner. If you hear it in time, pop across the road; not only will he see you earlier, he won't have to move out to avoid you.

"Close one eye when a car approaches--you'll retain some of your night vision.

"A flashing red light on a belt, or shoes that flash are useful aids to being seen. A small flashlight with a strong beam is helpful for you to see.

"When running at night, keep to known routes--you will have a better idea of where the hazards are. Run with a higher knee lift--this will raise your feet above many objects and surface imperfections. Land soft...ready to allow your leg to fold partially if the surface surprises you...prepare to fall and roll.

"Street lights can help--but they are likely to lead you through heavily polluted areas. Running indoors is an option for many, though once or twice a week is most people's limit. Some of Part Two will work well inside.

"Any moron who wears a musical device deserves what he gets. The only place where it's reasonably safe to use is at a populated track. A populated track has at least ten people actively exercising...giving all present some degree of safety. If music listeners stay out of the inner lanes, and obey the other track rules in part five, they should remain safe."

"Many people think it's cool, listening to music while running," I said.

"First, people should never do something because they think it's cool. They should do it because they want to. Second, there are too many noises in your society as it is--constant nagging intrusions on your auditory systems. Give your mind a break--take in the silence--listen to the background churning of your brain--think your own random thoughts for thirty to forty minutes."

*   *   *

"David," he said some weeks later, "I've had you avoid hills for the most part. Now it's time to introduce them into some of your runs--you need to get used to the slightly different running action they require. Don't go for anything too demanding, but include a few hills in new routes you plan. Get used to running them economically. Shorten the stride length a bit; if necessary, reduce the leg speed also. Shuffle up with a low knee lift and a relaxed lower arm action. If you get very short of breath, stop and resume at a slower pace.

"Hills will slow you down. As with running itself, you may take several attempts to find the right speed for each type and length of hill. The aim should be to run well within yourself and accelerate to your normal pace over the top. In time, you will get your leg speed back.

"We've applied a stress to your body five times a week; your body has adapted to that stress: we can now increase the stress.

"You can build up the time to forty minutes for three of the runs and thirty for the other two--using the same basic schedule as on page 13. By this stage you might like to consider an additional method to assess the pace to run at."

"You mean instead of the talk test?"

"In addition to the talk test. Your people, like mine, generally accept the talk test as a fair indication of the speed to run at, in order to gain some training benefit. This 'training threshold' pace can be confirmed by use of a number of simple formulae. The starting point is your pulse at rest. This one is my favorite."

He then directed me to a slip of paper with the following.

(200 - pulse at rest) x 60 % + pulse at rest

Examples

Heartrate at rest 80:

200 - 80 = 120

120 x 60 % = 72

72 + 80 gives a threshold of 152 to be maintained throughout the run.

Pulse at rest 70	target in run 148
60	144
50	140
40	136

"Other formulae take account of age. Most reduce by one, the target pulse for each year above a certain age--thirty is the most popular age. A fifty-year-old with a pulse at rest of 70 would have his target pulse reduced to 128. As you become fitter, this age allowance is reduced until you have the same target as a thirty-year-old. The target should only be used as a guide--the talk test is the most important at this stage.

"For the time being, check your pulse five minutes before the end of a run. Do this is on a flat section, and don't increase your speed prior to the check--it will give you a false reading. Just stop running...count your pulse for ten seconds while walking, then resume running at a slower pace to finish the run.

"The number of beats in ten seconds, times six, will give a fairly accurate figure. Try to be within 12 beats either way of your target. More than 12 above target, and you're really doing a part three type run. More than 12 below may not be giving you sufficient stimulation for your endurance to improve."

"What about a heartrate monitor?"

"What about them?" he replied.

"Do you recommend them?"

"As I'm not sponsored by a heartrate monitor company, and I don't sell them, I've no need to strut them to the readers of this manual.

"New runners should read wide on their subject. Take certain advice with a mineral from your oceans."

"Huh?"

"Take some advice with a grain of salt.

"If a successful athlete swears by a fruit, or a certain type of energy bar, or specific protein or carbohydrate source--it's safe to say the person is receiving an incentive for the endorsement."

The alien doesn't want you spending much money at this stage. He wants your time and commitment, not your earnings....Or as he said. "Too many of your people spend vast sums on exercise equipment that they use only minimally."

Then he continued. "Carry out the pulse test at the ten and twenty minute stage of a few runs. You may be starting out too fast and slowing down as the run proceeds.

"Another way to recognize you started out too fast is if YOU hear your feet hitting the pavement. It can indicate your form has broken down. Walk a while--then get your form back at a slower pace.

"A heartrate monitor can be an aid to keeping you at a sensible pace. This steady running sets you up for faster running later.

"Believe you can do it," he said. "If you believe you can run for 40 minutes, if you believe in yourself, you can achieve anything. Simply add a minute or two every few days and you will soon reach the goal.

"When you've achieved the 40 minute goal, increase your pace to run at 65, then 70 and 75 percent of maximum heartrate--one each week at each level of training.

"I'll see you next week," he said. Then, added:

"By running 5 times a week over different terrain and distances you've vastly improved your endurance and strength. Our patient build-up will pay dividends when you move onto the quality work I'll outline next. Progress may have seemed slow at first, but you will soon reap the rewards of your patience".

Lyme Disease

This annoying "non plague" is not a serious danger to runners--you just need to know a bit about what the bacterium does and how it gets transferred.

It does not kill...but if untreated, it's unhealthy for you.

The disease has been in the country for at least a century.

Deer do not give people Lyme--but the deer tick is the carrier of the bacteria for Lyme.

Because it only feeds once a year, the deer tick is unlikely to give Lyme to you.

The tick takes about 24 hours to cement itself to you...then it will take a blood meal. Check your body twice a day for ticks, stay on trails, wear white to easily spot them, and enjoy your running.

Only a few states have more than a hundred cases of Lyme...but what if you're one of the people who gets it.

A bull's-eye shaped rash (*erythema migrans*) of several inches and flu like symptoms are typical.

Confirmation is by a simple blood test.

Treatment is easy and successful...take your antibiotics correctly.

Need more details--a concise essay on Lyme was in Bassin Magazine, May/June issue 1992.

PART TWO

STYLE AND SPEED

This second part will get your body used to running fast. We will develop this slowly to avoid undue strain, in part because it may involve adapting your running style a little. Three different sessions will be brought into the weekly schedule.

The more you train, the more important good form is in reducing your potential for injury, while improving the use of the limited oxygen supply. The best mechanical efficiency for you--which generally means *smooth* running--equates to faster races.

CHAPTER THREE

ONE HUNDREDS
&
FARTLEK

Although the alien's visits would grow further apart as my running knowledge increased and his information gathering grew wider, it was indeed the next week when he returned and started me on my speed-running. Some people call it speedwork. Doubtless influenced by the guru's views, I think anything with work in its structure creates negative feelings. Fast running is play at its best. Just watch a few puppies chase each other--they'll stop, check out a few smells while recovering, then chase again.

"Physical stress reduces mental stress--but not, unfortunately, the other way around", says a weekly note in a training diary. In fact, physical stress--exercise, only helps you cope with mental stress. The act of finding the time to exercise, plus the exercise itself, takes you out of the stress cycle. Don't allow exercise to add stress to your life.

Keep your speed sessions fun; they should not be intense. Do them in natural surroundings when possible; minimize distractions. Now, here are the alien's initial words on running faster.

"You've given your heart, lungs and leg muscles a solid foundation of steady running--now you can move onto faster running. When your friends can manage several thirty minute runs a week, they could introduce one session of fast running per week. Upon reaching the magic forty minute run, as you have, you can increase to two speed sessions a week. This will stop you from doing too much speed work early on.

"Although an untrained person can sprint for a bus, it's unwise to run fast until you have first trained slow. Endurance must come first. Then use this phase to build more endurance while playing at speed."

"You mean fast running will give added strength and endurance?" I asked.

"Indeed. Very quick results are gained from running short distances many times within a session. Some people use it as a means to get fit before steady running. For those with a reasonable level of fitness from non-running activities before starting to run, that's fine. But for someone who started unfit, steady running is a vital base. You don't build a house without a base; I hope readers won't run at speed without first laying down their base. If you have decided to go straight into fast running as a means to get fit, a steady run should still be done on alternate training days.

"Muscles thrive and improve if stimulated in the right way. Running fast in short sections is good stimulation--it doesn't over stress the body--yet allows the body to work harder. The heart, being a muscle, also improves. The muscle itself becomes larger and stronger. Each heartbeat pumps more blood. Your people call this the stroke volume. The result...running muscles receive more oxygen and energy containing blood each minute."

"You mentioned the lungs just now."

"Good listening: First I want you to do the following session of speedwork.

"Your first session should be in a quiet area. You'll need about 100 meters of reasonably flat and even grass. After warming up with ten minutes of easy running, discard the outer level of gear or kit. Stride out a little faster than normal...progressively build your speed. Maintain good speed for about 50 meters then ease off--decelerate, if you will. Walk a few meters until you're breathing easy--turn and repeat the stride back to your gear.

"You should do about ten minutes of these strides; work up to the full 100 meters at speed. As you progress, experiment with your running style. See what happens when you work your arms harder, or pick your knees up a little higher, or take short, quite rapid strides.

"Don't get too much out of breath at first. Enjoy the session, and use it as an appetizer for the next one.

"You are looking for smoothness in your running...devoid of jerky movements. The smooth, economic runner will use less oxygen at a given speed and ceteris paribus (all other things being unchanged) will run faster.

"On a windy day, continue the experiment. Run some strides with the wind...relax, stretch out and fly along. Then try running into the wind--lean into it and take shorter strides--use a forceful action. Pump the arms a little extra by pushing them backwards--allow them to come forward to their natural height before forcing them rapidly back again. Lower arms go forward and back, not across the chest; elbows close to your side, flexed at 90 degrees. Keep the shoulders above the hips to prevent trunk rotation--don't hunch forward or pull shoulders back. Keep that heavy noggin of yours nicely balanced above your hips too.

"If running into the wind, keep the knees low. This will reduce your stride length, ensuring that you are not in the air too long on each stride. The less time in the air, the less it has a chance to push you back. Make the calves propel you forward...not upwards. Just like flying in a plane, the energy cost of being in the air is huge. A half-inch too high in the air can cost you ten per cent of your energy--so decrease your vertical bounce--run forward with each stride, not up. This sort of training will take on a new meaning in Part Four.

"One of the best surfaces for fast running is where field hockey is played. The even surface and short grass is better than football fields...except those few weeks pre-football season when the new year's grass is at its peak condition before practicing tears it up. Artificial surfaces are good year round; be aware of the slope or camber though. Running across a severe slope is bad for the ankles and all joints north; run up over the center of the field from the sidelines.

"A good way to do the 100s is to run from corner to corner across the field. This will give you about 130 meters. To recover, walk or jog the side of the field. As you get fitter, you can jog the end of the playing area, which is a little shorter than the length. This session is particularly good in the depths of winter when many paths are too muddy for fast running. But don't deny yourself too many part four sessions by avoiding the mud."

"As I said before, lung capacity also increases. The action of breathing deeply many times a week has improved your diaphragm...which is the main weapon of breathing. The auxiliary breathing muscles--the muscles of the abdomen, chest, including the intercostals--are also developing more strength and endurance. As a result, you're finding steady runs easier. Breathing in takes muscle action--expiration is mostly passive--a result of those muscles relaxing.

"One irony of life on this planet, is that people who smoke tobacco and other leaves or animal products develop--at least temporarily--huge lung capacity. The deep inhalation they take works the muscles of breathing to the maximum. Of course, every time they smoke, they kill a few more lung cells. Just like brain and muscle cells, lung cells are never replaced.

"But smokers aren't going to be reading your journal, so I'll get to my point."

"Which is?"

"You should do smokers' exercises...but devoid of the leaves. Once or twice a day, practice breathing deeper than you normally would. Sense your interior stretch receptors sending messages as you fully expand your chest...taking in pint after pint of air. Adopt a good upright posture for this exercise. The typical lung capacity, or vital capacity is 4.8 liters. Do these exercises to ensure you get the maximum capacity genetics has allowed you. Train your lungs.

"Let pleasant thoughts pass through your mind as you do these breathing exercises--the lovely wife you will be seeing later; the trees and flowers on your next run; the way you will answer questions at the next committee meeting (oops); your running style compared to a faster runner; choosing the one TV show to watch before or after one of your other hobbies this evening. Build up those intercostal muscles just like you do the leg muscles--strictly speaking...they are all running muscles.

"We are also increasing the number and size of bacteria in your muscles."

"What," I said, shocked.

"Well...retired bacteria. Little organelles you call mitochondria are the energy factories which enable your muscles to contract. They take fuel (sugar usually) and fuel (oxygen) and...with the nerve to ignite...wham...you get energy. The steady runs and gentle speed stuff has increased the number and size of your mitochondria, and increased the capillaries to bring the fuel. Your muscle fibers have grown...you have more power."

"Running fast will require slight adjustments to the format of training sessions. I advise a warmup of ten to fifteen minutes steady running, followed by the exercises from chapter one. The warmup procedure prepares the muscles for working hard. Muscles are more efficient when warm; they are less likely to strain. Speedwork can then be done with minimal injury risk.

"The third part of the session will be five to ten minutes steady running. Take care with your cooldown. Don't come to a sudden stop--fast running leaves harsh chemicals in your system. Get in the habit of doing easy running after all speedwork. Then repeat the gentle stretching. The more blood you can move through your well exercised muscles after a session...the quicker they recover. However, sore muscles need rest too. A walk may help; as may a warm bath and use of liniment.

"As your speed increases, you will feel more relaxed and enjoy your running much more.

"But find the speed that feels natural to you...you're less likely to get hurt. Find a comfortable stride rate and length--then as you work on one aspect of your form at a time, your entire form will become smoother. Think about being graceful.

"You may strip down to shorts for the speedwork, although you should feel relaxed with a track suit bottom. The main consideration will be the conditions. Having raised the body temperature slightly in the warmup, you must maintain it. In winter--or on windy days all through the year--this can require two or more layers on your top half, and a light covering on the legs to keep the chill off.

Fast running will improve your flexibility. Power yourself forward with the calves to extend the stride.
But land close to a point under your center of gravity, with a flexed knee, to prevent pounding. Float as if on hot coals.

"If the temperature is below about 40 degrees, or warmer but windy, the cold becomes a potential danger. Treat cold with respect... collapsing when training hard in winter is not unknown. Plan ahead. On very cold days, the recovery should be short, to prevent the body from cooling down. The fast part will need to be slower to ensure you can recover.

"After doing the session of 100s a few times, you can move onto one of the most enjoyable types of training. Use an area of varying terrain--a park or forest is ideal. After the warmup and stretching, run round the park at an easy pace, doing strides of 50 to 200 meters as and when you like. Continue with easy running or walking between efforts. Stride up some small hills, and ease effortlessly down others. This is speedplay or fartlek, and is of most use when feeling run-down or tired. Just put on your kit and go--get in touch with your inner child...to keep running fun.

"If the surface is uneven, your muscles compensate to keep you balanced; rough ground will make you work harder to achieve the same speed, so early sessions can be shorter. Let the ankles roll with the terrain, building up the small muscles of the legs. Later, increase the duration of your run on this surface".

From Coach Roy Benson.

The purpose of David's first three chapters is aerobic conditioning to develop base endurance.

How...easy running and short strides at 65-80 percent of max heart rate...for as many times a week as you can handle without getting injured...for as many weeks as you can tolerate before moving to the next training phase. Don't move to the next part until you have at least 12 weeks of base.

Adaptations

increase maximum oxygen uptake

increase efficiency of running--you move in a fairly straight line

flexibility, strength, and coordination improve from the aerobic speed work

increase muscle metabolism of fat--conserving sugar
increase muscle and connective tissue strength
increase fast twitch muscle use--they look and behave more like slow twitch fibers

Specifically

Diaphragm and rib cage muscles improve...therefore move more air...more oxygen is available
More red blood cells are produced
Blood volume increases...giving Carbon Dioxide waste a greater reservoir to be excreted in. (Red blood cells bring most of the Oxygen in; the blood plasma takes most of the Carbon Dioxide out.)
More and bigger mitochondria in the muscle cells
Myoglobin--which carries oxygen to the mitochondria--increases
Stronger heart with a lower resting rate decreases the effort needed for a given speed
The "other" muscles of running are stronger
This means you can run faster before forming excessive lactic acid
Or...*Endurance* increases...that is, the ability of your muscles to repeat a movement over and over again at a submaximal workload for a prolonged period.

Benson has 30 plus years experience as a coach, including 10 at the University of Florida. He was president of the Florida Track Club that placed Gold medalist Frank Shorter, plus Jack Bachelor and Jeff Galloway on the 1972 Olympic team. Benson coaches privately and through his Nike Running Camps. Fax (404) 255-0731

CHAPTER FOUR

TWO HUNDREDS

"After several weeks of 100s and fartlek, you should be ready for more formal speedwork. This will involve timed efforts over a set distance. Find somewhere you can run without interruption for about 200 meters. One side of a small sports ground or a section of good forest path will be fine. After the usual warm up and a few relaxed strides of fifty to one hundred meters you can start the 200s.

"Stride as you did previously for the 100s. Walk back as a recovery and repeat--but this time, just a little faster. Don't commence a stride if your pulse is above 120 per minute at the end of the recovery. Time each one. When your times are increasing, you've had enough. Pace yourself to do ten efforts. They should not be eyeball-out efforts because you will be lucky to manage two of these. Check your pulse at the end of a couple--say the forth and sixth--it should be twenty to thirty more than your normal running pulse. Don't take it beyond this for several sessions.

"When you feel tired, think about your rhythm....Run smoothly. Cut out exaggerated, unneeded motions.

"When your body is used to this session you can increase the speed. Try running the first few in the same time as (say) the third fastest from the previous session. You should still be short of a flat-out sprint. When you get fitter, you can take your pulse higher than the earlier guideline--up to 85 per cent of your maximum heart rate.

"By now you may have had one or two ignorant people telling you to 'get your knees up' as you run by. Or perhaps they have a point. Surely only sprinters have a high knee lift--a forceful action which will see them through one to four hundred meters. Yet if you look at a good middle distance runner, you will see the knee fairly high...especially in the final lap."

"Can knee lift be relevant to me also?"

"Although all you want to do is run five miles at a respectable speed, not a sub 3:35 1500 meters or a 46 seconds 400...knee lift is relevant.

"A highish knee lift enables the lower leg to swing through under the knee much faster to start its next stride. The higher the knee lift, the faster the lower leg will swing through, and the longer the stride. Next time you get shouted at, say 'thank you' while going on your way!

"Your knee lift will be lower at longer distances, but a respectable one will help. Care should be taken not to overstride however--injuries to the back of the legs are one indication of this. These injuries are caused by early fatigue and loss of muscle efficiency. An improvement in flexibility of the hip may help.

"An oddity of running, is that when your foot hits the ground, it should be moving backwards, even though the body is moving forward. In overstriding, the foot is still traveling forward as it strikes the ground. The heel then acts as a break, causing stress and damage on every stride. In order to avoid this damage, find the stride length that suits you. Your stride will possibly increase as you become stronger...then decrease again as you find its natural length.

"Once you've improved your speed, you can make the session help your endurance. Endurance is improved by reducing the recovery period. Instead of walking back, jog slowly. A second option is to jog away at the end of each strider, then turn around to jog back to where you finished, and run another strider the other way.

"Remember to keep good cadence while you're working on your endurance with this session; don't allow your leg speed to decrease.

"Check your pulse a few times at the end of the recovery. If it's not down to 120 per minute you should increase the rest period. The heart recovers about 60 percent of its composure within one minute. To ensure this session prepares you for the stresses of racing, aim to get the recovery down to that minute.

A fortnight's (two week) schedule might look like this:
Sat -- 40 mins including 20 mins fartlek in woods
Sun -- 40 mins steady run at 65 % max heartrate
Mon -- warmup, 10 x 200 meters 200 slow jog recovery
Tues -- rest
Wed -- 35 mins including a few small hills
Thur -- 40 mins steady
Fri -- rest

Sat -- fartlek in a park, striding up and down gentle hills
Sun -- 40 min steady
Mon -- 35 min steady
Tues -- rest
Wed -- after warmup, 20 mins of 100 meter strides on grass--work on relaxed high knee lift action--jog back recovery.
Thur -- 40 min at 75 percent max heartrate
Fri -- rest

"One problem of fast running...it puts additional stress on the body. You develop strong running muscles, but you may create an imbalance. The antagonistic..."

He looked intently into my face.

"...no David, they're not angry at you. An antagonist muscle is one that complements the work of another muscle. You humans miss-named them. You should have named them complementary muscles...not antagonist muscles."

I guess I looked it, as he said.

"No need to be confused. Let me give you an example. The calf muscles work very hard in several phases of the stride--though we tend to think of them mostly in terms of the propulsive power at push off, or toe off--anyway...they become very strong. The calf is the agonist or prime mover. The calves, complementary muscle at the shin is relatively weak. The Tibialis Anterior...the muscle in front of the Tibia bone of the lower leg doesn't work against the ground. Its resistor, its complementary, is the calf muscles themselves. Once the calf muscles have finished contracting at push off, with the foot (hopefully) at full extension, the calf muscles...muscle fiber by muscle fiber...relax. The calf muscles gradually return to their resting length. The toes and the rest of the lower foot moves back to its neutral position...but not merely by the calf muscles relaxing. The tibialus anterior muscle comes into play. It contracts, speeding the foot back to a neutral position."

"Shouldn't take too much effort." I said. "I suppose that's why they remain relatively weak."

"Yes. That's part of why these complementary, or to your specie, antagonist muscles are the first to strain. To avoid this, you should consider the following exercises, before and after running: Do each for one minute to prevent injury to these weak areas."

He then described the following:

* To **strengthen the shin muscles**--sit on a table, legs hanging down. Dangle a 5 to 10 pound weight from the toes; lift the toes upwards to raise the weight. Hold for 10 seconds and repeat four times.

* To **avoid knee problems**--position as above, raise the leg to the horizontal, hold ten seconds and repeat four times.

39

* **Low back pain**--do sit-ups, with knees bent and heels touching the buttock; build to one minute of a steady flowing action.

* **Hamstrings**--lie face down; curl the lower leg to touch the buttock.

* **Glutei's**--or for the rest of the book, gluteals--kneeling position--raise each leg alternately as high as you can; hold up for ten seconds; repeat four times per leg.

* **Achilles** trouble--faster running may have resulted in a tender achilles tendon due to the heel tab on your shoes digging into it on every stride--bruising results. Cut off the tab. Take a few days off running to let the swelling subside. Read the section on overpronation (Chap 19) regarding the Achilles, before running again. Do the calf stretches of Chapter One.

"You may only need one or two of these exercises. Listen to your body. Try to spot its weak points. Don't let an ache develop into a minor injury."

MORE ON FORM

He watched a few more of my speed sessions. One day he said. "Slow down fella, your form's all to pot."

Pointing out my defects, and of other runners that we came across...he added this advice about running style:

"You need to run more upright...perpendicular to the planet. Don't run as if you're about to sit down...with your weight behind you. Run tall and proud. Bring the hips forward...good. That brings the center of gravity forward my boy--over the midfoot, where you should land on each stride."

He advised me on the others one at a time. We suggest that you adjust your own form as needed--one aspect at a time.

"What do you know about pendulums?" he said one day.

"They swing?"

"True. How fast do they swing?"

I thought for a while, picturing various clocks and one in a museum. "They vary...they each have their own speed."

"Good. Their speed varies according to how long they are."

"That's nice," I said...and waited.

"Your legs are pendulums. The axes are the hips.

"You can decrease the length of the pendulum--thereby increasing its speed potential--by making your foot hug the buns on the swing-through.

"On every stride, lift your heel close to your buns.

"One way to practice this is with bun flicks. Run along for twenty seconds and flick your feet rapidly up to touch your bottom. Take very short strides forward--moving up the track or field is not the main purpose. Some people call this exercise high heels because you flick the heels up to your buttocks. Others call them butt kicks.

"Next, use the quadriceps and the iliosoas muscles (hip flexors) at the front of the leg, to whip the leg through. To prepare for this, practice high knee raises while running on the spot or moving a few inches at a time up the track. Bring in rapid arm movements to increase your leg speed. After three or four 15 second efforts at this, practice running at moderate pace while whipping the leg through. Your knees don't need to be high at the front like a sprinter--leg speed is the key.

"Practice these two separately, then together as you hug the buns with your foot AND pull the leg through fast.

"Anything for the toes?" I asked.

"As I've said before, the toes are very important for propulsion. Most of the muscles for running are involved in setting up the calf muscles to propel you forward. A good push off from the toes is best achieved by extending the trail leg to its fullest.

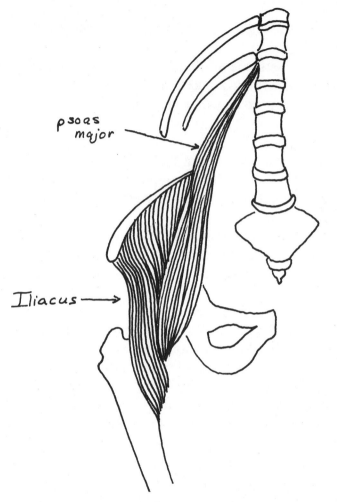

psoas major

Iliacus →

These hip flexors are described on page 41

"Push off from the end of the toes--you'll need to maintain good ankle flexibility for this to be done--then pull the leg through fast as I said a few moments ago.

"Now the arms. Move them smoothly; feel in control. They help your legs to know where they are in the stride cycle. Don't allow the arms to go too high in the front--just high enough to stop the shoulder roll.

"Keeping the arms smooth will also decrease head roll. Head movement is rarely a good thing. Head rolling toward the finish of speedwork is wasteful of precious energy and will slow you down. Keep the neck and shoulders relaxed. You rarely see world record holders with head movement. The eyes should not wander much either, except to take in the periphery.

"Keep your arms bent at about 90 degrees. Avoid bringing them across the body...the arms need to go straight back and straight forward just like your legs do. Your legs should not kick off to the side either.

"Relax your hands...stay loose.

"Use a natural style. Think of being at ease...at play. Let the feet roll you down the path.

"Don't land daintily on the toes. Do land softly on the outer mid-foot or outer heel. Then roll inwards and off the toes.

"Land with a slightly flexed knee; don't lock the knee.

"Good flexibility will help you.

"Don't copy sprinters.

"But don't shuffle along either. Hug the ground as you propel yourself forward in the horizontal plane...not the vertical.

"Don't overstride. Too long a stride makes you lose momentum. Taking strides a few inches shorter can help you run faster. The quads want to devour the ground...let them, but keep them in check.

"Find your ideal stride length which will change according to your running speed.

"Practice making your feet go straight forward, rather than throwing your feet to the side each stride, which makes the hip swivel. Practice running in a straight line. Remember school math. A horse pulling at a 30 degree angle exerts less force than one pulling at five degrees. Run straight for less waste and more speed.

"David, think of an aspect of your form for a few minutes on every run. An efficient running style will save you energy and decrease your potential for injury. The more practice you have, the more efficient you will become. You will get faster.

"Some people run a little differently because of their body shape, their biomechanics. If readers feel awkward using the style I've described, they should use what feels natural to them. A leg length operation or orthotics may cure them, of course. If you want to improve, seek out experts to check for leg length differences.

"An orthotic will enable some to run with more efficiency...with less effort. You should all aspire to run fast with minimal effort.

"Stop the speed session for a minute when your form deteriorates. Gather your mental energy and do four more strides to practice form with a tired body. This will help you maintain good form at the end of a race.

"None of the speedwork at this stage should be flat-out fast--that will come later. Stay in control at speed. Although I encourage you to do those four extra strides, don't discourage yourself by doing long, hard speed sessions. Tendons, ligaments and bones need to catch up to the lungs, muscles and blood supply."

"Use the mouth to breathe," said the alien, "the orifice is bigger, and you don't have to worry about it being stuffed up. The length of tubing (deadspace) is less. Forget the 'in-the-nose...out-the-mouth routine.' You don't have to concentrate on it if you mouth breathe. Take rhythmic long deep breaths because 150 cc of tidal breath is deadspace--a section of air which goes in and out with each breath, yet is not replaced. You don't wear a mouthgard, so you don't need tape on your nose to breathe right."

"When I told you to slow down, it wasn't just your form I was worried about. I wanted to stop you getting injured. Your muscles get tenderized by the pounding of fast running if you're not careful. Speed running will strengthen the muscles and connective tissue, but a bone takes three months to mend...it will take just as long for the full physiological changes to take place after training.

Before leaving he said. "When you've got used to running fast for short periods, you can move on to a more challenging type of training as described in the next part."

The shuffle debate.

Beware of too high a knee lift. You may run faster by keeping your feet closer to the ground. High knee lift will waste energy...you go vertical instead of horizontal. The *shuffle* is a ground hugging style which is more economical for many people. You still push off from the toes properly, but keep the foot close to the ground in all phases of the stride--saving energy with less vertical bounce. Yes...the stride will shorten, but leg speed can be increased to compensate. Practice raising those feet so they barely slither above the surface...No forward lean. Run tall with rapid strides. As you set off, think short rapid strides and feel the cadence change.

PART THREE

SUSTAINED EFFORTS AND RACING

Racing requires a constant fast pace. So far, you've developed endurance with steady running, and some speed with short strides. Now we will combine them as a prelude to races of a mile to 10 kilometers.

You will need the manual for this.

Ethos of running.

At first, any running, getting comfortable with exercise, confirms your self-worth.

Now, you'll gain a greater sense of self as you seek quality.

CHAPTER FIVE

LONG REPETITIONS

It was Sunday. About time I saw my guru, I wanted to say to my wife. But our health insurance doesn't cover psychiatric institutions...so I told her I was popping up into the hills for an easy run. "Back in an hour and a half," I said as I picked up my keys.

"Are you going out to practice?" she asked.

"Yes dearest," I replied, smiling. "One day I'll get it right."

Then...to myself added, "Ball players practice; runners train." Perhaps I was getting too serious about this sport.

Twenty minutes later, I did a few stretches and exercises with the emphasis on getting the shin muscles warm. Despite the guru's advice, my speedy stride and fartlek sessions had given me shin pains in the first two weeks. Decreasing my stride length to land softer, as if on eggshells, combined with toe lifts and ankle rotations, had cleared the discomfort.

As I eased into the run I reflected on the last eight hours. I'd related to the relatives; I'd been Christian to the religious and otherwise; I'd been mechanic to the machines; I'd mown the lawn, and done several other things that make weekends satisfying. This pre-dinner activity was the only one I didn't share with others...unless my reluctant friend opted to show.

I've been here every fortnight for ten weeks now. Surely ten weeks was enough to develop speed.

"How you'll doin' Davey boy," he said as I reached the five minute point. "I likes the way you start your run ladde...nice and steady like." He paused as I converted the words. "Don't ever give up yer speed-meister-work matey. I'm not a one to insult that fine animal, but as a runner, you be a sloth. But there's a much work we can do for you."

"Have you eaten *Treasure Island* per chance?"

"Yes me boy...and a good read it was as I studied the south of this fair country."

"Do you think your masters will benefit from the learning?"

He opened his left eye, then raised his right shoulder as if a parrot had just taken flight from it saying. "Precious little, David. But I have my coaching to keep me sane. And I'm off to Africa tonight. The Valley of Rift."

"The Rift Valley you mean."

"Absolutely. Now then, I watched you do some of your strides. Your arms hardly flap at all these days. How do they feel?"

"My arms feel fine. No aches at all."

He gave what in his galazy may have passed for a scornful look.

"Okay. Okay. The strides were fun...leg speed is developing. The quadriceps objected to coming up higher, but they're used to it now. The hamstrings and my butt were tender after I got carried away doing the 200s. I won't do that again."

"Try not to run more than a second faster than previous sessions for 200s. You have years to make progress.

"Are the shin exercises you do effective?"

"Yes they are. Now. What's next?"

"Don't be too eager my friend. You have to think of your bones. Osteoblasts are busy depositing a matrix which is calcifying by the day--making your bones stronger. Osteoclasts are shaping this new bone. Don't rush into still harder training. First promise you will take things gradual like."

He seemed to realize I meant it sincerely...despite the fact that I all but blurted out the child like, "I promise."

He paused as we came to the best overlook on the course. We looked into the green valley--home to one and a half million humans--then continued along the trail as he told me the following.

"To date, you've been running at speeds which enable you to provide all the oxygen requirements of your body as you run. So-called aerobic running--the muscles working with sufficient oxygen.

"However, when you run fast for long periods, the oxygen system will not be able to keep up--part of the long repetition or race will be run without oxygen being used to breakdown all the fuel into a usable energy source. This is anaerobic, or running without oxygen.

"In practice, the aerobic system will provide as much energy as it can--only the deficit will be made up by the anaerobic system. Both systems operate at all times, but the anaerobic system becomes more important for sudden intense efforts, such as running fast up a hill. In a race, the anaerobic system will be supplementing the aerobic system, even if providing only a few percent of the total energy needs.

"Anaerobic running produces lactic acid. The acid accumulates in the muscles and contributes to the heavy legs feeling--the wastes contribute to your fatigue--a factor causing you to slow down. Television commentators often say things like-- 'he's running in treacle; rigor mortis has set in; the monkey's jumped on his back' about runners in that highly anaerobic event...the 400 meters.

"To delay this anaerobic poisoning of the muscles, I had you develop your heart and lungs with steady running...then further stimulate them with the strides over short distances at a moderate effort.

"These two forms of running have developed your aerobic system to good effect...though it'll be years before you reach your maximum potential. I can't stress how important it is to go through the first two parts of this manual. At ten weeks each, they've given you an excellent base from which to proceed.

"So David, continue to be patient with yourself."

Then he addressed the potential readers of this journal, saying:

"If you have *not* developed decent background fitness by running at least a month each of Part One and Two's training sessions, or you don't have a history of regular running, please wait before proceeding with the sessions in this part.

"Those who do have the background fitness, can proceed to develop the body's ability to run anaerobically...by introducing sessions that create a build up of lactic acid. The acid is not dangerous, it is merely a natural--though to you, a slowing--by-product of fast running."

Looking at me as I rounded a turn on that Sunday run, he said:

"Your first stage is to run moderately fast for three to four minutes...and do so several times within a training session. The recovery between efforts will be a walk at first.

Later, when you're used to the session, you can jog. However, the jogging should last as long as the fast part. This type of running is quite hard on your entire body--not just your muscles."

He moved in close to my side and whispered in my ear.

"David--running fast creates extra stresses on the body. It's not only the muscles that feel the strain...Joints, tendons and ligaments experience additional work. You can lesson the strain on these parts by aiming to run relaxed...in control. Just like in the strides of Part Two, land soft rather than pounding. Run on soft surfaces such as packed dirt or sand, grass, or synthetic tracks. Run within your own body limits. Lesson the risk of injury by holding back."

He moved a few feet away, surveying the track ahead of us.

"Parts of this trail would do nicely. Another good area to run these repetitions would be the edge of a large recreation ground. Run two thirds of it fast and use the other third as the recovery. Or you might use the length of a favorite piece of road--do avoid concrete though...it's six to ten times harder than asphalt.

"It helps to use permanent start and finish points to aid your timing. Timing reps make it easier to monitor your progress. A large tree or the corner of a building are effective points to use.

"After warming up for at least a mile, do the usual stretching. Run a few relaxed 50 to 100 meter strides. Then start the first of your three minute repetitions. Not too fast, but you should be feeling quite tired by the end. Your pulse will go higher than in your previous speedwork--85 to 90 percent of your maximum is okay; with your good overall fitness, it should soon return to 120 per minute. Once it's done so, you're ready to go again.

"Do a second repetition while thinking about your running style. Try to keep a steady rhythm going...especially the second half. Let the tension go from the shoulders, maybe drop the arms a little--but keep them moving fast and allow your legs to carry you through.

"The leg muscles should feel a little heavy with the wastes of anaerobic running, but after an active rest, you should persevere with the third repetition.

"This time, start a little slower. As you reach halfway, pick your knees up to extend the stride. Don't extend it so much, and go so fast, that you collapse on the ground afterwards. Complete the session with a significant amount to spare. The real work will come in later sessions, when you aim to improve your times, and reduce the rest period--but in alternate months.

"The first time you do this session should be after a rest day. If you're very stiff afterwards, you've overdone it. As you found with the 200s, any new type of training is hard to judge at first. In fact, if you think you were too fast on the first repetition, consider calling it a day. Perhaps do half a dozen short strides to unwind.

"A week later you can repeat the session...maybe judge the pace better. As with the 200s in Chapter 4, aim for your times to improve during a session. Don't run a fastest time by ten seconds first, to be followed by slow efforts.

"After doing the above session twice, you should find yourself a second area where you can run fast for five to six minutes."

I interrupted his flow.

"Should," I said, "You sound like a mother. What about saying might like to, or, you could find yourself an area that takes you five to six minutes to run?"

"Well," he countered, "I could be wishy washy about it I suppose, but the English tend to be more definite in their instructions. As I first learnt your language on that little island, I do tend to use some of their mannerisms."

Then he dug inside my cerebral cortex with:

"When I say a definite statement, don't think of it as definitive on the subject. Do as you think fit. Read other experts on the subject. The heavens know I *have* made mistakes."

Though by his tone, he felt he'd made precious few.

"If you want to substitute might or could every time I say should...you are of course welcome to old boy. I have the experience in these things you know, but running is democratic. Running is an experiment of ONE after all. I'm still willing to advise you, just use whichever part of my advice you feel is appropriate."

I made a circle with my hand, signaling him to continue.

Devoid of malice, he said. "Do two efforts of this five to six minute route or loop. Try to run the first half at close to the speed of your three minute route...then keep it going an extra two minutes.

You will need a longer recovery period--up to ten minutes is fine. Jog or walk to stay warm for the second effort."

He gave me a sly look.

"You might like to try a 9 to 10 minute loop, but to be honest, few runners find them palatable. Most of them think 10 minute reps take them too close to those high plains cities."

"Oh really," I said.

"Yes. Most runners feel a ten minute rep is too close to Purgatory, and likely to place their sanity and enthusiasm in Jeopardy."

"So you think six minutes is the maximum?"

"I think six minutes maxes out most runners. Though I entreat you and your friends to do 10 minute efforts one day.

"Another problem, you see, is that long repetitions are hard work on the body and on the mind. For this reason, long reps should be done only once a week. Alternating the area and the length of the repetitions will give you variety."

He whispered in my ear again.

"It's far better to get faster by two or three seconds per repetition than to go slower for each one as the session progresses. Going faster within the session makes you feel in control.

"Going slower for consecutive reps makes you feel bad and uncomfortable...demoralizing you for future sessions of this type. You'll dread the sessions; then you'll avoid this type of training. You're likely to experience some sessions where you slow--just use your head to keep these to a minimum."

"To race fast you must train fast; but this fast running must feel relaxed. Maintain your form--be economical--like you were in Part Two. Try to gain a sense of relaxation at speed...at what will soon be race pace.

"Every time you do this session, you further train your muscle fibers to buffer the capacity for operating in the presence of lactic acid. You also push back the anaerobic threshold. The seven minute miles which were at your threshold a few weeks ago, will soon be under your threshold.

"Some people say soreness after these sessions is due to lactic acid remaining in the muscles."

"Whereas--"

"Whereas, the soreness is from micro muscle fiber tears...which will heal and result in stronger muscles if given sufficient rest. You could lie on the grass for half an hour after the last rep (something you might be tempted to do if you've run them too fast) and all the lactic acid would be gone...absorbed by the system. However, it's still better to do a cooldown to bring a steady supply of blood to the muscles. Walking is fine if you're too pooped to run easy--any gentle activity will reduce the potential for stiffness.

"As you learn how to pace yourself, the times for these weekly reps will decrease substantially at first. The next level of improvement will come after your buffering system has adapted--the decrease in your times may not be as profound, but it will confirm you're getting training benefit from the reps. Restrain yourself from racing them...and move onto the next chapter."

Use your head!

CHAPTER SIX

TEMPO RUNS

"When you've done long repetition sessions for about six weeks, you should be ready to bring in a sustained run once a week.

"Sustained running, like its name implies, is fast running, sustained over a longish period of time. Another name for it is Tempo running--you maintain a fast tempo. The initial target is to run for 15, building to 20 minutes. The pace will be faster than your steady runs, but slower than your long repetitions.

"You will run at 80-90 per cent of your maximum heart rate...again, you will be pushing back the lactate or anaerobic threshold. Cruise moderately hard on these runs. Stay focused on your form...the toe push off, the amount of knee raise, stride length, correct arm swing, and relaxed breathing.

"Heartrate is the key. The pace should feel harsh but you must feel in control. Conditions--internal and external--will determine how fast you run on a given day.

"For instance, one of the problems of sustained running is overheating. For six weeks, you will have worked for three to five minutes with a rest to recover. On hot days, this also lets your body dissipate some of its heat--to cool down. Even at close to freezing point, you may find these Tempo sessions are best done sans sweats or tights to allow for additional cooling.

"On real hot days, be prepared to run these sessions a little slower. If possible, adjust the time of day you run to take advantage of cooler conditions. See Chapter 16 for coping with climatic changes.

"As usual, bring in the new training gradual like. After a warmup, stretching and short strides, take off your excess gear or kit. Start off on a set route or loop, perhaps one that would take you 25 minutes at a steady pace. At the beginning, your speed should be barely faster than your 75 % max H.R. run. After five minutes, increase the pace a bit...then increase again at say eight and eleven minutes...but still remain slower than your long repetition speed of the previous few weeks.

"Don't push yourself to collapse. Run at a speed where you feel as if you're under a minimal amount of pressure. Enjoy the sensations from the body as it copes with the run. Feel your old ticker gently pounding in the chest--letting you know it can handle the effort. Enjoy the feeling of those muscles working below full power, but at great effort all the same.

"If you can hear your feet hitting the ground, it can mean your form has broken down due to fatigue; ease off for a minute to correct your form. Whereas on your steady runs you will have two gears in reserve, on these runs you'll have only one in reserve.

"Your heartrate should be about 85 per cent of your max--just below the highest it gets to in long repetitions. After 15 minutes, ease off for the warmdown.

"This first attempt can be a target for a time trial in due course. Well before time trialing though, try your next sustained run with a different approach.

"A week after the first tempo run, assess the pace you think you can carry through the length of the run. Set out at this pace with the aim of maintaining it. Mile markers can help you judge pace, but

---

The PH of muscle effects the muscle enzyme activity; running at threshold pace teaches your muscles to buffer the acid. In fact, psychological fatigue is likely to make you stop exercise at this intensity before your muscles are actually pooped out.

While production of ATP (energy) is twice as fast using anaerobic pathways, it is only one sixteenth as efficient as aerobic sources. On that basis, perhaps you should restrict yourself to 1/16th of your miles at this pace. However, because most of this running also stimulates better aerobic pathways, you can safely do 10 to 15 percent at this pace. Keep most of the other mileage at 70 percent max HR, plus or minus 5 percent.

unless accurate, they will give a false indication of speed. Don't get too engrossed in the watch. Use it to help judge the pace, not to race against. A set point, about halfway, will be of more use than mile points. You will soon get used to how an even pace run feels.

"Most coaches agree that you will find this comfortably hard pace instinctively with practice...yet the pace will vary week by week according to other things in your life. Don't fight the watch.

"Improvement of your times will come with patience; by a good running style and even pace, rather than by blasting out too fast.

"Find three routes if possible. By alternating clockwise with counter-clockwise, you will only need to run each loop a certain way once every six weeks.

week	route
one	1 -- steady start getting faster
two	2 -- even pace quite fast
three	3 -- steady start getting faster
four	1 -- even pace quite fast
five	2 -- steady start getting faster
six	3 -- even pace quite fast

"One of the routes should include a few hills if possible; the others can be mainly flat. The intention of the tempo run is to prepare you for the stresses of a race...by raising your anaerobic threshold.

*   *   *

Thinking of the six weeks, I was reminded of my vacation. "What shall I do when on holiday?" I asked.

I think he went starry-eyed...if such a thing is possible for him. He said, "So many of your people go on vacation and stop exercising. Vacations are an opportunity to engross your exercise...you don't have those 40 to 60 hour work weeks to distract you. Plan for running to be a natural part of the vacation experience. Running is an excellent way to view a new area.

"If you believe exercise is the healthiest thing you can do for yourself--and as a non-smoker...exercise is--then you should still run five days a week while away from home. Get out the door...the most difficult step sometimes...and run without a clear idea of where you're headed. Of course, it doesn't hurt to check a map first. See some of the sights. Slip in some fartlek, long reps, or 20 minutes of tempo running if the terrain asks you to.

"Plan for your runs. It will do you and the family good to manage without you for an hour a day."

He paused.

"As I mentioned earlier, you're training at Lactate Threshold; you're running in oxygen debt because you can't get enough oxygen into the blood stream to prevent formation of lactic acid. Get away from the family for an hour; let them breath also.

"This tempo portion should comprise no more than 15 percent of your total miles each month.

"In a race, you'll have to take hills in your stride, so practice a relaxed economical way of running these as I described in Part One.

"After a few weeks, you can increase the tempo part to 20 minutes."

When we reached the car, he handed me a piece of paper, saying, "This is a sample three week schedule. Change anything you think is inappropriate for you."

I gave it a quick look, and recognized the sessions we'd talked about, then tucked the paper in my notebook. Here it is:

Note--fast running is preceded by warmup, stretching and strides.

Week one

Sat -- long repetitions, 3 x three mins
Sun -- 40 min steady
Mon -- 40 mins including 20 mins fartlek in woods
Tues -- rest
Wed -- sustained run--even pace, quite fast. See how long you can think about your form before you lose your concentration. Then settle into the realistic mode--think about your form for one minute, twice every mile; one or two aspects per session.
Thurs -- 40 min steady
Fri -- rest (always)

Week two

Sat -- long repetitions, 2 x five mins
Sun -- 40 min steady
Mon -- 100 meter grass area, 20 mins of strides--working on relaxed high knee lift action, jog back recovery.
Tues -- rest
Wed -- sustained run--steady start, getting faster. Should feel fairly hard, but please run smooth.
Thurs -- 40 min steady

Week three

Sat -- 10 x 200 meters, jog back recovery
Sun -- 40 min steady
Mon -- 35 mins including 15 mins fartlek in woods
Tues -- rest
Wed -- long repetitions 2 only x three mins relaxed
Thurs -- 30 mins steady--prior to race or time trial Saturday
"Note the routine...long reps Saturday; short stuff Mondays; rotating the sessions as discussed earlier...you don't have to think about what training to do.
This schedule covers all energy systems--more on that in Part Five.

"The easing off over the second half of week three will freshen your legs for a race. You should race only when your body is used to the increased training load--perhaps after six weeks of the sustained (tempo) training. This happens to be two full cycles of three weeks."

He slipped between the closed door and its frame as I prepared to drive off.

"What about the 10 minute reps?" I asked.

"That's up to you David."

Progress, I thought. Now, here are his racing tips:

"Racing is a high stressed Tempo run...or a day at the park...depending on your attitude.

"At this stage, you can consider any distance from a one mile fun run to a ten kilometer race as far game; the latter should be treated with great respect because it entails running fast for much longer than you are used to.

These last pre-race days are tough!

"Having entered the race, ensure you don't over-train in the final days of preparation. Rest is the most important element over the last four days...hence the reduced load on Wednesday and Thursday in the schedule. Plan your running gear and travel arrangements in advance to avoid last minute worries."

He gave the following guidelines as we neared my house.

"The day before the race--check your race clothing; use your most comfortable shorts and singlet; use good shoes, but not brand new shoes. Racing flats are not obligatory.

"4 hours pre race--last meal...light and easily digested--cereals, toast, scrambled egg whites if the race is in the morning. Try a small but early lunch for an afternoon race. Over-eating can slow you down. It can give a nervous stomach too much to work on.

"2 hours prerace--check in, or collect your race number if necessary. Find a course map and check the route for hills. Drive around if possible. This will help you decide how fast to start. An uphill in the first few hundred meters would suggest a steady start. After the hill, you can stretch out and overtake many who died (ran too fast) going up it. Be cautious of steep downhills early; they demand as much respect as uphills.

"Note the finish area because it's good to know where the last half mile is if that's your planned place to make a move.

"1 hour to go--relax...time for a drink of water if it's hot: if it's not hot...time for a last drink of water. If hot...consider the option of a steady start.

"30 minutes to go--ten mins at easy pace to warmup. Then find somewhere quiet to do your stretching exercises. If you become a club runner, a person doing forty to one hundred miles a week, you will most likely commence the warmup about fifty minutes before the race, by 'jogging' three miles.

"10 mins prerace--a few gentle strides. Do them near to the start. Try not to do them into the wind or up a slope...conserve your energy. Arrange for someone to look after your sweats (if you needed them in the warmup), which you will strip off just a few minutes before the off. If it's a big race with time targets on display, go to a realistic target based on slightly faster than the pace of your sustained runs, but slower than your repetition sessions. No time targets on display--start nearer the back of the field than the front.

"Avoid starting off too fast. The adrenaline flowing makes this hard at times, but it pays dividends if you can achieve it. The legs soon get tired--filling up with the wastes of anaerobic running--resulting in a labored action. It is much better to run at an even pace, though the first and last mile are likely to be faster than the middle section.

"Don't take too much notice of your mile or kilometer times, or splits. Even when the entire course is accurate, many of the intermediate mile signs are wrong. Perhaps the error was because they were put out the morning of the race, based on a car's odometer...or attached to the lamp post nearest the actual point. They may have been moved slightly, or obliterated by Joe public.

"Used as a guide, mile markers are useful; within a hundred meters, most are correct. In a ten kilometer or five mile race, the two or three mile, or five kilometer point may be the most benefit to you. If you can think straight, average your mile times to give a more accurate picture."

Just before I pulled into the garage, my friend said, "see you in about three months," and vanished.

Before this goes to the printer, I'll add two more items.

The first is use of a 400 meter synthetic track for the long repetitions. His preference was for track running to wait until part five. I see no harm in doing say one in four of the long rep sessions at the track from the get-go. Half-miles and miles are the most logical. The main advantage is that wherever you are in the country, most tracks are the same size--give or take two meters (440 yards is about two meters longer than 400 meters). Tracks aid pace judgment because you can check lap splits on each repeat. Note the track etiquette in Part Five.

The second related to quiet. He recommended choosing a time of day when your repetition area has fewest distractions for you. Avoid popular dog walking times; school chuck-out time; busy trails at the weekend. While it's easy to cope with people in a park when you're doing striders--it makes no difference which part of a field you use, or whether it's 100 or 150 meters; you'll just change the distance according to the available area that day.

But for long reps you need tranquillity. Don't let others add to your running stress--after all, running is supposed to decrease life's stress, not add to it.

There's more on racing in Part Six.

As the little alien said at some stage. "Try to race every three weeks or so, at a variety of distances up to ten kilometers. This can include local cross-country, road, and open track races. After a few months, you can consider increasing your training along the lines in the next part. Then attempt longer races, or aim to improve your performance over the short distances. When you feel relaxed at this level...when you're ready for the next challenge...simply turn to Chapter Seven."

FIFTEEN WEEK SCHEDULE

FOR THE

MILITARY or PUBLIC SAFETY FITNESS RUN

Or FOR YOUR LOCAL 5 K RACE

The three mile timed run typical of most military, police, fire and other public safety departments is not a challenge to the recreational runner. But it can be tough on non-runners because they are:
> * in poor overall shape--whether doing the test for the
> first time, or doing their annual re-test
> * or they are somewhat muscle bound in the upper body
> * are often overweight
> * have a tendency toward strength or anaerobic ability

Let's look at these in turn.

* Poor fitness level.
Don't kid yourself. You know how often you've exercised in the last 9 months while flying a desk. Read Part One of the book; then get your gluteal (butt) muscles and the rest of your body out there, and start at the level which won't kill you. Build up to three to four miles, four times a week.

* Naturally muscle bound.
The other aspects of the fitness test will be easy. While getting ready for the run, ease back on any gym or weight work. Use your arms to practice an economical running style.

* Overweight.

Can't get away from this one--fat will slow you down. Decrease your intake by 500 calories a day, and you will lose a pound per week. Second helpings; desserts; second and subsequent beers; regular soda; cheese and mayo on a hamburger...cut some or all for significant calorie savings. The exercise you are doing will help, too. Read the diet chapter.

* Anaerobic or fast twitch muscle fibers.

These can be taught to work with oxygen. The steady runs will educate them to some degree.

After at least a month of steady running you can move onto interval work...a type of training which has been around for decades, yet still isn't used by most militaries.

Run an easy mile. Run twelve times one hundred yards; use meters if you prefer. Do them at a good pace, but not an all out sprint. Jog back between strides to catch your breath. Run a mile to finish off. Next time, do 16 efforts. Alternate these interval sessions with an easy run, so that you run fast twice a week.

After four sessions of 100s, do two sessions of 200s...eight the first time, 12 the second. Then for two more weeks:

Day one...20 x 100 meters

Day two...easy run

Day three...16 x 200 meters

Day four...easy run

For the final six weeks before the test, keep the two easy runs. The third session, do eight 200s plus ten 100s. Do it as a continuous run with 100 easy between efforts.

The first session each week will be long efforts. Your preparation should include 800s, 1200s and 1600s; these are half, three quarter and mile repeats.

Week one. 3 x 800 at 10 seconds per mile faster than target pace for your test. This will increase your maximum oxygen assimilation ability--it'll open up your lungs. Take a good rest between efforts. If it matters to you, this is VO2 maximum pace...check the index.

Week two. 2 x one mile at 10 seconds per mile slower than target pace. Doesn't sound right, does it? Trust the coach--world record breakers train at this pace. It will be your anaerobic threshold pace, which as plenty of Ph.D. types will tell you, helps you to run the test better, despite running the session slower than target pace. Actually, the threshold is closer to 20 seconds slower than test pace, but we want you to keep the session closer to your target pace.

Week three. 3 x 1200 at target pace. This is to check your pace judgment. If you get the first lap wrong, make half the adjustment in the next lap, and get it close to perfect on the last lap. Five minutes should be enough rest.

Week four. 4 x 800 as week one.

Week five. Repeat week two. It's ten to fourteen days till the test. We don't want you to increase training this week. We don't want you to overtrain. Reduce the other session to 6 x 200 plus 6 x 100.

Week six. Two 1200s at target pace.
cut a mile off of each easy run.
Day four do 4 x 200 plus 4 x 100

This avoids over-training...still a common problem of public safety test takers. Rest will give you a 10 percent increase in your potential performance. Meaning you'll begin serious hurting at two and a quarter miles instead of at one and a quarter. You have a greater chance of success if rested.

In case you want to save time by not reading the book, those mile repeats were at about 10 kilometer race pace. People training six days a week will usually do this session at 15 k pace, or another 15 seconds per mile slower--but they'll do four or five of them. Every other session, they will do the four miles as a continuous run.

The 1200s are target pace for pace judgment, confidence and it happens to be 5 k pace--close enough to VO2 max to get most of its benefits.

The 800s are at VO2 maximum, that is, two mile race pace. Heart, lungs and the rest of the circulatory system work at their maximum capacity to achieve this speed. But you'll still go into oxygen debt; wastes from anaerobic work will contribute to your feeling of fatigue.

The ifs...if you had 25 instead of 15 weeks to prepare, you'd use fartlek (Chapter Three) for variety from the 100 and 200s; include some resistance type sessions from Part Four, and some 300-400 efforts borrowed from Part Five.

---

if you've got 15 weeks

At least four weeks of steady running to get the heart ready for:

Five weeks of twice weekly short intervals...100s and 200s; then:

Six weeks of long repetitions.

25 weeks...as above...then

Five weeks of hills or other resistance training once a week.

Three weeks of 400s, alternating with two weeks of 300 meter reps once a week.

And rest up for the test.

ACTIVE SITTING

Back problems. Looking for a new workout. Try sitting on balls.

All baseball teams have to provide the visiting teams with one; Tom Kite used one for his rehab; the Swiss swear by them; hyperactive kids learn better while sitting on them.

"Static sitting (using a chair) is a terrible thing for our bodies," says Joanne Posner-Mayer, a Denver Physical Therapist. "Sitting on a ball keeps your muscles active while you work, bringing your back and torso into alignment. You can do strengthening and stretching exercises; work the postural muscles; build tonic endurance; and do aerobics with the ball."

These sturdy vinyl spheres, made in Italy, are available from 30 to 200 centimeters, or about one to six and a half feet in diameter. Weighing 1-2 pounds, yet withstanding up to 660 pounds, the only risk of breaking them is if you spray the floor with tacks, or leave the ball in a car.

It is important that the ball be sized correctly--so the hips and knees are at 90°. Keeping both feet flat on the floor is advisable at first, though eventually your sense of balance will allow other "poorer posture" options.

Ball $20-35. Exercise video $30 from Ball Dynamics at 1(800) PLA BALL (752-2255)

PART FOUR

GET STRONGER

You get stronger by running more miles; by running more difficult miles, and sessions which improve fitness without running. Combine the three to maintain your enthusiasm and improve. This extra strength and endurance should one day enable you to maintain your current three mile race pace for four and then five or more miles.

Hills are the icing on the cake.

"Later, the strengthening phase will become part of a yearly cycle.
"While hills and other running is best...supplement it with weights and cross-training:
"The best training for running however...is running."

CHAPTER SEVEN

MILES

"The five day a week runner," said the Guru, "will gleam the occasional nugget from the rest of the book. He or she should use anything in the following pages to make running more satisfying. Most of the possible health benefits ARE achieved by the millions of runners who exercise about three hours a week as shown in the first three parts of the book. Though cardiac events will continue to decrease, there is probably no need to increase your training--the closest you get to immortality occurs at about 40 miles per week.

"If you do increase the training load for an extension of your pleasure and faster race times...expect to feel some fatigue and discomfort while looking for progress. Aim to end every run looking forward to your next run. Don't do a particular session to exhaustion. You get better by using a variety of sessions placed closer and closer to each other, rather than by running one particular session to exhaustion. You should feel exhilarated after a session...not dead."

He said those things as a caveat to this part, about mid-way through our Monday discussion.

I'd taken a day off--and with most people working, I had few distractions. I'd done my hundred meter striders after work on Saturday...saving my long repetitions for today. The beach beckoned, and who was I to fight. Low tide was at 10 a.m., a perfect time to run. And the perfect beach. Miles of sand with minimal slope...or camber, as the Guru calls it.

No chance to get over engrossed with the watch either. The restrooms are mobile; the houses too far from the compact sand I use;

so, other than the pier, I have no set points for this session. I won't run fast within a mile of the pier anyway. Once that far away, the leisure walkers of which I used to be a member, have thinned to a dribble. Most people are satisfied with the two mile round trip.

Which is good for me.

Three weeks ago, after ten minutes of running, I'd made a double line, a ditch with my heel, from the ocean edge up about 15 meters. Another five minutes of running and I marked a second line. These were my start and finish points. A pretty arbitrary distance of course, but it took a little over three and a half minutes to do each rep. I did two with the 6-8 mile per hour breeze...which was like running in a vacuum...it felt very hot. The middle rep was into this breeze, which combined with my speed, gave a pleasant cooling rush of air across my body. The middle rep took five seconds longer, but it felt more comfortable.

Today I had my beeper watch set at four minutes. I figure I'll do two going south, then one rep coming north.

A minute into the rest after the first effort--my stride length ahead, and two strides to the right--the Guru materialized. If he had any, his feet would have been in the water.

"How was Kenya?" I said.

"Poor but happy. Chasing worthless assets is not the route to happiness."

"Too true," I said. "That's why I took an extra day off."

The **sarcomere** is the contractile unit of muscle: It's all or nothing. The sarcolemma either fire the sarcomere to contract or it doesn't. The total amount of a muscle's contractive power is dependent upon how many of your sarcomeres contract.

Increased training will boost the number of sarcomeres which can contract at one time, and increase the frequency at which they can contract.

Each sarcomere, or muscle contraction unit, is joined indirectly to bone. The transition of muscle to tendon--the so called Muscle-Tendon unit--is very susceptible to injury.

Increase training sensibly to keep these millions of tiny units intact.

"You're ahead of your time, David. If only you'd realized this before you took on the mortgage."

"I've got that in hand also," I replied. Now here is his advice. "The main problem of upping the mileage, is the increased risk of injury. The knees or calves which can handle 25 miles a week may need help and nursing along to handle 40. Refer to parts 2 and 7 if you have any problems--it may only take one exercise done daily to strengthen a weakness.

"The first stage to getting stronger is a slight increase in mileage. I'm a realist, David, I know people will read the entire book before they've finished the practical for Part One. I suspect many of them will increase their long run to fifty minutes during Part Two, and to sixty minutes in Part Three.

"But you my friend, you don't have the complete book in front of you. You will be going at my pace. This extra running will be the foundation for your future quality work.

"Your options are several: You can add an extra run on your rest days...Tuesday or Friday in my schedule. These runs should feel like rest; they must be very easy. *Polepole* as they say in Swahili."

"*Polepole*? Meaning what?" I said.

"Slowly or strolling. The Kenyans who run 46 minutes for ten miles, do prodigious mileage at eight minutes per mile. Don't be frighted to run slow."

"After running polepole for a period, you can *upesi* the pace again."

"You mean, up the pace, my friend."

"No. *I upesi* means fast. But we aren't doing speedwork in this part, so lets stay with the slow stuff until you get a *nguvu*...strong. Strong muscles and ancillary tissues make for fast running."

"So I *upesi* the pace in the next phase."

"Perfect. Now, in addition to adding Tuesday or Friday runs, you can increase the length of your two steady runs. You can also add a longer warmup and more efforts in your speed sessions. Most likely, you will do all three...just do it in rotation to keep yourself below your injury threshold level. Let your body adjust to the new demands you're putting on it. Aim to increase your running by about one and a half hours per week over three months.

"The first hour of the increase will probably be in the length of your two steady runs. An additional five minutes every fortnight will be enough. One hour should be the norm for these runs, though you should make the Sunday run ten to fifteen minutes longer than the midweek run. Sixty-five and fifty-five minutes would give a good balance.

"This is a long time to be on your feet. If you run too fast, it will wear you out for the rest of the week."

"So I ought to imagine I'm carrying a pole which will keep me running slowly...thus avoiding any inclination to *upesi* the pace."

"Yes." He gave me a strange look. "But stay relaxed. The easy pace can initially be slower than you've been used to--closer to 60 percent max H.R. After a few weeks you'll ease back to your former pace--and maintain that pace for an hour.

"It's the last quarter of these runs which are most important--where you reap the gains. You'll have to use more of your fast-twitch muscle fibers late in the run. You are educating them to become endurance muscle fibers. The longer you run, the more your fast-twitch fibers will come into play.

"You're educating the muscles to use fat as its energy source--but you'll only do this by training at modest speeds--about 70 percent of maximum heartrate. Fat use requires 10 percent extra oxygen compared to sugar use--a factor in hitting the wall in marathons.

"Set a sensible pace and maintain it for the entire run."

"You might want to feed your muscles, too."

"An I.V. straight into the muscle...there's a concept." I said.

"Take fluids orally--" he said "--every fifteen minutes from the time you leave the house. A five percent sugar solution works best...it's absorbed faster. This would be a half-strength sports drink--one day my friend, I swear a company on this planet will get the concentration right!

Fat for fuel--saving the glycogen in the muscles.
You'll need to do some runs without taking in sugared drinks to get the full benefit from these runs. Keep your food handy, of course, in case you come up empty in the later miles.

71

"The weeks you don't increase the length of your steady run, you can increase the amount of the other sessions. The fartlek session can go up to 30 minutes...but again, be conservative with the pace. A few weeks later, add another repetition to your three minute area...or if you're up here on the beach, add a minute or two to the overall amount of the speedwork. Two times one minute, after you've finished your four minute efforts would be good. Then move up to four long reps the next time.

"Work towards fifteen minutes of speed; alternate three times the five minute area with five times the three minute area.

"The 200 hundred meter efforts can be increased to 16 by adding a pair each time you do the session.

"When you've got used to these changes, increase the length of your sustained runs toward 30 minutes.

"Having done some races, you can use an additional measure to guide your speed on these tempo runs."

"Which is?"

"Ten to fifteen seconds slower than 10 k pace. Or 20 to 25 seconds slower than 5 k pace."

"Hold on," I said. "Slower than 10 k pace to improve my 10 k race times."

"Yes." Came the adamant reply. "Tempo runs slower than race pace develop stamina and a sense of pace, which will give you confidence. This comfortably hard pace as we called it in Part Three, raises your lactate threshold--the threshold at which you produce excessive lactic acid, and you will be able to run faster without getting tired."

"You mean my race times will improve?"

"I believe that's what I just said: Comfortably hard equates to about 85 percent of your maximum heart rate. In a few months, you may find 90 percent max to be comfortable. If it feels right, then run at the higher heartrate."

"Overall, this will represent a fifty percent increase on your previous level of training...do bring it in *polepole*. Do bring it in slowly. A sixth run of 20 to 30 minutes will help you get used to the extra load. It will also be a part of the increase.

"Remain patient, David. Runners, like cultures, are not made in a day. Build slowly to allow the body to adapt. Try to increase the training for two weeks, then consolidate, perhaps resting up for a race."

As I started my second indeterminate distance rep, I asked if racing every two weeks was okay.

He said. "Racing that often ought not to be a problem, but don't expect to improve each time."

He saw my puzzled look.

"You can't completely rest up every two weeks. If you did, you'd never have time to do the running you are pretending to rest up from.

"I suggest you take it a little easier before each race...just the last two or three days...cutting down by 25 percent. About every six to eight weeks however, treat a race to a fresher body. Spoil yourself all week by resting or peaking for it.

"Part Six gives you many ways to rest up for a race."

Maybe he realized that I was pacing off him, because he eased back level with me.

"When training by yourself, you can benefit by pretending you have a partner running alongside you, setting the pace. This takes the pressure off of you mentally, allowing you to run as you feel, easing along in his wake if you're going into the wind, or at his side like we are: You might allow him to analyze your form like--"

And as I entered the last 90 seconds of the rep he said...

"--your head has begun to roll side to side a little. Keep the eyes focused on the ground...about twenty-five meters ahead. That's it. That's the best position for your head...but you should allow your eyes to wander to the periphery.

"Relax your fists. You need to hold your fingers very lightly curled--slightly flexed as your medical people would say--a neutral, no muscular effort position. A clenched fist uses energy; a clenched fist transfers its stress to the shoulders...which also tighten. Save all the energy for your legs.

"I'm only going to tell you those two things about your form to-day--I'd like you to think about both during your last rep. Then in future sessions we'll work on other aspects of your style."

And so we did. But this chapter is about strength--the rest of my defective form, and other people's defects, were covered in Part Two.

Jack Daniels on Anaerobic Threshold.

Call them what you will--Fast Continuous Runs, Sustained Runs, Tempo Runs, or Cruise Intervals...but call them often--train at anaerobic threshold (A.T.) twice a week--it packs a punch to help you race faster.

A.T. is the pace or intensity beyond which blood lactate concentration increases dramatically, due to your body's inability to supply all its oxygen needs. As you get fitter, your red line rises from about 80 percent of maximum heartrate to 90-95 percent.

Physiologically, threshold training teaches muscle cells to use more oxygen--less lactate is produced. Your body also becomes better at clearing lactate: Race day red line speed rises.

How long? 20-25 minutes at 80-90 percent of max heartrate--or...divide into long reps.

This pace will be...comfortably hard--a controlled pace--you'll need to stay focused.

Maintain the effort level...not the speed. Your speed may vary according to conditions.

Do them on good trails, road, treadmill, or the track.

Too fast is no better than too slow. 10 k pace is 90-92 percent of max heartrate for most...it's above the red line. 10 seconds per mile slower, or 15 k to 10 mile pace is about 86 percent of max, and probably the best pace to do these runs.

Tempo:

* Improves concentration...you can't just float; so pay attention to form.

* The run is controlled...heartrate and perceived exertion set your pace.

* Difficult to overtrain...you are at pace for twenty minutes, as determined by heartrate, not by your, or a training partner's desire to run a definite speed...don't race it.

---

*Can be used even when fatigued...your threshold pace may be slower.

Endure threshold's mild discomfort at least weekly.

Jack Daniels, Ph.D. Exercise Physiologist, coach of Cortland State's successful cross-country team. The person who coined the phrase "cruise intervals," running long reps, at moderate intensity, to improve anaerobic threshold.

CHAPTER EIGHT

TOUGHER MILES--RESISTANCE TRAINING

"Once you're used to the extra mileage, it will be time to make some of the miles harder. This involves the introduction of resistance training: Running on terrain that is strenuous if you try to maintain the same pace--such as hills, mud, or running repetitions into the wind. The sand dunes to your left are superb, but deep sand running above the high tide point is effective too.

"Running in mud is not tough if you simply maintain the same effort level. You will run slower at the same effort level, yet your legs will get stronger. But first the hills.

"The slow runs, at 70-80 per cent of your maximum heart rate will develop your aerobic base or ability some more; but these runs do little to develop the neurological pathways needed for fast running. You need to do some fast running also. Hill repeats are a great way to do your speedwork.

"You already cope with hills within training runs, so the first type of resistance training is to augment the hilly circuit once a fortnight with hill repetitions. Find a hill which is reasonably steep, but still runable...three to four degrees is good, but steeper may give you faster rewards. You will need 100 to 400 meters of hill for these sessions.

"For this session, ignore the efficient way of running hills. Hill reps require a different action...an exaggerated running action; though inefficient in a race, it's perfect for our present purposes. Use a section of about 100 meters for your first session.

"After a normal warmup, you can start the first of about ten repetitions. Run up the hill with a high knee lift and sprinters type arm action. The legs should not be going too fast...the emphasis is on lifting the knees higher than in normal runs...but landing softly. Land closer to your toes than the heel of the foot...midfoot is ideal. You will run more like a sprinter in these sessions than at any other time.

"On alternate reps, shorten and quicken the stride. One rep for strength and speed; one rep for speed and strength.

"Pick a focal point close to the top of the hill, much further than your usual 25 meters ahead. This helps to prevent you leaning forward. You need to be perpendicular to the surface in hill repeats.

"Walk down the hill for recovery and repeat the run. When you feel tired, or cannot fully recover in the rest period, stop. This becomes the target number for future sessions.

"Hold back on the first session. This type of training puts extra stress on the Achilles tendon and calf muscles. The quadriceps may also ache a little after, as may the back...gentle stretching should clear these aches.

"The second time you do hills, try about eight repetitions of 200 meters. The third time, try five at up to 400 meters.

Treat them with respect. Increase the amount and grade gradually. Take care of the Achilles. Hills are not about suffering. The entire session should be no harder than a tempo run.

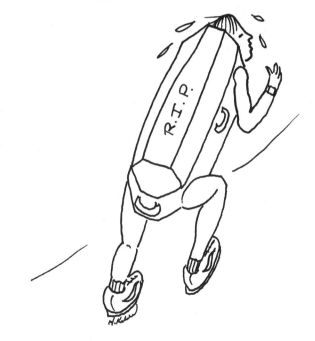

He dies going up the hill.

"With the 400s, finish the rep just over the top of the hill--practice accelerating as the gradient decreases. You can also practice this on your long or tempo runs when you're feeling fresh...pick the pace up by ten seconds a mile for 20 strides before settling back to your regular speed.

"As you get used to hill repetitions, you can increase the quantity of reps and the speed. Always aim to run hills faster than in a race...using the rather unusual running actions described above.

"The number of repetitions is up to you, David, but the overall effort involved should be no harder than a session of long repetitions would be. You may find 25 of the short section of hill is about right; 10 or 12 of the long section may be its equivalent. These are only targets for the long term. For now, build the session up until it lasts thirty minutes--including the recovery sections. Aim to do 10 minutes of reps.

"As you get fitter, the recovery can become a jog...thus reducing the resting percentage. But land gently on the way down.

"A fun way for you to do hills is to split it into sections. Stride up the first section of say 150 meters--jog or walk up for thirty to sixty seconds--then run the second section. You will have a longer recovery going back to the start to repeat the reps in pairs or triples. You might run six sets of two efforts in a session.

"When you can handle hills well in training, they will seldom be a problem in races. In a race or tempo run, always run them with economy...using a low knee lift and short but fairly rapid stride. Tuck in behind someone, get 'pulled' up the hill, then find that other gear you've been practicing as you accelerate over the top.

"Hills will improve your racing speed by building strength in the quads, hamstrings, buttocks, calves and back. It will also correct your form--you can't run hills well with bad form. Hills increase your anaerobic efficiency. Bigger quads result in fewer knee injuries. Hill reps cause few injuries...there is much less shock per stride."

"Enjoy the hill David. Always enjoy the hill. Don't fight it...work with it.

"Doing a lot of distance can decrease your stride length. Even though you will be doing repetitions, 200s etc. the hills will open your stride. Just remember to exaggerate the knee lift and the arm swing, while pushing off with the toes and calf muscles.

Hills for strength.

Must be run properly with an exaggerated knee lift for the best effect.

Types of hill: short, medium and long. Seek a variety, otherwise you become brilliant at one hill, but rarely see "your" hill in a race.
* Split the hill into sections for short recovery sessions.
* Mud and sand hills for added resistance and heavy shoes.
* Accelerate over the top to practice race situation.
* Technique for hills in a race--relax... then accelerate.

Hills increase muscle elasticity and the range of motion at the foot and ankle--vital to you running faster.

Run on the softest surface you can find--it reduces the long term joint wear and tear; reduces bone and muscle injuries in the short to medium term.

The least friendly surfaces are concrete, to asphalt, to dirt, to grass, to sand, in that order.

"In several ways, you do resistance training every time you run. For instance, the action of moving through the air takes effort. You've found out how much easier it is running with a slight breeze behind you? How much effort do you save when running just behind someone in a race? Not much, surely. The one second you gain for every 400 meters may not sound huge...but it's worth 25 seconds in a ten kilometer race. The five seconds faster which you ran with the wind on your last repetition session, would be worth fifty seconds at 10 k.

"However, we are not after easier running. We aspire to make a given session harder. At this stage, you'll get more benefit from running three hard miles into the wind than by running with the wind.

"By running into the wind, you can make a session of one or two hundred meter strides harder also...and gain more fitness from it.

"I introduced this type of running in Part Two. Now you can extend it to make a full session rather than as part of one. It's wonderful to do a whole session into the wind--a special high results from beating the elements. You might do the occasional stride with the wind to relax you both physically and mentally though. One in four, where you simply run at near maximum speed with very little effort, will do wonders for the psyche...and for your concentration in the rest of the session.

"When running with the wind, you should of course work on your style. Are the knees up high enough to give you a full stride? Are the calves and foot hugging the hamstrings and butt as described in Part Two...to reduce the pendulum swing? Are you using your ankles and calves to the limit? Do your shoulders roll because you don't use the arms much?

*   *   *

"The third type of resistance running may require some effort to find...particularly for the keen road runner. It requires a soft surface (even a heat wave won't make the road very soft). Sand, dirt, mud, snow or soggy grass work well. All these terrains require you to make more effort to run at a certain speed compared to a firm surface."

The Triple Benefit.

1/ The surface "gives" therefore you have to work harder at push-off.

2/ The feet will have to be lifted above the surface before the real stride takes place, the knee lift is therefore higher--otherwise you would fall.

3/ Wet or muddy shoes require still more effort to raise.

The result is less pounding on the body because you are running on soft terrain, and increased leg-muscle strength giving greater speed potential.

"Cross-country racing is perhaps the best way to find this type of training. Unfortunately, many courses are mainly flat, dry recreation areas--they have great speed potential, but few strength building attributes. However, on the off chance that you come across a real cross-country course, part of your training for these races should include various muddy or other terrain to build up strength and get you used to uneven surfaces.

"Most sessions involving repetitions can be done in a muddy area--part of a favorite course--sections of a muddy lane or the edge

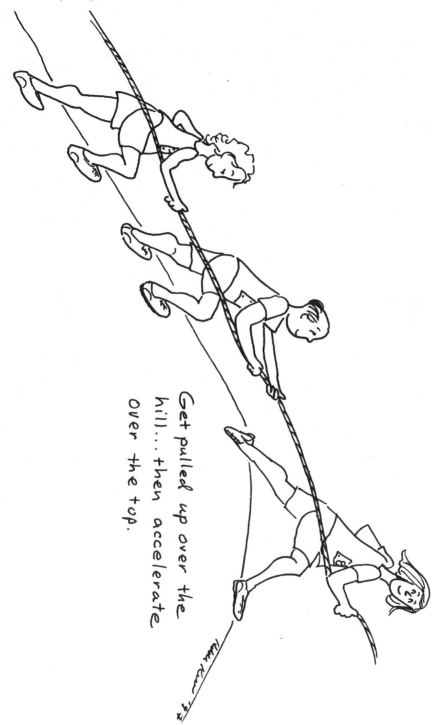

Get pulled up over the hill...then accelerate over the top.

of a plowed field, for instance--all will make you work harder. A low lying area which floods can come into its own at certain times of the year--take the opportunity when it arrives. Know where the ditches are though. Fartlek is a good mud session too--steady running on the firm parts, efforts of fifty meters upwards where it's soft.

"Seek out mud during part of at least half of your runs. One hundred yards of mud will keep you working for several more hundreds as the mud comes off, or for the rest of the run if you are lucky.

"If you have the good fortune to live close to oil tanker washout areas--"

"You mean where tankers illegally clean their tanks out with sea water?"

"Illegal eh. Oh well, until these people grow a conscience, we'll take advantage of the oily beaches they produce. During fartlek or rep sessions the oily substance will grip your shoes, making them heavier; every grain of sand will be heavier. These subtle slicks are another great training tool for you.

"Snow provides other chances of improving strength while creating a break from the normal routine. Four to eight inches of un-trampled snow is an excellent, if short term training area. Once it has been pushed down and had a frost, it becomes treacherous and your enemy. But when the thaw sets in, the slushy area can again be used for training.

"You can run through a foot or so with the high knee lift of a hill session. Do efforts as you feel inclined, with easy running through the lightly covered sections. Or do a more formal session of timed repetitions if that's what you feel like. Many people prefer a relaxed approach--not too hard because it is often very cold--just lift the knees up for thirty to sixty seconds as you go through the part of the snow which appeals to you. Be prepared to fall flat on your face as you step into the occasional deeper part. Just roll with it and play.

"Snowshoe running gives a double bonus:
The shoes are heavier, and
The surface gives...reducing the pounding.
Use it for aerobic base work, plus some bounding for strength and power when conditions allow.
Use ski poles if you want an upper body session at the same time.

"You can try boots in snow conditions--for extra grip and to make the legs work still harder. Some runners use them throughout the year to maintain strength. If you find enough mud, snow and hills, you may not need boots in your training--but do consider them. If worn only once a week for an easy run, friends who keep mainly to the roads would gain significant benefit from boots. Boots keep your feet warm too.

"Inclement weather can get out of the routine of doing a similar session on a certain day each week. Instead of long reps every Tuesday, you might do snow running or fartleks where you go hard into the wind...then rest as you run easily down a sheltered street.

"For the few weeks when much of the country has bad weather, treat every day you can do some running as a bonus. Be prepared to miss days when conditions are at the worst. Most days, you will only need to reduce the session a little, perhaps to two-thirds of your normal run to avoid the chilling danger of being out too long. Keep to fartlek where the surface allows you to run fast, or steady runs. Refer to Parts One and Six for advice on keeping warm."

"These harder miles will make you stronger. Your race times will improve provided you remain injury free and give yourself sufficient rest.

"Resistance running on soft terrain has a positive affect on joints and tendons. There is less wear and tear. You avoid repetitive use syndrome because each footstrike is a bit different. This gives a more equal use of the joint surfaces.

"Many coaches believe the body wears out slower when training on soft terrain than it does on hard surfaces. This could be a mali-

---

"I once saw an article about addiction to exercise in a Sunday magazine. It said if you exercised in atrocious weather, you were probably addicted. The picture next to the article showed a well dressed runner cruising through the woods. Yes, there was snow on the ground, but it was not snowing. It looked as if her legs had only one layer of lycra. It was not cold enough for her to cover her face, and it was warm enough that she did not wear gloves.
A gorgeous winter day: Perfect for a run."

cious rumor put about by the cross-country lovers. Or perhaps you should try an experiment, David: One Saturday, with the pulse at 85 % of max, run five times three minutes on a road circuit. Record how you felt afterwards. Give your aching muscles a score on a one-to-ten basis. Score your aches Saturday evening and Sunday before, during and after your long run. The maximum score would be fifty.

"The following Saturday, do a similar session on a muddy circuit--or at this beach--same time, same number of repetitions, same pulse target. The two sessions should have taken a similar amount of effort as the pulse target was the same...but the muddy section covered will be a little shorter. Now--compare the feeling of tiredness the second week. The main difference will be in how you feel during the Sunday run that follows this session."

Remembering my Part Two speedwork...he winked at me.

"The shin muscles are renowned for liking the soft surface."

Then he discussed one of his favorite coaching debates.

"Some people say run on the pavement uphill to get better traction; then run downhill on a soft shoulder where possible, or in the ditch if safe to do so...for shock absorption."

"I know how keen you are on absorbing shock," I said.

"Yes...but I'll deal with the uphill part first.

"The purpose of running hills is to make you stronger. The softer the surface, the harder you will have to work...you'll get still stronger."

"So do hill repeats up a muddy track, or soft grass," I said.

"Indeed you should. Wearing appropriate shoes, run the hill reps on the softest terrain you can find. Sand-dunes are the ultimate.

"Strides in the deep sand above high tide are useful, too. The deep sand makes you adjust your position on every stride--you get a whole body workout.   "Make the hills hard to run.

"Time to be controversial," he said.

"Not you, surely," I mocked.

He gave me a knowing look. "Run on a hard surface downhill. Not all the time. I don't want runners to take this the wrong way. Most of the time soft is best...we all know why. But once a week, run on the hard surface to encourage bone growth. If you don't run on asphalt once in a while, you may feel awkward in road races.

"On steep hills, use a switchback path to lesson the load going down. Consider switchbacks going up; consider also, running straight up the steepest part. Be aware of potential Achilles problems...ease into the session."

"Running hilly loops make you work both of the calf muscles. The gastrocnemius dominates uphill, whereas the soleus comes into its own during downhill running.

"When running on hard surfaces, you are constantly 'taking something out of the body;' mileage done on a soft surfaces usually 'puts something in.' The more of these good miles you deposit, the more you have to draw upon in races.

"Look at Part Six for bounding."

After three months, your schedule will look similar to:

Week One

Sat--3 x 5 or 5 x 3 mins hard, alternate the surface when soft terrain is available. Gradually reduce the rest period.

Sun--Long easy run of about 70 mins if you want to race up to ten miles. Alternate with 85 to 90 mins if you intend to race 20 kilometers or half-marathon.

Mon--45 mins. Include 30 mins of fartlek--efforts up hills and through mud if available.

Tues--A recovery run--gentle 20 to 30 mins.

Wed--After a warm up, sustained run of 30 mins, steady start, increasing the pace during the course of the run.

Thurs--The second long run--about 55 to 60 mins--just a little faster than Sunday's pace, but much slower than yesterdays.

Fri--The constant; it is always rest--which can be an easy run

Week Two

Sat --30 mins of 100 meter efforts--some into the wind, some with the wind.

Sun--Long run as last week but a different route.

Mon--Sustained run--even pace for about 35 mins including a few hills which can be taken as if in a race. (Relaxed up the hill, pick the pace up over the top).

Tues--Recovery rest or easy run.

Wed--Long repetitions as above.

Thurs--Steady run up to 55 mins.

Week Three
Sat--Low key race or a time trial over a favorite route of four to six miles.
Sun --Long run.
Mon --Easy 20 to 30 mins.
Tues--Hill session, building up the number of reps as described in this chapter.
Wed--Long run 55 to 60 mins.
Thurs--Long repetitions as above.

Week Four
Sat --16 x 200 meters pretty fast--reduce the recovery over the months.
Sun --Long run, but 10 mins shorter than usual.
Mon--Sustained run of 25 mins--no hills, steady start, building to a good finish but well within yourself.
Tues--Rest or 20 mins easy.
Wed--Long repetitions, either 2 x five mins at same speed as two weeks ago; or 3 x three min repetitions, the first 10 seconds slower than usual, the second at normal speed and the third with a slightly faster second half. As on Monday, run well within yourself.
Thurs--Steady relaxed run up to 45 mins ready to race Saturday or Sunday.

This is the base schedule for the rest of the book. Parts Five, Six and Nine sessions are slotted in as appropriate.

If you must do the same type of session (say) every Tuesday, make the session more interesting by varying what you do the day before. Cruising the four mile tempo is easy after a gentle fartlek session, but what about the day after 5 x 1,000 meters...or hill repeats?

Don't lose sight of legspeed during this increased mileage phase. Maintain, or improve legspeed with the following from Jack Daniels, Ph.D. Exercise Physiologist and coach .

Stride Frequency

The best rate is between 90 and 95 steps with each foot per minute for most runners.

Long strides can cause great impact on each step...at best it slows you down; at its worst it increases injury risk.

Fortunately, stride length is related to stride frequency. Increase the frequency to 90 plus per minute and the stride has little choice but to decrease. Overstriding is cured.

The Nuts and Bolts.

At a track, count your strides for a minute; repeat several times to get an accurate figure.

Increase stride rate with:

 * Rapid, short strides for 30-60 seconds. Set the watch beeper and count the footfalls.

 * After a few weeks....Long reps at high legspeed. Count them each minute; increase cadence if you are below 90 a minute. Shorten the stride length to ensure the workout is manageable for the rest of the body.

 * Hill reps. A short hill. 100 meters at fast leg action going up.

 * A gentle grass hill. Stride down at rapid cadence for 200 meters at a time.

 * Then...All runs. Use rapid, shorter strides.

Stride rate already in the 90s...land light, with relaxed steps. Imagine running on eggs; step on them, but immediately push off, without breaking any..

It shouldn't be long before your body gets used to the speedier stride. As you gain in strength, most of your old stride length will return...but your body should be ready for it. A forty-five minute 10 k runner can improve by one minute if stride rate increases from 90 to 92 per minute.

CHAPTER NINE

CROSS-TRAINING
(Training when you are angry ?)

"You can improve leg strength without running. I mentioned swimming and bicycle riding in part one to get the body in shape before running. They are also an aid to extra strength without the wear and tear effects of landing on the ground thousands of times in each run.

"In addition, stair climbing, rowing and the sundry ski machine family can give you a useful workout. Cross-country skiing--which works the buttock muscles too much for my liking--so don't overdo it--and snow shoe running are a sub-specialty of course. Most of the machines enable you to exercise with less body weight on the legs...and in all except a poorly aligned machine...less pounding on the joints.

"Cycling and stair climbing will build up the muscles required for running hills. By choosing an easier gear on the bike, or less resistance on the stair climber, you can improve your leg speed. Beware of knee problems with the stair-climbers; many an orthopods business increased when these machines became popular. Swimming enables you to improve your cardiovascular efficiency while exercising at a low work rate. Adjust your breathing to say six or eight strokes at a time."

"How often should I do this cross-training?"
"Once a week is insufficient for each individual type of exercise. For instance, if you choose to swim every Wednesday, you'd find it difficult because your muscles never build up enough for it. Do it often enough so the cross-training exercise is not unusual or hard on

you. Every four to five days will work. Six or seven sessions a month at each of two exercises for 20 minutes each."

I felt perplexed. "But that's another 14 sessions a month."

"There you go...Homo Sapien thinking again. You won't need to add extra sessions. You just lengthen some of them."

"I have my emergency quarter in my shorts. I'll buy."

"I recommend you do two exercises--one should involve significant arm work."

"Cycling and stairs are strictly the legs aren't they?"

"You got it. Rowing, ski machines and swimming use the arms more."

"So I need one from each group?"

"And after an easy 20 to 30 minute run...do 10 minutes at both exercises."

"Is there any point in exercising for ten minutes?"

"That is the point."

"Huh."

"Ten minutes at low intensity will be as enchanting as spring. When you're ready to increase the cross-training to 20 minutes for each exercise, go ahead.

Advantages of Biking

Increased flexibility

Overall conditioning will improve...with minimal jarring on the legs

Decreased incidence of injuries

Move faster--good on hot windless days

Build muscles for running hills

Used properly, you give the legs a rest--do it closer to 60 than 80 percent of maximum heartrate.

Fast leg turnover

Helps people predisposed to knee injuries, especially the wide pelvis portion of your people

Maintains, or if you have been inactive, restores strength lost through aging

"The mistake many runners make is in replacing running with this cross-training. Unless you are doing over 50 miles a week, replacing is sheer folly. You need the physiologic, the psychomotor practice of running to improve your running. Substituting cross-training won't cut it. There is also the problem of the heart over-taking the body."

"What do you mean."

"Cross-training increases your cardiac ability--tempting you to run too fast. Your joints and running muscles may not be ready for this running stress. The body may break down. Besides, I didn't see a single stair climber or ski machine being used by the Kenyans.

How to bike

Look and plan ahead to avoid accidents and red lights...slow early...spin while approaching

Always stop at red lights and stop signs; they are for your safety.

Roll your head a few times every 15 minutes to avoid a crook or aching neck

Use a low gear and fast cadence

Make knees track up and down; do not splay out

Pull up and push down on the pedals

Ride with a recreational cycling group for your longer rides; make it a social session once a month.

When you want a hard workout

* attack the hills...the entire hill, or as one to two minute spurts with cruising up in between

* Anaerobic threshold--do 5 to10 minute efforts at 2-4 miles per hour faster than your steady ride pace; or 80-90 percent of maximum heartrate.

* VO2 Max--do 1-2 minute efforts at 95 percent max heartrate.

Pedal (freewheel with no resistance) when going downhill to flush wastes out of the muscles, while bringing in fuel. Coasting downhills without moving your legs will leave you stiff when you try to start peddling at the base of the hill.

"That said, if a four day week runner commenced two sessions a week of say...15 minutes rowing, stair climbing, biking and swimming...his or her strength and endurance would clearly increase. Unless this extra exercise constituted over-training for the individual...race times would improve also...at least compared to remaining inactive on those two days.

"They will make even more progress if they do a half-hour run, followed by two of the other exercises. The choice depends on how much a person enjoys running. It's nice to exercise in the gym occasionally--with other people around you--but you can do all your runs with people if you feel that particular desire. The trouble is, you end up spending more time arranging to meet these people than is worth the effort. If running with other people fits your schedule, don't avoid it...but don't press for constant companions either. You need to do your own running remember."

"I have company twice a week."

"Sounds good. You'll appreciate company in the next phase...but lets get back to cross-training."

"Okay," I said. "How is non-running training best used?"

"Cross-training is best used when you have nearly reached your limit with running. That may be at four days a week, or at 70 miles a week.

"The exception is cycling. An hour or so of biking at good leg cadence will build the quads while stretching the hamstrings. Done twice a week, this will stabilize the knee.

"Otherwise, to make you a stronger runner, cross-training is over-rated. To get you fit or healthy enough for running as in Part One, or to maintain your fitness, it does wonders."

"I recall what you said an overweight person might want to do before running in Part One. But how about the maintaining fitness angle?"

"There's been a whole load of cutsey studies done (in your galaxy and mine), attempting to show fitness can be maintained by cross-training. Most are done by people for higher degrees. Like those higher degrees, most are pointless. They follow few runners for a minimal number of weeks.

"It doesn't take a triple digit IQ to realize that someone can maintain 90 per cent of his fitness for a few weeks, by running hard

91

three times a week; or by running once and cross-training twice. The main reason these people stay fit is because of all the rest they are getting. The extended rest allows the previous 6, or 8 or 12 months training to take effect."

"You feel pretty strong about this don't you."

"Yes I do. I've yet to see a study lasting long enough to make meaningful conclusions."

He moved on to a related topic.

"Weight training should be considered as the frosting for building strength. Though hill repeats are more specific to running than weight training for the lower legs--running posture and muscle co-ordination is hard to replicate off the hill--I'll still tell you about weight training.

"For those who contemplate racing distances below 5,000 meters, it's an essential ingredient of the schedule. Many runners move up in distance because they lack speed--yet some of these people would have developed good speed if they had done weight training in the first place. Speed, you see, is dependent upon strength.

"Calisthenic exercises...using your own weight, pull-ups, push-ups and sit-ups, are a good start. Do two sets of 10-12, plus back-extensions, bench press and neck exercises. Do hamstring curls and leg extensions of course. Do calf raises with straight and bent knees. Add the lunges and other exercises in that nice Volleyball essay of yours (Part Ten). Use free weights because you'll use many muscles to keep yourself balanced. Machines are more specific; they allow you to build the complementary muscles. Do many reps with light weights.

"When lifting free weights with a barbell, stand with a half inch weight or other item under the heels. This will help you avoid falling."

"What are the advantages of weight training?" I asked.

"By working the major muscle groups...legs, hips, back, arms and shoulder, you will decrease tiredness at the end of races--because your arms are not tired, your legs won't slow down. It will aid you in the final sprint; it will also enable you to run faster in the first 98 percent of the race. But don't try to build bulk; bulk will slow you down.

"You can't turn fat into muscle; you can't create muscle. You can only make the muscles you have grow and thicken.

"People may have noticed their muscles decreased in size during Part One. This was because they were losing the fat layered within a muscle group. After losing some weight, the muscles became more defined. Now they may appear to be blossoming into the muscles of a person's youth.

"Muscle fibers never disappear from your body, but they do get weaker as you age. They atrophy from non-use. Weight training will help you maintain a higher percentage of your potential strength in later life...especially the fast-twitch fibers. Strong muscles decrease your risk of injury by stabilizing the joints.

"One of the simplest exercises," he said, "is to stand with your feet 18 inches apart. Hold a small--to decrease air resistance--one pound weight in each hand. Move the arms forward and backward in a running action. Speed it up until your arms are at sprinting speed...then ease off. Do four sets of 30 seconds, three times a week, and see what happens."

"Remember also--weight training, used along with exercise machines, is a good way to get out of the elements in winter.

You don't need bulk. Use something under your heels to help you balance.

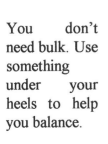

The pool...or other body of water.

"Swimming--backstroke and freestyle (front crawl) are probably best because butterfly puts too much emphasis on the arms, and breaststroke can cause knee problems for runners. Some runners take a while to develop arm strength for swimming, yet all you need do is float on your back and kick with the legs. Use the arms at slow cadence; strength will come. You also need to cultivate a feel for water--by swimming with good mechanics. Get some coaching early.

"Some people find running mile after mile boring, others find swimming length after length boring. No scenery, no gentle hill climbs--but then again no cars or dogs to bother you. By alternating back and front crawl, the speed and the amount of strokes in each breathing cycle, relaxation and form, 40 minutes in a pool will soon pass. The first and last few minutes will be easy as a warmup; the real work is done in the middle half an hour. To avoid bumping into people, check with pool staff for lap swim times.

"You can also run in the pool. Some people like the relaxation of a flotation device around the waist; others argue you can work harder without.

"Homo Sapiens is a strange beast. Immersing yourself in water lowers the heartrate. Your maximum exercise heartrate is therefore lower...by 5 to 10 percent. One way to get over this, to make your pool sessions more worthwhile, is to exercise at 5 k effort level. Do 5 to 10 times one to two minutes of swimming or running, or both, for

Pool running is an excellent choice:

* on hotter than normal days--substitute the pool, or do part of the session there.
* for second runs in a day;
* for the session following a particularly hard run,
* or after one done on a harder surface than normal,
* and especially after a grueling race.
* for putting your joints through a fuller range of motion than when on land,
* and, during injury recovery--hips and ankles especially.

94

a great workout. Start with 5 at one minute--perhaps taking two minutes rest. Increase the frequency and duration until the total at 5 k effort moves up towards 20 minutes.

"The resistance from pushing aside water while you run matches the energy you save by being non weight-bearing. Forty wet minutes equate well to forty dry ones. However, the calves are underused in the pool; do a couple sets of weights for them, and for the shin muscles.

Bicycling

"Cycling requires more planning than pool sessions. You can use the machines at your sports center or gym, preferably in conjunction with circuit or weight training. The other options are an exercise bike of your own, or high clouds forbid, you could buy a road or mountain bike.

"An exercise bike needs an even spread of effort on each pedal revolution. It needs a tension adjuster so the load can be increased. You runners require a tension at which a fast leg speed can be maintained--90 to 100 a minute, for a longish period--thus developing cardiovascular efficiency and endurance...rather than the bulk which a lower cadence would produce.

"A road or trail bike need not be expensive--runners' needs are less than a competitive cyclist's. Fact is, a heavier bike will allow you to achieve the desired heartrate at lower speeds, and possibly be safer. But consider the style of brakes...stopping distance varies.

"You only need ten gears--cost is the same as 'top of the range' training shoes, (or two pairs of most runners' shoes). The only other equipment required are cycling shorts and additional protection for when you fall off. How much is up to you, suffice to say that speeds can be high. Grit in gloves is better than grit in your skin.

"A helmet to protect your noggin is a must.

"In winter, the bike can be used on an indoor cycle trainer, thereby avoiding the cold (an even bigger problem than when running, due to the speed of air flowing across your body) and wind.

"Outside, traffic can be a problem. Look well ahead to avoid the prates (fools), who possess a driver's license. By timing your arrival for the right moment, stopping at traffic lights can be minimized. On wide, safer streets, they also allow for interval training. Take note of the smog essay in Part Ten.

"Wear intelligent (I mean bright) clothes, and treat vehicles for what they are...dangerous weapons which kill tens of thousands each year....Treat pedestrians as a hazard too, and you should not go far wrong.

"Cycling is good for developing the muscles that work opposite the main running muscles. These fighting fiends (antagonists) tend to be weak and can tear as a result. With cycling, these muscles, like you, become less tense and can therefore stretch more. You improve flexibility and decrease the risk of injury. You may be surprised at how far you need to raise the saddle over the first few weeks, as your hamstrings go back to something like their full length."

"The first time you do this phase will take at least three months. The next part is in some ways easier. I think hill sessions are the hardest form of training...though don't think for one moment there aren't other challenging sessions ahead.

Before leaving he said. "Once you've built up your total training time beyond five hours, with sufficient mileage to be able to run up to a half marathon race, you should return to getting something extra out of it. More speed will enable you to feel greater relaxation in the early stages of a race. This will lead to a further improvement in your times. But do this strength work first. When I see you are ready, I'll meet you to introduce Part Five."

"Every month should contain some type of strength training. Even racing months. If your winter had you doing hills every ten days or so, you should still do them every 21 days in the racing season. Two-thirds of your winter session at faster speed is a fine way to prep for a race...but not in the seven days before the *most* important race."

The leg press has many uses. A low foot position allows you to work the calves. Straight legs for the gastroc, bent legs for the soleus.

The higher foot position is more conventional, and allows you to work most of the bulky leg muscles. Use slow movement so you work the muscles when the weights are returning to the starting point--you don't just train while pushing your legs out straight. Keep knee flexion to 90 degrees or less, to avoid pressuring that joint.

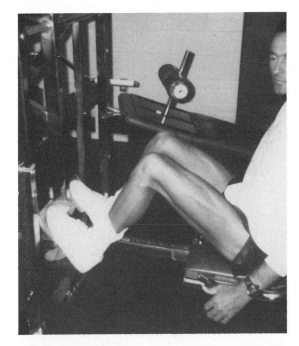

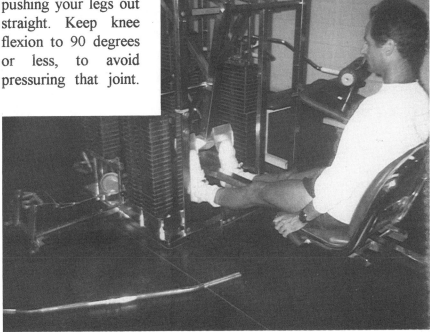

Don't forget our favorite muscles--the **iliosoas.** Three or four times a week, stand by a support and swing your leg forward to thigh height. Then swing it behind you to about 45 degrees. Some call this the hip pendulum swing. It's a good injury avoidance exercise; it builds those flexors and the butt muscles. Be rhythmic, don't roll, and keep the knee bent at about 90 degrees. The supporting leg will need to be straight.

THE ZEN FACTOR

You don't have to sit under a tree for days to become enlightened like Buddha did, though restful days might do certain runners some good.

Avoid endless suffering in life by eradicating all cravings. Don't crave a new personal record too much; just let it come of its own accord as you enjoy running different types of sessions, while avoiding injuries in the long term.

Contemplate your training from time to time - adjust it where necessary and enjoy your lifetime activity. Above all, remember the four noble truths of Buddhism.

1. Run long - twice your normal, once every 10-14 days.

2. Run quite fast, but be able to talk in two - three word sentences. Run at this speed for several long efforts totaling 15 minutes or more; or for 20 minutes continuously.

3. Run many fast but efficient strides on grass, sand and up hills to improve your style. Find out the best arm movement, back-kick and knee-lift for YOU. Practice different stride frequencies. Then practice the same art doing one session a month of 300s, of 400s and of 600s on the track.

4. Rest before and after races. This can involve doing 10 x 300 three days pre race instead of your usual 15 reps.; or running an easy 15 miler the day after a 10 k race.

PART FIVE

TIMED FAST RUNNING

BETTER KNOWN AS INTERVAL TRAINING

The emphasis of Part Four was again on strength--building a base from which to develop additional speed and endurance. This phase will take your speed sessions which you did in Parts Two and Three to a much higher level, resulting in substantial improvements to your running economy.

Pleasure Versus Pain

"Your planet's coaches are years removed from the 'no pain no gain' philosophy: yet you still need a balance between comfortable running and moderately stressing runs.

90 percent of your miles must be a joy, including most of the interval session.

The first quarter of your reps will be easy. The last 100 or the next few reps will feel difficult. About halfway through, and half of each rep feels tough...you'll have a mental battle to keep going at times. The final quarter of your reps may seem hard once you've done 25 % of the rep, but these are the ones which will make you stronger.

Get through the session by thinking about your form on each rep; do each rep at appropriate pace--a pace which allows you to run at least adequately, or perhaps well, the next day.

On long runs, you should not feel tired until the last few miles. You may have an occasional bad patch, but most of it should be enjoyable."

CHAPTER TEN

INTERVAL BASICS

Although he'd watched me on a weekly basis to check my progress, it was several months before I saw the Guru again. I was practicing tennis, doing lunges and flexibility stuff when he arrived to let me know it was time for the next phase.

"The speedwork introduced in Part Two," he said, "is a form of interval training. Interval training involves a series of efforts with a rest period--the interval--which develops speed, a good running action and endurance at the same time. So far, most of it has been in a relaxed form such as fartlek or strides of up to 200 meters on grass or road. We shall now turn our attention to an, at times, more stressful type of interval work involving distances based on 400 meters.

"You know by now how much stress you undergo in a session of long repetitions--keeping up a good pace for several minutes. Provided you allow your body sufficient time and rest to adapt, this is good stress.

"By comparison, your short strides required less concentration, despite the fact that you were running faster. Because you will now be running fast for longer than previously (up to twice as long) in the new interval work, it will place more strain on you than before...this is precisely what you need."

"So in essence," I said, "we're going to marry the stress of running fast, with the stress of fast running for a long time."

"Kind of. I prefer this approach," then he whispered in my ear:

"We WILL bring the fast running together with a longer distance--so you'll maintain fast pace for longer than you've been used to. But think of it as a chance to enjoy the thrill of going near full throttle for an extra 200 meters, rather than feeling the need to pressure and strain your way through the longer distance at full speed."

"You mean, if we think of these sessions as exhausting, they will feel hard and stressful."

"Whereas, Davey, if you think of yourself as being vigorous, the session will feel less arduous. It'll be more like asking someone for a tenth date."

"Rather than the fear of asking for a first date."

"Yes. Anyway....I'll be bringing in the 400s so gently, it will seem more like a twentieth date. You learn more each time--you get to know the terrain (the track) better."

"The track," I said. Here's what he had to say.

"These sessions will frequently be done on a track--tracks create a more reliable yardstick to assess progress. To some people, running around a track is boring: but trust me, it's worth the effort once a week.

"Of course, some people find any running boring; but those who've made it to this level should be able to handle one day a week at the track. Note I'm not talking of three days a week here. Running in a group; exchanging views; and the varied sessions, can give immense satisfaction."

I asked him if there were any other advantages to track sessions" He gave the following:

1/ Same distances all over the country...within a couple of yards or meters.

2/ An even flat surface.

3/ You get away from traffic, dogs and pedestrians...

4/ With like minded people, who have a respect for each others efforts, at whatever standard they are running.

"Various people using the facilities does create problems," he continued. "You need to obey a few rules. You may need to buy a permit to use the track...or pay a daily fee. Make yourself aware of changing room protocol. The shoes you wear on the track should be clean road running types. If the warmup included mud sections, finish off through some grass to clean them up....Or put on a clean pair for the session.

"Be aware of the college or high school's time to train; there is a chance you'll be unwelcome. If you run fast enough, you can ask to join one of the groups--don't even consider racing them.

"Run at the back of the group, or to the outside of the lane, halfway down the line of runners. If your pace judgment is superb, you could offer to lead a rep or two--make sure you do it at the right pace. Help the coach with his or her difficult job, rather than adding to their problems."

"What you mean is, wait until you're experienced before trying to join this kind of group."

"Generally. In some places they'll be pleased to have a relative novice join in, perhaps with the second or slower group. They'll appreciate an additional adult to guide the group."

"What about those track rules?" I asked.

*   "Always look both ways before walking across the jump runways.

*   "Also look both ways before stepping onto the track from the inside or the outside. Look behind before you change lanes.

*   "Always give way to someone who is running--sprinters tend to use lanes four to six of the straights.

*   "The inside lane should only be used for 600 meter or longer repeats. This will ensure it doesn't wear out too quickly. This phase is mainly about 400 meters or quarter miles--referred to (oddly enough) as 400s or quarters. We will use lane two. You will start each repetition at the echelon or staggered start of the 400 meter race.

*   "The general rule of the track is that slower runners give way to faster runners. When you are running your repetition, however...simply run your repetition. It's up to the faster runner to overtake you by running wide; there is no need to give way. When you're jogging or walking the rest period, you must always give way to those who are training. When getting lapped in tack meets, give up the inside lane to faster people.

"Your options during the recovery (the interval between efforts), are for you to move to an outer lane if it is not being used by any-one, or to jog on the grass inside the track. You can rest at the side of the track--starting the next effort after a set time or when your pulse has recovered to a certain number. But the body recovers much better if you keep moving at a respectable jog...within three minutes per mile of the pace you do your reps at. The movement helps the muscles to get rid of the accumulated wastes. If you're the only group or person using the track, ease one or two lanes out from the lane you are using; move back in fifteen meters before the next effort.

"At some facilities, you will hear people shouting 'TRACK' at the top of their voices. This is to warn someone to move off the track as a runner approaches. It is very annoying and stressful to be forever shouting at people to move....And none too comfortable if being shouted at, either. Once concentration has been lost in a hard session, an athlete can soon get in a foul mood at having his session spoiled. He's likely to make others feel uncomfortable. Track sessions should be fun...don't add stress to the session by getting in people's way."

He then listed some danger areas to watch for.
* 1/ In the spring--runners who haven't seen the track for 6 months--some, if they ever knew them, will have forgotten the rules.
* 2/ Overcrowded track--as more people get agitated, some may forget to look before changing lanes.

Rest

Generally, you should take less than 90 seconds rest during interval sessions. The greatest stimulation of heart development occurs in the first 10 seconds of the rest period. If you're running reps at the appropriate pace for you, it should only take 30 seconds for the heartrate to get below 130. The extra minute is for your mind, not your body. There is no need to wait for the H.R. to reach 90. 110-120 while maintaining a decent recovery speed is better.

* 3/ Groups being coached--moronic yes, but they often hover around at the end of repetitions checking times. Ease to the outer lanes people, or the inside, off of the track--let the next group go through unhindered.

* 4/ The new track person who has not developed the sixth sense which allows him to see everything and know what every other person is doing. Just kidding--stay out of lanes one and two and you'll soon get the hang of it. Slip into lane two for the 400; ease back to lane three for the rest....Simple, isn't it?

"Visit the track sometime and see the rules being used--or not being used--as the case may be. Introduce yourself to a group who are at a similar standard. Then join the group for a few sessions to get used to the track. Introductions are best done before they train...during the warmup; or after they've finished training...joining them for the warm down. See what you can learn from them--including their mistakes.

"You need a good base before commencing serious speedwork.

"Serious," he said, almost to himself, "I'm not saying you can't smile--your comedians smile, yet they are serious about their work.

"You can and should enjoy these sessions. If any running is going to get you high...these sessions will.

"Back to the base work theme. Many people find they run a 5 k as fast at the end of winter...filled with sessions such as twenty slowish 400s...as they do when peaking for the short races by doing eight fast 300s. The secret is that the runner is strong. Don't lose sight of the strength phase. Keep medium to long runs and the bulky yet modest pace interval sessions throughout the year.

"The strength you attained in the last part will allow you to do race pace training; the strength facilitates your shift to speedwork.

"Your first session should be either 100 or 200 meter strides--not excessively fast or too many. Get used to the track surface, running perhaps half or less of a session the others are doing (if joining a group). It's far better to enjoy a few half sessions before pushing yourself into new territory--in terms of speed or number of repetitions. This is not a new session to you of course: but it will feel different to doing it on grass.

"After a few weeks, you can increase the length to 300 and then 400 meters at a time. The recovery should be the same distance as the repetitions--walk if necessary, but a jog will be better when you can judge the pace of the reps. If a similar standard group is not available, you can join a group which is slightly faster than you. The essential thing is...don't attempt to race them. If they are doing 10 x 400 meters, you could do ten at 200 meters. Rejoin the group at some stage before they start their next effort.

"You don't even have to run WITH them. You can let them start their effort--and a few seconds later start yours at a slower pace. That way, you won't be tempted into running the first fifty meters too fast.

"As you get fitter, try 250s and then 300s with them. Then you might like to do two out of every three over the full 400 meters. Take a complete rest while the group does its thing on each third rep. Remember always--YOU MUST DO YOUR TRAINING, NOT SOMEBODY ELSE'S. When you feel ready to tackle their full session, do so, but build up to it slowly. Being around faster runners can help you--but training sessions are for training...and joking...not racing."

Training on your own, or in a group, here's his guide to progressing over ten weeks.

* Week one--Bends & straights, stride along the straight and jog the bends at a steady pace. Eight to twelve laps--giving sixteen to twenty-four striders--should not feel too exhausting.

* Week two--As above but on two days.

* Week three--One session of bends and straights. One of 16 x 200 meters with 200 interval recovery. The surface may tempt you to run faster, hold back to decrease the potential for injury.

* Week four--As last week--judge the pace better. Aim to run the last five, one second faster than the early ones.

"Nothing you haven't done on trails or grass so far. By now you should be used to the surface...you should be comfortable with its softness and with the presence of many other runners." That was what he said. I'll add that if you've been doing the 200s on the track already, you can move straight to week 5.

* Week five--One track session. 10 x 300 meters. A little slower speed than the 200s; take a 300 recovery. Run two straights and one bend for the repetition; two bends and a straight for the recovery. This will make it easier on your ankles and joints up to the hips--there is a tendency to lean into the curves.

* Week six--200s, but the recovery can be at a faster pace; making them shorter in terms of time. Bends and straights--stay relaxed, the speed will come.

* Week seven--10 x 300 again. Pace judgment will improve with practice, aim to run them fairly even. A session of bends and straights--either increase the number of laps by two, or the speed a little.

* Week eight--Nirvana...8 x 400 meters with same jog recovery. You will need to run a little slower than your 300 pace to enable you to keep going the extra 100 meters. Even with a full lap recovery, this session is quite hard. Aim to maintain good form for the entire lap...assess yourself in each hundred. Ask...is my form going? Quarters have the advantage that you start and finish each effort at the same place. A session of 200s, getting a little faster, will complement the 400s.

* Week nine--300s; perhaps increase to 12 efforts, or improve the speed. Bends and straights or a fartlek session of short efforts.

* Week ten--Back to 400s and 200s. "Once you are completely used to the surface, aim for only one session to be done on the track each week. More than one session, and you may become stale, losing interest in track work. The week you do 200s on the track, do a session of longish hill repetitions. Or use a watch with a beeper to do a session of one minute efforts with a minute rest...on grass, or paths and road. The week you do the three or four hundreds on the track, re-visit short strides on grass or paths. A mixture of track and hill sessions or fartlek gives you two sessions of short efforts a week.

"Do retain a tempo run or session of long reps each week.

"To make progress...the speed, or number of efforts at 200, 300 or 400 that you can do at a given speed, will continue to increase over a period of years--improving your endurance and running economy."

"What about the science behind intervals?" I asked one day.

"First the non-science," he said. "Interval training is precise...you can measure your progress. Intervals fine-tune your body; they help you get the best out of yourself. The real progress is measured in racing though. Don't just become good at interval sessions.

"These intervals, provided you practice good form, will improve your running efficiency...enabling you to race faster.

"They will improve your strength and therefore your stride length or frequency--allowing you to run faster.

"They improve your neuromuscular coordination even if you forget to work on form.

"You can run 10 k at 10 k pace...and it will feel easy. Yet the next day, you won't feel as if you did a 10 k race. I shouldn't kid you too much. You will feel as if you trained very hard, perhaps as if you'd raced four miles. With good base, you can do an intense workout, yet you won't feel as if you've punished yourself.

"You can talk during the intervals. Some days there's little talk; others, a lot.

"Your speed and economy improves. Your pace judgment improves.

"Once you've learnt how to do them, one session a week of intervals can be done anywhere.

"Intervals are progressive. You apply a load--your body adapts--you're better able to handle that load a few weeks later...provided you include sufficient rest.

"Those runners with superb speed, a high natural ability to run at 800 or mile race pace, should probably work on their endurance to maintain the fast pace longer--do more anaerobic threshold and steady runs to improve endurance.

"Those who feel super relaxed at 15 k pace, yet lack speed, should do strength and speedwork to develop their mile race potential to the best. Increasing VO2 max will benefit them at the longer distance races.

"However, train at your weak area in moderation; continue to practice your strengths. Adhere to the general rule of alternating 15 k pace with 2 mile pace speedwork, and you won't go far wrong."

"You can run at the pace of race distances you've no desire to race--and it will improve your times at distances you do race. Example...you may never race at two miles, but reps at this pace will help your 5 and 10 k times.

"You make huge early gains...provided you have enough background endurance.

"This economical or controlled running is great preparation for races.

"It's easier to concentrate on fast running when you race.

"You can train at 90 percent max heart rate with minimal risk of injury...to your mind or your body.

"You can feel as comfortable in the last 400 meters as you did in the first 400.

"However: Don't jump straight into long sessions of intervals. Don't feel wasted afterwards.

"Make sure the last reps are as fast as the early ones."

He paused.

"And the scientific?" I asked.

"Won't make you run any faster."

I gave him a look.

"The body's ability to process oxygen improves. Your VO2 max goes up. You breath deeper."

I gave him my sternest look.

"Your aerobic capacity goes up. Your anaerobic buffering system is enhanced; some would say your lactate tolerance goes up....it is difficult to avoid running part of your repetition at or close to anaerobic pace.

"Your leg turnover also goes up."

I repeat the look.

"You can run longer before you reach oxygen debt...and you're better able to handle that debt...at a given speed. You race faster.

"Just make sure you do short and long rep interval sessions at all race paces. For example, do 400s AND miles at 5 k pace; do 300s AND 1,000s at two mile pace.

"If in doubt...do any reps faster than the pace you intend to race at...five to ten seconds a mile faster...it's that simple."

How to use interval training to drop your 10-k time from 48 to 46 minutes.

There's no single correct formula for interval training. Training benefits can be achieved over a wide range of paces. An Interval workout is a function of several variables:

Pace; length of runs; recovery time...and

total workout volume

can all be adjusted in a variety of ways to produce sessions that are challenging, stimulating and even entertaining.

Choose a pace that enables you to run a total of 8 - 10 repeats of 400 meters with recoveries of 1:30 to 2 minutes (or slow 200 meter jogs). The pace of your repeats should not slow; nor should you be totally exhausted at the end of the workout. Initially, try a pace of about 1:48 per 400, which is slightly faster than 5-k race pace of 23 minutes. If you progress to 1:44s at the same effort level as your current 1:48s , you should have a good shot at running a 46 minute 10-k....Provided you also have sufficient mileage and endurance from your other running.

Don't limit your intervals to 400s. Workouts can include reps. at the same distance (e.g.. 6 x 800; 5 x 1000) or a variety of distances in one session (example:400-800-1200-800-400). For best results, aim for 5-k race pace or a little faster, and allow recovery equal to the time of the repeat just completed.

Adapted from John Babington's contributions to Runner's World, with permission.

John Babington is Wellesley College Cross Country coach; 1996 U.S. Olympic Women's distance coach; his athletes include Lynn Jennings...three times World Cross Country champion and Olympic Bronze medalist at 10,000 meters.

CHAPTER ELEVEN

LONG TERM PROGRESSION....

The Guru says progress can be achieved in many ways:
* Run faster in the effort
* Take a shorter distance recovery
* Put more effort into the recovery (jogging for a minute instead of walking)
* Or, increasing the number of efforts.
He continued. "The prudent runner will only change one of these factors at a time. One exception glares into my retinal vestige....Namely, when you go from summer training at 5,000 meter pace to strength training for the winter. If you've been used to doing 12 x 400 in 80 seconds with a 200 jog, it will not be hard for you to move straight to 20 x 400 in 85 seconds with a slow 100 jog. In fact, some runners keep the twenty 400s session once a month in the summer; it helps them to maintain endurance, and is a relief from pushing for the pace of the faster intervals.

"A runner specializing in the shorter distances will generally aim for a lowish number of quite fast repetitions--thus ensuring part of each effort puts him well into oxygen debt. He will increase the speed of the efforts until he is running faster than race pace...then steadily decrease the recovery period session by session. He may also reduce the number of repetitions to enable him to achieve the extra speed."

"What about the 10 k or 10 mile racer?"

"Upon achieving the required speed, they will decrease the recovery period, and then increase the number of repetitions."

"So he'll run the repeats at the same pace," I said.

"Yes. Once target pace is attained, aim to do more repetitions at that pace.

"You see David, one of the aims of interval training is to get the body used to running fast for a long (overall) period of time. Interval work allows you to do huge amounts of mileage at fast pace--yet without wearing yourself out. Achieve the target speed, then emphasize improving endurance at that speed."

Both specialists could progress along the following lines at first.

Week 1   8 x 400 in 72 secs 400 jog
Week 3   10 x 400 in 72 secs 400 jog
Week 5   12 x 400 in 72 secs 400 jog
Week 7   10 x 400 in 72 secs 300 jog
Week 9   12 x 400 in 72 secs 300 jog
Week 11   8 x 400 in 72 secs 200 jog
Week 13   10 x 400 in 72 secs 200 jog
Week 15   12 x 400 in 72 secs 200 jog

"For the next two sessions of 400s, it would be a good idea to consolidate your gains. Weeks 17 and 19 could be the same as week 15. Then move on to 8 x 400 in 70 secs with 400 jog (if requiring more speed); or increase the number of efforts if looking for greater endurance...only you can set the limit on the number. Each time you increase the speed of your reps, a greater proportion of the repetition is anaerobic. As you get stronger; as your muscles get used to the new speed; as your body learns to process more oxygen, (with a nudge from your steady runs), it becomes more aerobic. Over a period of months, the anaerobic training changes to aerobic training: You will be able to race faster.

"You'll find that while aiming for the 72s, some of your efforts will be closer to 70. If you make a conscious effort to run every fourth rep faster--that is, to intentionally run a 70--moving to regular 70s will come easier. The occasional faster rep also helps to break up the session."

"Avoid doing any session more than once every two weeks," he said.

"But you have me doing 200s on consecutive weeks."

"True. But that was to prepare you for the 300s; which themselves got you ready for the 400s. There is often an exception to a general rule.

"You need to avoid doing 400s or 200s week in, week out. Doing the same session will only make you good at running that session. The 200s and 300s do something for you which the 400s won't. Don't miss out on their benefits.

"Here's how your 1200s might progress over one year. It assumes you do them once a month--in winter, half the sessions will be away from the track.

"The runner does a 19:15 for 5,000 meters; her goal is to get under 19 minutes--and perhaps break six minute mile pace for the distance, or 18:39.

"In this session she'll train at close to current two mile pace early on--if she winters well, it becomes her 5,000 pace.

Month

One   4 x 1,000 in 3:45 (90 per lap) with 600 rest...gets you
        used to it.

Two   4 x 1200   4:30   600 rest

Three   5 x 1200   4:36   (92 laps)   400 rest

Four   2 x 1200   4:30; 3 x 800 3:00 with 400 rest...note
        you only start two reps after a 1200 with short rest.

Five   5 x 1200   4:33   (91s)   400 rest

Six   3 x 1200 and 2 x 800 at 90 per lap

Seven   6 x 1200 in 4:36

Eight   4 x 1200   4:30   400 rest

Nine   5x 1200   4:33   400 rest...last couple close to 4:30

Ten.   6 x 1200   4:36   alternate 400 and 200 rests

Eleven 4 x 1200 in 4:30, 4:29, 4:28, 4:27 with 400 rest

Twelve 5 x 1200 in 4:34, 4:32, 4:30, 4:28, 4:26 with 400 rest

---

"In practice, you may run 400s every three weeks. The 17 sessions will give you a full year of progression. Progress along similar lines for the other track sessions. Week two could be 12 x 300 meters with 300 jog; week four 12 x 300 with 200 jog and week ten 10 x 300 with 100 jog. The 300s will be run at perhaps the equivalent of a 70 second lap....When you move on to 400s in 70 seconds, it's a natural progression in terms of increasing the speed of the 400s because you run the extra 100 meters at the speed you had been running 300s.

"By the time you reach that level, you will be running your 300s comfortably at sixty-eight second 400 pace."

"Use the speed of your current 300s as your target for next year's 400s. Like in Part Three, your progress will be phenomenal for a while, but be prepared for it to slow as you get close to your potential--the potential at your current level of training. Keep the speed of reps in a proper relationship to your race pace. There's little point in running excessively faster than racing speed.

"Try running 200s at your best 1500 or mile speed; the 300s at 3,000 meters (or two mile) pace; with the 400s being at 5,000 meters pace. Gradually increase the speed so that 2, 3 and 400s are run at 800, 1500 and 3000 meter pace. Aim to run two or more times the distance of the race during these sessions. If you're running at 3,000 pace, aim for 6,000 in the interval session.

"There's a girl at the track who always runs 400s," I said. "She does different numbers of efforts at different speeds."

"She's one of those exceptions," he said. "I've observed her for some time..."

"And what do you think?"

"I think she's got those 400s close to an art form. First, you should be aware her other speed sessions include a hill which takes her four minutes to run up; a forest where she does mostly 150s during a fartlek session; and a park which takes seven minutes per loop--she varies her recovery to a quarter or half lap, depending on whether she is running the reps at 15 k or 10 k pace."

"You're saying her training is balanced then."

"Nicely understated my friend. The 400s complete the picture.

"She runs eight reps at 1500 pace one week, taking a slow 200 meter jog. The next week she does 20 reps at 10 k pace with a fast 100 jog. The third, it's 16 reps at 5,000 pace with a slow 100 jog. Her fourth session is at 3,000 pace...she does 12 with a fast 200 rest.

"There's also a guy who finishes his run at the track."

"You mean his steady runs?" I said.

"Yes. He once told a friend he'd stopped doing intervals because he'd heard you should end the session when you begin to lose form...when your style goes. He did two reps well...then lost form. He would stop after three reps."

"Sounds like he started off too fast," I said.

"He did. But that's only my first point--" the Guru added.

"--I believe you should do several reps while you are tired: You need to practice relaxing at speed while tired. This teaches you how to run fast in the middle to the end of a race. It will give you added confidence and improve your concentration.

"A few one hundreds after a session of short reps, or a couple 400s after long reps, is a great way to finish a session. Run relaxed with tired muscles.

"It's also a good way to prepare for increasing the length of your interval session. You may have noticed the 800s after the 1200s in month four and six above. She could simply do 4 x 1200 each month at the beginning of the season, but add a 400 at the same pace each session. After three months, she'd be doing the four 1200s plus three 400s. Month four she could do an 800 plus a 400; then the fifth could be five full reps. Repeating the process with the 400s will allow her to reach six 1200s at the tenth session.

"Anyone can run a fast quarter...just watch the start of most races. Few are efficient runners in the 16th or 22nd quarter of a 10k.

"The less you want to give up an easy run for speedwork...the more you will probably benefit from that speedwork. Don't sprint. Don't rush. And don't make it hurt...too much.

"But do practice running economically when tired."

He paused a considerable time after telling me the last few sentences, then said.

"I told you there are four ways to make progress with your interval work at the start of this chapter--by changing the speed, the recovery distance, the intensity of effort during the rest, or increasing the number of reps.

"There's a fifth way to improve fitness. You can simply maintain the same four sessions in rotation every month--no changes at all. As the months go by, these sessions will become easier to you; the run on the following day will feel easier; you will have the desire to run faster on those recovery days. Pretty soon, you will be doing a mile or two at close to tempo pace on those recovery runs without attempting to. Instead of the interval session making you feel worn out for the run which follows, it will make you feel bouncy and ready to cruise at good pace. Instead of avoiding hilly loops, you'll search them out.

"One day, you may want to make one of the four changes to your interval session, but you could have already found the ideal pace and length of session for your body ."

PRIORITY ONE....INCREASE YOUR VO2 MAX. By Frank Horwill

What does VO2 MAX mean? It is the amount of oxygen we can breath in one minute while working at full capacity. It's a measure of fitness expressed in milliliters per kilogram per minute.

In the research lab. this is measured at a treadmill speed of 11.3 kilometers per hour. During the first five minutes, the treadmill is raised two degrees per minute (to 10 degrees). Thereafter, it is raised one degree for every minute, until the athlete is unable to maintain11.3 km/hour.

Experience tells us that a male athlete who can keep going 14 minutes or more will have a figure of 75 mls.kg.min. plus. A female who keeps going for 12 minutes will have a figure of 65 mls.kg.min. plus. However, accurate measurement is obtained by collecting exhalations from the athlete via a tube in the mouth, which goes into a Douglas bag (inventor...Professor Douglas). The contents of the bag are passed through an analyzer which gives an accurate reading. This is called indirect calorimetry.

VO2 max can be predicted with 95 percent accuracy by getting a group to run around a track on a windless day for exactly 15 minutes. The distance run to the nearest 25 meters is noted, and Bruno Balke's formula is used to predict VO2 max. After a base of 6.5, this follows a linear pattern of 5 mls.kg.min. for every extra 400 meters covered. For example, if 10 laps is run (4,000 meters), it predicts 56.5 mls.kg.min. If 11 laps, or 4,400 m is run, VO2 max is 56.5 plus 5 = 61.5. Twelve laps (4,800) will be 61.5 + 5 = 66.5. World class runners have a figure of 80 (male) and 70 (female).

The best way to improve VO2 max is to run between 80 and 100 percent of VO2 max. One hundred percent equals the athlete's 3k pace; 95 % equals 5 k speed; 90 % is 10k speed; and 80 percent equals his steady running pace which is between 20-25 seconds per 400 meters slower than for each 400 m of his best 1500 meter time. Thus, an athlete with a 4 minute 1500, runs it at 64 secs per 400; his steady running should be between 64 + 20 and 64 + 25 or 5:36 to 5:56 per mile. Anything slower will not be at 80 percent VO2 max.

Work physiologists believe training at 95 % VO2 max brings the best results, although one Russian physiologist of note--Karibosk, thinks 100 % (3 k or two mile pace) is better because it tunes up the anaerobic pathway. Note--3,000 m is run at 60 % aerobic and 40 % anaerobic.

Physiologists are agreed the percentages at the higher level (100 - 95 %) should be done for 3-5 minutes' duration, repeated many times in one session, with a short recovery; and the lower percentages (90 - 80 %) should be for 10-20 minutes, also with short recoveries.

Physiologists also believe steady runs should be at least 35 minutes to get a training effect.

Costill reports the volume of steady running alone at 80 percent VO2 max does improve fitness by as much as 12 percent to 80 miles per week. After that, there is very little return for the mileage expended. A good way of building to this volume is to add 5 minutes per day per week to the running. A 35 minute runner will reach 70 minutes after seven weeks. 80 miles should be achieved after another month.

In order for this mileage to be effective, it will be necessary for the runner to race or do time-trials at 3k, 5k and 10k, to ascertain the speeds required if these distances have not been raced before.

The best time to increase the VO2 max is in the winter months--it can be maintained in the summer by regular weekly sessions at 5k and or 3k pace, plus steady running at 80 percent VO2 max.

It should be noted that Sebastian Coe, who broke twelve world records in four years at distances from 800 meters to the mile, did a regular 5k pace session each week...and his weekly mileage for the year did not exceed 50 miles. The era of big mileage is over unless the 80 miles a week plus is FASTER, i.e. 80 to 140 miles a week is at 3k, 5k, and 10k speed.

Frank Horwill, whose system of training was used by Seb Coe, is a BAF coach. (The British Athletic Federation.) He was chairman of the British Milers Club which organizes quality races for the sub-elite. Regional races have a dozen or more invitees, at several distances, to take runners to their next level. To and beyond 4 minutes miles; to and below 8:30 for two miles; to and faster than 1:50 for 800. He is a frequent contributor to the British Athletic magazines.

CHAPTER TWELVE

PONDERABLES

One evening, while watching my 300s, the Guru considered a couple of our country's coaches ideas.

"I'll never understand," he said, "why your people suggest doing the same session six weeks in a row and then they stop. First the obvious."

"Why the same session."

"Right...breaks our rule doesn't it. Six consecutive weeks.

"The coaches argue that runners will make substantial improvements in economy but should only do 6 weeks of speedwork. They also say decrease mileage for these 6 weeks.

"Well, if you've never done speedwork before, the gains will be huge; add the resting up...you're bound to get faster.

"But it's hardly a long term approach. It's probably more likely to give you an injury too."

"So why not rotate the sessions like we do with 200, 300 and 400s." I said.

"Plus the fartlek and strides," he added. "And why stop after six weeks. You've just got used to the session, your running economy has improved, yet I keep seeing training programs which say do only six weeks. Just when you're beginning to benefit from reps, they say stop. For galaxy sake...why."

"Short attention span," I said.

"Don't you believe it David--your specie is capable of doing and enjoying track sessions year round."

"And you implore me to do so."

"Mind reader," he said.

"The mind is where the ability to do year round speedwork is. Take no notice of the six week, then take a break idea. Improve your endurance by adding more reps. Do get away from the track for a few weeks twice a year, but continue fast running elsewhere to keep your hard-earned good form.

"If you do the same session very often, the times will still vary according to how tired you are, (mental or physical), your food intake and hydration status, and the weather.

"Another thing that intrigues me is the tendency for your peoples' schedules to say that a long run should be preceded by a rest day."

"Sounds sensible to me," I said.

"It is: If you are going to run twice the distance you normally do...and at 30 seconds a mile faster than your usual long run.

"Your longest run is typically a quarter to less than a third of your average weekly mileage. You run it at an easy pace. The ideal is for you to do a good speed session on a Saturday...then follow it with the long *recovery* run on Sunday."

"Once you've got used to track work, you can transfer some of the long repetitions as well."

"Ha ha." I said. "We cheated. We've been doing one week in three on the track for months."

"I know," he said. "I'd prefer readers to wait though. It's tempting to spend just a few weeks at each level...with each phase. These scribblings are more of a lifelong philosophy for training. Venture into this level too early, and you're more prone to injuries."

"But do you think it was necessary for me to wait an entire year before trying four hundreds?"

"It's because you waited an entire year...building up the physiologic strength...that you've been so successful with your 400s.

"The three minute efforts (which even you dear boy, do off the track most of the time), might become five or six times 800 or 1,000 meters at 3,000 meter (roughly two mile) race pace--about 5-10 seconds per mile faster than your best recent 5 k. Gradually reduce the recovery to a quarter the distance of the rep--move down from 400 to a 200 recovery.

"The five to six minute efforts may become four times a mile (1609 meters) at 5,000 meters pace--also with a gradual reduction to a 200 meter recovery.

"The slower the race pace you are training at, the shorter the recovery should be. As little as one eighth at 5,000 pace; one quarter at 3000; half the distance at mile speed and the same distance as the repetition at 800 pace.

"And think about one aspect of your form on each rep."

"Long reps also give you a better chance to run with faster people."

"How so?"

"Let's say you're a 16 minute 5 k runner. At the track is a group of 15:25 to 15:35 runners. When they do miles at 5 k pace, you can do 800s at the same pace. You will be running at 3,000 pace though. You could also do a 600...rest while they do the middle lap...then do a second 600. They will pull you to good times. Sometimes you can lead the first two laps for them--but try to make it even pace. At other times, you can join in at the back of the group. When they do 400s, you can do 300s...as mentioned in chapter 10.

"This training at, or a little faster than race pace, prepares you perfectly for racing. That's why you were doing long reps in part three."

The best session

One of the simplest ways to improve VO2 max is to run long reps at 90 to 100 percent of max VO2. Alternate 1,000 meters at 2 mile pace with miles at 5 K pace. And do those long hill rep sessions. Match each of these three with sessions at 200, 300, and 400s to improve running economy. Provided you have good base at anaerobic threshold (15 k pace) and you retain your ability to run tempo, the VO2 training will give good benefits.

"Would you like to give some sample schedules with speeds?" I asked one day.

"I'd rather not," he replied. "I've no great desire to turn reams of trees into schedules for every level of runner. I think you're all capable of using the basic schedule in part four--then slot in the track sessions. Advance the speed as I out-lined above. 5,000 meter runners train at 2 mile to 5 k pace for 10-15 percent of their mileage."

"What about the speed to train at for ten kilometer races?" I asked.

"I'm not sure you want to get me on that subject."

"Why not?"

"We might use up those trees I was saving."

On a long Sunday run, he let me in on his opinions.

"Your elite runners," he said, "run two and a half seconds slower per lap for 10,000 meters compared to their 5,000 speed. Some of your clubs seem to think just because their runners take over 16 minutes for 5,000 that they can't aspire to a 33 minute ten kilometer. Yet they can. Most runners should be able to stay within three seconds per lap for twice the distance."

"That's only twelve seconds per mile." I said.

"It's the same percentage slowing as a 14 minute 5,000 runner." said he.

"Good point," said I.

"The real trouble with those comparison tables is they show what has been done, rather than what could be run at the longer distance. Just because the average person slows by five seconds a lap, or 20 seconds per mile, doesn't mean you have too.

"The problem is the statistics are swayed by the preponderance of runners who, except for an occasional random set of four hundreds, train at phase three level. Readers should not take this as an insult. More people exercise and enjoy level three intensity than level five, six and nine. But if you've chosen to incorporate the extra training of phase four and five, your goal must be to run within 12 seconds per mile for the longer distance--rather than the artificially low goals based on current average race times."

He went on.

"Then you have the mile to two mile situation."

"Which is..." I said.

"Many of your people under-achieve at two miles compared to their one mile time. The result is they also under-achieve at 5,000 meters."

"How much should they slow for double this distance?" I asked.

"You should be able to double your mile time and add 15 percent of your mile time, to find your two mile potential."

"That would be the same as adding seven and a half percent to my mile time, and then doubling it." I said.

"True. A 4:30 miler, to take an arbitrary threshold you humans are partial to, should be able to do a 9:38 two mile. A 5:00 miler...a sub 10:45 two. A 6:40 miler...a 14:20 two mile.

"I think the downfall is the same as above. People with good natural speed don't do sufficient training to make it up to their potential at the longer distances.

"You recall I said your 3,000 pace should be 5 to 10 seconds per mile faster than your 5 k pace. Take the middle figure...say 7 seconds a mile. The 4:30 miler, doing a 9:38 two mile ought to be capable of a 15:30 5,000. Check around your running compadres; see how many can do fifteen and a half minutes...yet many have 4:30 speed."

"What's the answer then?" I asked.

"The answer is in the preceding pages. Once you have found the speed you need...increase the number of reps to do more than three miles worth in a session. This way, they compliment the strength endurance work of Part Four. I'll have more to say about this subject in Part Nine."

Exercise Physiologists like to come up with new ways to express and test fitness.

Running Speed at Maximum Oxygen Use (RSMO) measures how efficiently you use oxygen. It helps us decide what pace to run at. But look at the name again!

RSMO is slightly faster than 5 K pace. You'll improve it by doing your regular VO2 max enhancing sessions.

Speed table 15:30 5k (4:30 mile, 9:38 two mile, 32 for 10k).

	Improves mainly Aerobic ability			Improves mainly Anaerobic buffering and threshold					
Rep of	200	300	400	400	600	800	1,000	mile	2,000
Recovery	200	200	200	400	200	800	200	800	400
Race pace	mile	2m	5k	mile	5k	2m	10k	5k	15k
Rep speed	34	54	74	70	1:51	2:24	3:12	4:56	6:40
# of reps	16	15	16	4	8	3	6	2	3
Build to	24+	20+	20+	8	10	4+	8+	3	4+
See	Note one...			three	two	three	two	three	two

Note One...You have to set the limit on the number of reps. A 5,000 meter person may be satisfied with 3 miles worth. He will probably race better if he does closer to 5 miles worth. The 10 k runner could ease through more reps at 10 to 12 seconds a mile slower; perhaps, quarters in 77 and 300s in 56; though half the reps should be at close to 5 k pace.

You can combine the sessions once a month. Eight each at 400, 300, and 200 will give four and a half miles with the pace going from 5 k to one mile as the distance of the reps decrease. You should be able to do all these speeds with a one hundred jog in due time.

Note Two...You've been doing this since phase three. Long reps at 5, 10 and 15 k race pace. The runners who think they never went beyond Part Three, still get most of the benefits of Part Five. Go from 15 minutes worth up to 25. Alternate:
* the three sessions between track and other training areas
* the three distances
* between aerobic and anaerobic sessions
* Match each session of long reps with a session of short ones.

Note Three...You did 200s at mile pace in the aerobic section; here are 400s which will be more anaerobic. Same for the 800s at two mile pace, and the miles at 5 k pace. Longer rest is needed due to the distance done at these speeds.

Final note...This table is based on a 15:24 to 15:30 5k runner. For the rest of you, your reps should be 2 secs a lap faster than 5 k pace to equal your two mile potential; 7 seconds faster than 5 k to match the one mile. Ten k pace is 3 seconds a lap slower than 5 k pace. Anaerobic threshold pace is 5-6 seconds per lap slower that 5 k pace.

---

12 KILOMETER TRAINING SCHEDULE

If you've raced several 10 kilometer events there's nothing special about a 12 k: You simply run close to your best at 10 k...and keep going another mile and a quarter. Your last effort (the sprint) will have to wait an extra mile and a quarter: Because the middle part of the race will be longer, it becomes more important to spread your effort over the entire race.

We could increase your training by 20 percent to help you to a better time, but that would be like telling you to double your mileage before entering a 20 k or half-marathon.

Instead, tweak your current mileage--adjust two of your runs.

First...the long run. If it's less than 10 miles, increase it by two miles. That's it. Same leisurely 70 to 80 of max heartrate pace, for an extra 14 to 20 minutes. Steal these miles from one of your easy runs.

Second...the key speed session. If you've been used to three times one mile (or 1,600 meters) do an extra lap of the track to make 2,000s. Run at the same pace, but with a longer recovery the first few times. Six 800s can become six 1,000s.

The weeks your short stuff is the key session, either do another mile of them, or do more of them at the fast pace. Take 400s. You can break up a session by inserting 8 x 200 a tad faster than the sets of 400s each side. Many people find 16 x 400 is too close to a cure for insomnia; the 200s will entertain you. Or, instead of 12 x 400 with every forth effort two seconds faster, do alternate reps faster.

Mileage will be the same, but the borrowed miles will mean two of your easy days are easier than previously. Keep your second or third speed session, and the medium length run to maintain a well balanced week.

Start this modified program at least twelve weeks before the race. You could increase your mileage of course, adding the 20 percent over the first month and maintaining that level for eight weeks. But do distribute those extra miles to the best affect.

Avoid doing any session more than three times during this period. Alternate the key session between long, short, and hill reps; and don't forget some fartlek.

The three to six seconds per mile slower which you will run during a 12 k, should help you feel more relaxed than in the rush of the shorter event; you should feel like you are cruising and in control.

PART SIX

RACING

With 15 to 30 races a year, you'll be learning all the time about pace judgment. In addition to rest, Chapter 13 will show you 10 ways to heighten your racing potential; Chapter 14--re visits long reps; Chapter 15 discusses ways to rest up for races; and Chapter 16 covers weather problems.

"You don't have to be a world beater to enjoy a good sprint at the end of a race--though some would say if you have too strong a finish, it could be because you didn't run hard enough in the rest of the race.

"If you're close to personal best speed for the distance however, your rabid finish is probably due to proper training and resting. Enjoy the satisfaction of beating the two or three people you've been running with and against for perhaps half the race. These extra places give you a boost."

CHAPTER THIRTEEN

TUNING UP BEFORE RACES

"The final phase to prepare for the perfect race is more rest, plus specific sessions to help you on race day. These special sessions will enable you to tolerate higher levels of lactic acid in your body and make you buffer wastes better. A pleasant side effect is you will feel more relaxed at high speed, enhancing your confidence.

"The first session is not revolutionary--do sprints of about fifty meters, but with a fast jog of fifty meters recovery. You could start with a mile of these efforts; build to three miles as you get used to them. You've been doing similar sessions to this in fartlek work, and bends and straights. Now, not only must the efforts be fast, but the rest must be fast so that your body is not allowed to recover completely--similar to the situation in a race where someone puts in a burst.

"While doing this session, think of the running as sprint...coast...sprint...coast. Don't ease to a jog at the end of each stride. The six minute mile 10 k runner should be sprinting at 5:30 pace and coasting at 7:00 pace.

"The 'coasting' section does not last many seconds--but nor does the fast part. The cumulative effect after a mile, or sixteen of these efforts is what you're after. Your net pace if you time the mile (don't even consider timing the individual 50 meter efforts) will be close to tempo run speed."

As I started the first of these sessions, the Guru repeated his main theme for this book: *build towards racing in a logical manner*, by saying:

"Most runners periodize their training. They gear the training to a racing season, or a series of key races. They will do perhaps six months of base mileage, a period when hills dominate, then three months of intervals. During each phase, they retain some of the other sessions--but they emphasize, like our chapters have, a different element in each phase.

"Now David, I know you're in good shape, but before the readers do the sessions in this chapter, they need to be in good shape, too. Three months of Chapter Five's intervals at least once a week, done at a variety of paces and distances, as in the table of suggested sessions, should be preceded by months of strength and endurance running.

"Wear racing or lightweight shoes to put you in the mood to go fast. Start modest...go a little faster each week. Remember track protocol. Unless you're doing a speed effort, stay out of the inside lanes. If you are doing a fast rep...faster runners must go around you. While some of these sessions will improve your racing, don't expect instant results."

After four sessions of the 50s at 10 day intervals, he felt I was ready for another layer of polish.

"Next, we'll reconsider sprint drills. You've been doing drills ever since Chapter Three of course, but here is a different one. It involves a few efforts of 150 meters working on a relaxed, fast running action. Speed up in five stages every ten meters, maintain at maximum speed for fifty meters or so, then run out (ease down) over the last fifty meters. A good surface will be required for this session--preferably not a synthetic track."

Pay attention to your body as you train and race. Top runners "associate" with the discomforts of fast running. When you feel like slowing because it's hard work to keep your pace, think about form and relaxation of all your muscles; think about your position in relation to the earth; to your fellow runner; to your fellow man. Relax your way through the second half of (the 600, or the 5 K) run.

Over the next few weeks he said:

"Lean forward while staying tall. Run off of your forefoot. Reduce wasted motion...keep the head still. Feel the surface, pull the surface back to you and devour the ground. While you should not land as far forward on your toes as an ostrich, emulate the way that creature drags
the dirt back and pushes off the toes with full extension. When your readers have mastered this session on its own, they should do four to six acceleration runs at the end of a track session once a week."

"Now you've found the extra legspeed, it's time to simulate a race day situation: get used to running fast when tired.

"My preferred way to do this is at the end of the even pace sustained run. About a mile and a half from the end, commence five quite fast, but not flat out, three to four hundred meter efforts with one to two hundred meters recovery. It may surprise you how fast you can run these, despite being tired from the first 20 minutes of the run. Some fatigue is mental. Develop the ability to get through this fatigue.

"After a 20 minute tempo on the track, rest a few minutes, then try 4 x 300 meters at two mile pace. You'll feel great.

"After doing the above a few times, take a look at your long runs."

"You aren't going to make me run fast on my easy runs are you?" I asked.

"Not much, I just want to bring in those fast twitch fibers on every SECOND or THIRD long run. Not every week. About two miles from the end of some runs, change up to 15 k race pace for half a mile--two times a quarter, or four times 200 meters works just as well. Run the fast part relaxed; then jog in the last part of the run.

"The third, and more controlled type of session for fast running when tired is a differential. The differential involves splitting an effort into two parts. The first part is run well within your ability, but fast enough to tire you somewhat: Then, with pooped out legs, you accelerate over the second part...increase pace by four or five seconds per 400 meters. Do fewer efforts with longer recovery than in your usual even paced sessions.

For example:

8 x 800 in 2 min 30 secs with half lap jog could become 6 x 800 first lap 77 secs, second lap 73 secs, with a full lap jog.

12 x 400 in 72 secs with half lap jog becomes 8 x 400 split 37/35, with a full lap jog.

Where does bounding belong?

Strictly speaking, this is a strength session. But bounding has a special relationship to racing, so we've placed it in this chapter.

On a soft surface or up a hill, bound forward with an exaggerated high knee-lift, and a fast running action. Bounce off the toes forcefully as you power your body up and forward--much higher and further than usual--then land softly. Do 20-30 meters at a time with a walk down or jog back recovery.

If you have wide stairs or steps available, do double leg jumps up them. Hopping is also effective, and allows you to isolate each leg.

Sand is the preferred surface because your legs struggle to propel you forward, and the arms work to maintain balance--you get a whole body workout. This arm strength will decrease late race fatigue.

Aim to stay tall and relaxed.

You'll develop your hip flexors, calves and quadriceps. These stronger muscles will increase your stride, your speed, and decrease the risk of injury.

Include a few minutes of skipping rope for the calves, but limit yourself to 10 minutes a week of these plyometrics. You want to build power to enhance your endurance--you get fast by being strong--yet you have to avoid the bulk of a sprinter.

Develop the strength which helps you to maintain form when tired. Leaning forward (when tired) is likely to strain the muscles at the back of the legs--the hamstrings and gluteals.

Don't start a bounding routine just before you do your racing.

"While doing these speed sessions, maintain your strength and flexibility work. Consider lunges, jumping and other cross training mentioned in the Volleyball essay of Part Ten.

"When doing resistance training, remember the resistance must increase as you get fitter. Find steeper hills; or run longer reps such as 1,000s at the speed of your 800s.

"Running up a slight hill costs almost twice as much energy as you gain coming down that hill. Practice both ways with relaxed form.

"Downhills teach you relaxation. Run perpendicular to the slope--work the arms to increase leg speed and stride. Do downhill reps of 200 to 400 meters. This is the chance to *upesi* the pace as the Kenyans say. Spring off your calf at maximum leg speed. Swing those legs through close to your buttocks.

"Start with two or three efforts...increase the number as the buttocks, hamstrings and calves get used to the effort and speed. This session gives the soleus a bonus workout."

After the downhill speed sessions, he enlightened me about wind.

"You can do long reps with the wind to help your legspeed, or while resting up pre-race.

"To improve legspeed, run the reps at what you consider to be your normal intensity...at long rep heartrate for those who use a monitor, while letting the wind push you to a faster pace. Stay relaxed though, or you will lose the benefit.

"Pre-race, you can run at your usual pace, but the effort will be easier as you are pushed by the wind. Jog back into the wind at easy effort.

"Run fresh in order to run fast. Keep the steady runs easy to allow recovery between speed sessions. Reduce the overall mileage by 10-15 percent in readiness for the final shine.

*   *   *

"After at least 8 weeks of this training, you can change the format of some interval sessions by breaking a session into sets. Run some 300s faster than you've been doing them; run at mile speed instead of two mile speed...but take shorter recoveries.

"You finally lost it," I said, "how can I run them faster if I'm taking less recovery."

"By doing a few at a time," he deadpanned.

"Start with two 300s, and take a fast 100 recovery between the reps. This pair is actually a set. You will then take a full lap of the track extra rest before commencing another pair, or set of 300s.

"In this special session, the first effort will seem easy; second and third 300s get progressively harder for you to maintain pace."

"I presume you want 'same pace' on these reps."

"Oh yes. The last 300 should be at the same speed, or marginally faster than the first. When you've done this session successfully a couple of times, you can try sets of three, four, then five reps. Five reps will give you a close simulation of a mile race. Don't do more than three miles of these intervals in a session.

"The short recovery means your lactate levels stay high in the muscles. This will increase your anaerobic capacity and lactate tolerance...the amount of lactate your muscles can hold before forcing you to slow down. Increasing lactate holding capacity before it grinds you to a halt, will allow you to maintain high speeds longer.

"The physiologists might say it increases your 'buffering system' or 'buffering capacity'. Like running at two mile pace, you breath deeper, thus increasing the maximum quantity of oxygen your lungs can take in, and which your blood has the opportunity to absorb."

*　　　　*　　　　*

Once I'd mastered the 300s, and occasionally, sets of three 400s at mile pace with forty seconds rest, he said he wanted to expand my horizon again.

"Next up is to run faster than mile pace. I don't want you to bash out rapid 200s like many of your countrymen do. They run at speeds they'll never attain in a race--partly because they take too much recovery.

"What you will do is 200s at close to 800 meter race pace. True 800 meter race pace is only one and a half seconds faster for 200 meters than your mile race pace...not the three to five seconds faster which many track people are _sprinting_."

"One and a half seconds faster sounds easy," I said. "Where's the catch?"

"First, you have to control yourself to that modest pace on the opening rep--"

"Because the recovery will only be 100?"

"Because my boy, the recovery will be 30 seconds."

"Wow. I can't jog a hundred that fast. It means starting at a different point on the track. How do I measure the second 200?"

"Thirty seconds will give you enough time to ease down after charging through the line at _real_ 800 speed; to jog round in a circle back beyond the start finish line; and get back to the start for the next rep. You will start each 200 from the point you finished the last one...the opposite side to which you started."

"Do you want me to aim for sets of five like with the 300s?"

"I'm going to have you start with five pairs of reps. You'll take three to five minutes rest between sets. The third time you do this session, do four sets of three 200s.

"Unless you intend to race 800 meters on a regular basis, I don't think there's anything to be gained by doing more than three reps at a time."

I'll never know if there was an advantage to sets of four 200s; he found it difficult enough getting me to maintain form on each third rep.

"I will not allow you to have wasted energy," he'd say...then point out one of the faults I did at such high speeds. We've discussed form before; this 800 pace stuff really showed my dis-coordination at speed. But we worked on it. After a dozen sessions I could run with good form at all paces down to the mile...in part he said, because we'd attempted to run relaxed at 800 pace.

The last 200 in each set was always tough; but it prepared me for one of the most satisfying training sessions...the thrill of running longer reps at mile and two mile pace.

Acceleration sessions

Instead of a mile race...try 800 meters at mile pace...take a full five minute recovery.

Do 600 just a bit faster...take a full recovery.

Do a 400 and a 300 at 800 race pace, then a 200 at 400 race pace. You should only need about three minutes between each.

Or, do one of Alberto Cova's sessions. This Italian dominated the mid 80s 10,000 meter track races with his final sprint, helped by doing 4 x 500; 5 x 400; 5 x 300; and 10 x 200. The two keys to its usefulness...100 jog between everything. They were not done as sets. And, pace came down from 5,000 race speed to mile pace at the end.

Start too fast and
your legs will explode.

CHAPTER FOURTEEN

LONG REPS REVISITED

Many months into the sessions of this part, after watching my 800s at two mile pace, he said, "I have two sessions to take your training to a new level. Three times 1,000 meters at mile race pace with 7-8 minutes rest is a good session about ten days before a 3,000 meter, two mile or 5 k race. Three times a mile at two mile pace with similar rest is great preparation for a five mile or 10 k race.

"Most middle of the pack road racers avoid track races. Long reps at high VO2 max give you the same advantages the European circuit stars have. They typically alternate a 3,000 meter race with a 5,000; or use one or two of each to prepare for a 10,000. So can you.

"Just pick a race eight weeks away and do your own variation of these sessions every 7-10 days."

* *6 x 600 meters at mile pace*
* 3 x one mile at two mile pace
* 5,000 meter race
* *4 x 800 meters at mile pace*
* 6 x 1,000 at one second a lap faster than 5 k pace (or do a second 5 k race; or a 10 k race at 15 seconds per mile slower than usual)
* 3 x one mile at two mile pace
* *3 x 1,000 at mile pace*
* Race the big 10 k

Note the way you are eased into longer reps at mile pace...with two supporting sessions between each mile pace session. You can also

From Harry Wilson

* Athletes usually need three attempts at a session before they can progress further. The first is an introduction--the second time is coming to terms--the third time is being in charge of the session...that's the time to move forward.

* During the last few sessions as you approach big races, you are not trying to run faster than before--you are trying to match your previous time...but in a more relaxed way. At the end of the session you should feel, "Hey, if I'd wanted to, I could run that session faster."

* Use heartrate to assess improvement and to measure the intensity of the repetitions and the recovery times.

* There are considerable differences in people's speed when they jog the recovery. You can't do much better than the exercise physiologists guide of:
approx. 180-190 beats per minute at the end of each fast rep, and 110-120 per minute at the end of the recovery.

* It's not just how high you raise the heartrate, but also how long you can maintain it at a steady high level.

The person who runs 4 one mile repeats at goal 5 k pace, is more likely to race a 5 k at that pace, than the person who runs 4 miles worth of 1,000 meter reps. Run the 1,000s a few seconds per mile faster, or take a shorter recovery, and you have long reps which complement the miles.

Harry Wilson...British Amateur Athletic Board Coach guided Steve Ovett to Gold Medals at 800 meters (1980 Olympics) to 5,000 meters (1996 Commonwealth Games), plus world records at the mile and 1,500 meters.

do as Harry Wilson suggests, and do the 600 and 800s for two or three sessions before moving the distance up.

"You will also do two other speed sessions between each of the above: one, a mainly aerobic session of 200-400s at mile to 5 k pace; the other at 15 k pace."

We'd been doing 400s at mile pace, and 800s at two mile pace for many months. We'd also done miles at 5 k pace, so he wasn't asking for a huge jump. In fact, with the speed from the short reps, plus the longer recoveries, the fast long reps became one of my favorite sessions...especially when he'd coached me on rest.

"The most important speed session of the week should be done with the freshest legs. If that is Saturday morning after an easy Friday, but before the commitments of the weekend, so be it. If it is Wednesday after a day at the work desk, and four days after the long run (which you maintain during this spell, though maybe a mile or two shorter), go to it."

Avoid Overtraining

"Easier said than done of course...you all have your own training threshold...which changes as you become fitter/stronger and mature or age."

"How do we do it then?" I said.

"Let's first examine the person who likes to race nearly every weekend. In urban areas, it's easy to find a quality race close to home for eight or ten weeks at a stretch. As alluded to above, some of these races should become the sustained or tempo runs. By running a 10 k race at 10-15 seconds per mile slower than your PR pace (on purpose, at even speed), you will be training at 15 k race pace or anaerobic threshold.

"But you can also race well for 6 to 8 consecutive weeks....Most years, after all, five or six of the biggest spring races are won by a single runner...who then takes a hiatus to train or return to his or her home-base.

"You avoid overtraining in these phases by eschewing speed-work between races."

I said, "So all I require is for my midweek training to include some quality to keep me fast, sufficient mileage to maintain strength, with enough rest to keep me fresh."

"Put like that, it does seem a lofty ambition...yet thousands of runners are doing it all the time. Take it a day at a time.

"The day after a race requires a rest type run. If the race distance was ten miles or more, a 30 minute easy run will be ideal; you can treat the race as the long run for the week. If the race was ten kilometers or less, most runners will run long but easy the day afterwards--at 70 percent of max heartrate. This is a relaxing way to get the race out of the system, flush the pipes out if you will. Provided you haven't got an injury, it will be of great benefit.

"Once recovered from the initial effects of the race, you have three days in which to do some useful training before resting up for the next race. A session involving short efforts, and one of long repetitions will be ideal. You should do three quarters or less of your normal amount: Allow the body to recover between race efforts. The midweek medium long run can stay, splitting the two quality sessions while you maintain stamina.

Running with headphones can be dangerous.

Schedule for Racing Weekly.

Day one - Race

Day two - Recovery run - long if race was ten kilometers or less, short if race was ten miles or more.

Day three - Rotate - Fartlek including a few hills, interval session 200 to 400 meters.

Day four - midweek 55 min run, a nice easy to steady pace.

Day five - long reps, a variety of distances: don't run more than 15 seconds per mile faster than your target speed for the next race: use the session to help your pace judgment.

Day six - Steady gentle run up to forty mins.

Day seven - Rest or short easy run.

"There is nothing magical about days three and five. They can be swapped. There are some advantages I like. The short stuff is done with post race tired legs, which is good practice, that is, running fast, with good form, on tired pegs."

"You mean legs."

"Same thing my boy."

"Anything else about the day three speed session?"

"Well, it's hardly a session. I'd want you to cruise through the intervals, though quite fast, but you will put more effort into your form than the actual speed. You'll be fast because you are fit. Unless you work on technique at this pace, the session will wear you down rather than get you ready for running relaxed in the next race."

"And what pace should it be."

"If you're racing 5,000 meters or below, include mile race pace. Otherwise, stick with the VO2 max stuff...two mile pace with a nod to 5 k pace."

"What are the other advantages of doing long reps later in the week?"

"Several inter-related things, really.

"It's four days post race, so the legs should be pretty well recovered--not that you'd want to race for a few days yet.

"You've done speedwork since the race, so you can handle long reps at any pace you like.

140

"By doing long reps three days before a race, you decrease the tendency of running ultra fast pre-race--something you might do if the short reps were on day four.

"This session will not help you in the coming weekend's race, but its training affect will aid next week's race. Yet it can hinder you--doing too much can compromise this weekend's race.

"You still have the option of training at anything from two mile to fifteen k pace. For example 4 times 800 meters at two mile pace or 3 times a mile at 15 k pace. By this stage, either session will seem like a rest day--they will be easy for you. They re-enforce and maintain your aerobic and anaerobic systems."

"We should rotate the sessions as in the previous chapter then, but do fewer reps."

"That's right: Just enough midweek to keep you ticking over as the anarchists might say; let the legs freshen up as the week goes by, and avoid blowing up in the next race."

"Fresh legs are less likely to blow up then?"

"Fresh legs and a well paced first half of the race will give you the best chance of avoiding blown muscles.

"Remember--the all-out efforts of racing each weekend are worth two or three hard training sessions. No matter how hard you try in training, it's impossible to get the adrenaline flowing like race day."

I said. "Those short recovery 200s got the adrenaline going; and those long reps at real fast pace did."

"That was the idea. Your friends should be aware of burnout from too many of those sessions though...and of over racing. One weekend off a month is the minimum in some peoples view; it allows you to put some background training in.

"On the non-racing weekends, the crucial session would be hills or other resisting surface...the type of training you normally avoid in the ten days pre-race.

"Many would argue that two speed sessions between races is foolish. If one is enough for you, don't be concerned that other people do two. You all have your own running potential to live up to...not somebody else's. In the beginning years, or in later years as

141

you age, one speed session may well be the ideal to maximize your racing fun and speeds.

"You often feel worse the second day post-race as the muscles go through the healing process. It takes confidence in your body to take it through the modest interval session on day two...which may make you feel stiffer than you did a few minutes after the race. Yet this modest session, followed by days three and four, will give the muscles enough active rest to keep you racing fit. The four easy days will enable you to race well for months, but then you should back-off from racing. Do one a month for a spell, using them at the end of an easy week, while back in base training."

Persevere with speed sessions while heavy legged. Rest towards the end of the week.

CHAPTER FIFTEEN

PEAKY ?

"One day, you will want to take racing to a higher level to prepare for the perfect race. You'll still use short races and long reps at one and two mile pace to help you, but the most important aspect of peaking for a superb performance is a four letter word...rest."

"But I've been resting every week, and before races," I said.

"Yes, you have. Now it's time for a prolonged rest.

"Instead of doing 10-15 percent less mileage for a few weeks while practicing those fast reps, you will decrease by 20, 40, 60 and 80 percent...four phases lasting one to four days each.

"Let's take a 35 mile a week runner. He or she averages five miles a day. Naturally, we can switch a couple miles around if needed.

	regular miles	decrease by %	to peak	
Sat	5		5	note one
Sun	9		8	note two
Mon	5	20	4	
Tues	5	40	3	note three
Wed	6	60	2	
Thu	5	80	2	note four
Fri	0		0	
miles	35		25	

Notes: One. At 35 miles a week, this session should normally be two to two and a half miles of quality--decrease it by half a mile. Three times 1,000 or 800 meters, or two by one mile with long rest would be good.

Two. Save a mile for Thursday. Go 10 seconds a mile slower than usual, on an easier course, at a cooler time of day.

Three. If you are used to speedwork on Monday and Wednesday, do a half speed session Monday (Five 400s instead of ten), and ten relaxed 100-200s on Wednesday. The one speed session person can save one of Monday's miles for Tuesday to give sufficient warmup and cooldown for say 3 x 400 and 3 x 200 and 2 x 100.

Four. Use the mile from Sunday to make it worth putting on shorts. Stride 75 meters four times to get you in pre-race mode.

"Bringing the average daily run down in steps is more profound for the higher mileage person. Take a 70 mile weeker; she rests up for a 10 mile race. Every three days, she will decrease mileage by 20 percent, but those miles can be used on any of the three days.

Days till race		Usual Miles	3 day decrease		New Miles	Daily Miles
			Total	by %		
13	Sun	15		0	15	15
12	Mon	9				7
11	Tues	10	(31)	20	(26)	8
10	Wed	12				11
9	Thur	9				6
8	Fri	6	(24)	40	(15)	3
7	Sat	9				6
6	Sun	15				9
5	Mon	9	(34)	60	(14)	5
4	Tues	10				0
3	Wed	12				3
2	Thur	9	(27)	80	(5)	2
1	Fri	6				0
Day zero						Race
	Total	140			(84)	

"By day seven, the legs should be feeling fresh. This is a chance to do three miles of good speedwork at 2 mile to 5 k pace, or a 5 k tempo. Don't overdo the pace.

"On day six, if you must go for double digits, don't go over ten miles.

"There are just enough miles on day five and three to do 4 times 800 meters and 4 times 400 meters respectively.

"Many runners will find it difficult to rest on race day minus four. Try a 30 minute walk instead; or do a three mile run if you must."

"Is there a less complicated way to peak for a race?" I asked him later.

"They're all variations on the same theme--a combination of reducing mileage and the amount of speed running, possibly doing the speedwork a bit faster.

"You can reduce your mileage by 15 to 20 percent for three to four weeks, finishing with about 40 percent of your regular miles. For example, weeks of 65, 55 and 40 for an 80 mile weeker.

"You can simply take a mile off each of your runs until you get down to say four miles for the last three days pre-race. If you average seven miles a day, you would need to commence the taper 6 days pre-race. A better taper would be achieved by coming down a mile every two or three days. Remember: the body takes time to make use of the rest; just like it took time to adapt to the training."

"How you organize your speedwork is just as important. As your mileage decreases, the length of the reps should decrease. By implication, the race pace you train at will decrease--Speed increases. The last four sessions, done at two to four day intervals according to the schedule you've been used to, might be:

* miles, 1,000s, 600s, and 300s.
* The pace will probably be 15 k, 5 k, 2 mile and one mile.
* The total amount of your reps for these sessions might be 5, 4, 3 and 2 miles.

"Another approach is the opposite."

"The opposite again," I was smiling, "how does that work?"

"It depends on which factor we change."

"I suspect we decrease the mileage," I said.

"Yes, we do. But we run long reps at fast pace early... then drop to short reps at slower pace. The last four speed sessions could be:

* 3 x one mile at 2 mile pace
* 4 x 1,000 meters at 5 k pace
* 5 x 600 meters at 10 k pace
* 6 x 400 at 15 k pace

"This scheme would discourage you from burning yourself out just before a race. All runners have an innate natural speed after all; though the last two sessions are slower than 5 k pace, the legs will still be capable, indeed, well rested to race a 5,000 meters. You will be fresh because you sauntered through the last two sessions.

"Note the amount of fast running comes down from three miles to only one-and-a-half at the end. Because you are running slower, you could do three miles at each pace, and it would still qualify as resting up. For psychological reasons, and to bring in those fast twitch muscle fibers, I recommend you finish the sessions with four 100s at mile pace.

Watch your eating.

While few of us neglect to look at what we eat before it goes in our chewing hole, the Guru wanted these thoughts passed on.

There is a tendency to put on weight while resting up for a race.

A. You're not dehydrated. Runners tend to be chronically dehydrated. The easier, shorter and non-run days allow you to correct this imbalance.

B. Less suppression of appetite due to easier training. Of course, some runners' appetites are never suppressed.

C. You have more time for food. Fewer lunch hour runs. You finish those short runs before the family has sat down to dinner--instead of halfway through it.

D. You think you need more food or energy.

FACT: Resting up allows the muscles to get a full store of glycogen for their race. You'll need fewer calories, especially from fat.

If you overeat, it will be like strapping a two to four pound bag of sugar to your waist.

"Instead of the table above, the person who averages ten miles a day could do eight miles for three days; then six for three days and four on the last three days prerace. Added to these nine days of resting up you'd have to consider the long run. Reduce it by 15 to 20 percent two weeks before the race...which is the day before the first eight miler.

"One week prerace would have been a six miler. Allow yourself 65-70 percent of your regular long run.

"The last fourteen days of our seventy weeker, would be: 9, 12, 9, 8, 8, 8, 6, (60). 6, 10, 6, 6, 4, 4, 4 (40). Retain fast running on your usual days."

"Some people get good success with the double peak system. They rest up while finessing their speed for a race--run the race--then take an additional easy week before racing again.

"Most of the six or seven days between races will be easy runs of three to four miles...assuming it is half or less of what the athlete normally does each day. The sub 30 mile a week person will not run on these rest days.

"Two days after the race would be a long run; do 60-75 percent of your normal long run.

"Four days after the race would also be three days before the next race--"

"So I'd do speedwork...a half session at two mile pace to blow out the gaskets."

"Quaint expression. I think blowing your gaskets out would be a bit too strenuous. Though you will be shifting, don't do much of it. Then race again. You can do this three or four times before going back to base training."

"While there is no golden session, no magic bullet in this sport, resting up, combined with the techniques in the first pages of this part, should help you race faster.

The most important thing is to rest, while doing sufficient running that you do not de-train.

Research

"Your people amaze me," he said one day, "for their propensity to quote erroneous research."

"Would you like to annoy a few Ph.D.s by giving specifics."

"The most often miss-used piece of 'research' showed that runners who did intervals every day for 6 days before a race--five times 400...decreasing to one rep at the end of the taper--while cutting mileage by 85 percent, improved their race performance by 8 seconds per mile."

"That's a huge increase. Where is the problem?"

"There are three. First...a person new to interval training makes huge gains in running economy when introducing this session. Most runners working through part 5 found it very easy to up the 400 meter pace by 2-3 seconds per lap after just two sessions. This alone would account for more than the 8 seconds per mile improvement.

"Second...The reduction in training by such a proportion, would also (on its own) give a substantial boost to race times. But why mess up a piece of research, why waste the money by changing two factors at once? How can you keep a straight face while claiming the improvement was due to either rest or speedwork?"

"Especially," I said, "when we know either will help you to run faster!"

"Which highlights the final point. The control group. Or as my bosses said when I passed on the info, 'the non-control group.' They did not make any changes at all in mileage, not even the 15 percent drop we recommend in Chapter Thirteen; certainly not the 40 percent or so we have been alluding to in recent pages. And they made no changes in speedwork at all. They didn't cut a mile off the session a week before the race, didn't do a half session three days pre-race. They didn't train at 5 K, 2 mile then one mile pace for the last three sessions. They just did their regular sessions as if they were in the middle of a winter build-up."

"So they stank in the race."
"Right." He said. "The control had no hope of performing better than in an average race. They were no fresher than if they were going out for their normal Saturday session at threshold pace, yet the researchers pitted them against people who had practiced running economy on fresh legs. A super-rested Chapter Fifteen runner, versus a Chapter Eight runner."
"No contest." I said.
"Mis-used research" he replied.

Hungarian coach Mihaly Igloi had huge success with his athletes pre and post Iron curtain problems. His emphasis was on stress tolerance. Fellow Hungarian **Janos Ronaszeki** followed similar principles while running professionally in the 1970s.

Janos says that you can do huge sessions such as 10-12 times a mile if you have sufficient background mileage. He added that:
Gym work is important age 16-22.
Once strength is developed, light speed training can commence.
You cannot run hard without base...the injury risk is too great.
Most people doing 10 Ks should probably do 3-5 miles of repeats.
Do them on a soft road or surface.
Include half miles and quarters.
Do a few strides after the repetition session.
Tailor speed sessions according to your needs and your health.
Be brave enough to take rest days.
Take one easy week in four; cut mileage by 40 percent.
As you get older you will need more rest.

Janos lives and runs in Glendora, California. He coached many runners in the late 1980s, and ran a 2:46 marathon in his late 40s.

CHAPTER SIXTEEN

RACING PITFALLS

How to decrease your exposure to dehydration, hyper and hypothermia.

Hypothermia--Coping with Race Day Cold

"In a design fault of its maker, the human body is more efficient when its temperature has risen slightly--to about 101 degrees F--this is why you need to warm up before hard sessions and races.

"On cold days, you must stay at this temperature--dress to keep it in. You may require tights or lightweight track bottoms for the legs; a long sleeve running shirt with club vest on top and possibly a T-shirt between. Make sure two of these tuck into the shorts...many shirts shrink over a period of months.

"Synthetics are better than wool. Use lightweight gloves. To avoid over-heating, these can be dropped off at a friend's feet if the race has circuits; or you can arrange for someone to be at, say, the three mile point in a long road race. Or drop them off at the one mile point, and pick them up in the warmdown.

"Except in long races, avoid the cold drinks on offer. Dehydration is rarely a problem in winter...unless you were drinking alcohol the previous evening, or forgot your fluids in the morning. A warm drink half *and* an hour before the start may be required if the race is more than ten kilometers.

"Avoid standing for long periods before the start. It will make you tired and allow you to cool. Go to the start area at the last practical moment after your warmup. Wear a disposable top layer and stay out of the wind.

"Provided you start at a realistic pace, the cold should not be a problem. Even pace is vital; if you slow during the second half, cold soon gets to you. If you have any doubts about your fitness, give cold race days a miss. The onset of a cold or throat infection must be treated seriously, give the first aiders a break--stay at home."

Hypothermia...technically, a body temp below 94 degrees F.

Some people exhibit the following signs at higher temps:

Fatigue--extremely tired, more so than usual.

Cold--the whole body may feel chilled, sweating ceases.

Shivering,

Slow pulse

Lightheaded--not high, just silly...leading to

unreasonable behavior--loss of temper, perhaps violence--and of course, the runner insists he or she can finish the race.

Slurred speech--as if drunk. Less alert

Loss of body actions--the running becomes a stagger or shuffle--wanders across the course.

Can lead to complete collapse.

Treatment:

Get yourself or the person you have spotted with this problem out of the cold and wind.

Remove wet clothing. Wet skin can lose 25 times more heat than dry skin. Replace with layers of warm clothes.

A shower or bath can restore warmth to the body--but great care is needed. A cold drafty shower room is of little use, but a shower or bath where the temperature can gradually be increased as the person's own temperature rises is recommended. Use 100-105 F. No heat pads--there's a high propensity for burns.

Do not rub the body to warm it up; gentle massage may be of use. Putting feet or hands into warm water or in a volunteer's armpits will help--blood flow to the extremity will then increase, take in the heat and take it back into the central core. Tingling on re-circulation is good. If no tingling, or the skin is still numb when warm...see an MD.

Give warm drinks, plus a simple energy source such as chocolate. Then hotter, nourishing drinks once the body can handle them. Soup should be kept at hand for this.

If able to, keep the person moving--they generate their own heat.

Use warm blankets or the heat retaining foils such as mylar.

No alcohol. Alcohol doesn't warm you...but it can kill you by further dilating skin blood vessels resulting in loss of still more precious body heat.

Exposed skin can freeze; the lungs cannot be hurt by running in the cold air--though if conditions are extreme, a cold air mask from a pharmacy can be a useful aid.

"Respect the cold but don't be frightened by it. Heed the wind chill factor. While 40 to 60 degree windless days may seem the ideal for setting good times, many personal records have been set as a light snow is falling amidst runners with three shirts on."

Running in the Heat

"Only about 25 percent of the energy you use for running makes you move....Most of the rest is wasted as heat. Fine in winter--but getting rid of internal heat can be a problem in summer.

"Losing this excess heat requires
1/ a temperature below your body's--so you don't absorb more heat from the air.

If you take a 9 day winter trip in the south--starting with a race on the first day, remember to do your 8 high mileage days at modest pace. Days 2 and 3, recover from the race. You could do anaerobic threshold on the 4th and 6th day, but leave your VO2 max session for day 9. If you've had months of steady running, do it at 5 K pace; don't push for 2 mile pace. Expect to feel wasted for a day afterwards...which is fine, you'll appreciate a couple of very easy days on return to colder climes. It will take you at least a week to recover from the 9 days training; for your body to benefit fully from the vacation's effort.

Attempting a track session, free of encumbering track suits, at one to two mile pace early in the week, can invite a frustrating vacation. You don't go south to lounge around by the pool.

2/ air movement, the body moving or wind.
3/ air that is able to take up more water--to evaporate the sweat. When there is near 100 % humidity, little sweat will evaporate.

"The worst situation is a high temperature, high humidity day with the wind from behind going at the same speed as the runner.

"When training in even modest temperatures, sweating occurs, and blood vessels near the skin dilate to allow heat to escape. This takes blood away from the muscles and takes fluid out of the system: The result is dehydration and a decrease in performance because the heartrate must increase to maintain the same volume per minute through the muscles...enabling you to maintain the same exercise intensity...but if you are already at your maximum, it won't be able to.

"The body will try to adjust. Urine output decreases, blood volume increases; sweating becomes more efficient. But it takes two weeks or so to adapt to the heat. Avoid the harshest workouts. Do your anaerobic threshold as reps with two minutes rest in the shade instead of as a tempo run. Do them based on heartrate, not pace; you'll be closer to half-marathon pace than 15 K.

"Plan your racing to decrease heat problems. Atlanta doesn't seem like the ideal place to race in July, yet many do so without problems. Adjust the time of your runs to prepare for hot and humid conditions--or wear an extra shirt at your regular time. If you live in a cooler part of the country, a lightweight track suit will stimulate the body's response to racing in the heat. Don't overdress though; do at least half your mileage free of these encumbrances. It's probably best to run in the sun to get used to the heat...and for the delight of feeling it on your SPF 15 protected skin.

"Hot weather running is a form of resistance training...and I'm not talking about that slight increased resistance of the air you must part as you run. You can train at a lower speed for the same heartrate--just like you do at altitude. At slow speeds, you are less likely to get a muscular injury. But stay well hydrated.

"On a long run at modest pace, say 70 percent max, you will be able to maintain pace--but as the run proceeds, as you become more dehydrated, you'll be working at and then beyond 80 percent of max heartrate. Yet the damage to your legs will be at 70 percent max speed. You have an altitude training effect from the dehydration--something you should avoid because of its potential harm.

"Most races start before 9 a.m. On the big day, wearing your lightweight running vest which the breeze goes through, you can concentrate on the race. Clothing should be loose and light in color. Drink sufficient fluids before the race; even sprinters have poor performances due to dehydration--from lack of fluid before the start. Avoid standing in direct sunlight pre-race. Find a breezy, shaded spot.

"For races of more than ten kilometers, get used to taking drinks on the move. With plastic cups, this is best done by taking half a cup of water, cover most of the top with your hand, and pour a mouthful at a time. Some people take a straw with them to make it easier. Sponges can be used to cool the head, neck and main muscle groups (thighs). Beware of getting all your running stuff wet; shorts and socks can become uncomfortable.

"As with cold days, even pace is the aim. When the temperature or heat index is real high, start off slower than normal. Stay out of the sun. Gentle stretching will suffice for the warmup; do a few gentle strides without tracksuit and you'll be ready to go.

"If you misjudge the pace, you must consider dropping out. Although you will feel bad at the time, you will feel better than if you'd ended up in the first aid vehicle with heat exhaustion. You can have your good run another day. The other reason to drop out is to avoid the plodding and suffering for the last three quarters of the race. This will leave a mental scare of greater magnitude than dropping out. Give your ego a break...drop out if you need to.

"Most of the above is relevant when training. Arrange long runs around drink sources. Wear a fanny pack water bottle holder if needed...hand held water bottles affect form.

"Part of the course should be in shade. There should be several cut-off points so that a run can be shortened. Listen to your body. Is it over tired from the previous day's training, or are you at the beginning of a slight illness? In the former case, a long run at a sensible pace will be ideal; in the latter, a shorter run or rest is required.

"Eating smaller, more frequent cold meals can help during a hot spell...preferably, with cold drinks. Stay in a cool place before and after exercise to help prepare and recover respectively.

"Avoid chronic dehydration by checking the color of your urine. This will usually be dark or orangy after a session, but should return to its normal pale yellow within a few hours.

"You may like to use one of the electrolyte drinks on the market, but a good mix of several drinks should be sufficient. Fruit juice, tea, coffee, milk, (beer has many things in its favor as a source of electrolytes and energy, but alcohol dehydrates--consumption should be reduced prior to racing in hot spells). You can decrease alcohol dehydration by matching each pint consumed with a pint of water....Don't use it as an excuse to do the reverse.

"Use caffeine in moderation.; and drink caffeine free stuff to flush it out."

Heatstroke & heat exhaustion--the first is simply an exacerbation of the second. Official temperatures are 105 and 102 F. But you may get heat exhaustion at 101, or with your training (but don't bank on it) 103.

"The body will feel hot with pale, clammy skin. Thirst, headache and dizziness are typical. Other signs are similar to hypothermia concerning how the body feels and reacts. The result is loss of coordination and confusion. If the high pulse rate does not decrease on cessation of exercise, and if sweating has ceased, total collapse can follow.

Drinking water.
Dehydration and raised body temperature lead to a decrease in performance. Heat injury risk increases. Drink water or a 5 percent sugar solution before, during and after exercise. Drinking fluids has a more profound effect on your cooling system than pouring it over your head. If copious supplies are available though, a dunking can help. The first cup goes inside...always.

155

Treatment.

Get out of the sun.

Stop exercising.

Cool the body. Get more air contact--face the breeze, or use a fan. or have someone fan the person. Removing the shirt is optional. A cold wet shirt can aid heat loss. Apply cool water by sponging; use ice if available.

Give cool drinks--sips only at first as vomiting can be a problem. A cool bath or shower is excellent, if available: It must be supervised. Keeping the clothing on is not a problem. Walking the person into natural bodies of water is often an option.

Low blood sugar may be a concurrent problem; simple sugars may be required. A small amount of salt may also be needed to replace what's been lost in sweating. As a general rule, extra salt is not required once the body has got used to warm weather running: though minimal salt (half a teaspoon in a pint of sugared solution) can be given for the initial muscle cramps.

Cool fluid is the important thing. Get them to drink as much as they can tolerate without becoming nauseous. Don't exercise to the point of nausea in the first place.

If the pulse rate doesn't decrease, the runner should be taken for first aid or medical attention.

"Don't let the above put you off running and racing in the extremes of this country's climate. Unless you have a weak heart, you should cope well with all but the very worst days. Indeed, some people thrive in such conditions. Most just have a slight decrease in the standard of performance. Running within a minute of your best time on a hot day could be the equivalent of a personal best in ideal conditions."

Wearing a cap with a bill shades your eyes, reduces squinting, which tenses the face muscles and can spread lower. It also improves your form.

A cap will make you look up. It makes you run tall. It can help you run better.

Treadmills are useful to avoid heat or cold. Set it at a two percent incline to compensate for the air resistance you won't have indoors. Make sure you have a fan...it's easy to overheat in a stuffy 75 degree exercise room. Dress appropriately.

"The biggest problem with treadmill running is the tendency to cheat the machine. You soon realize that if you bounce up higher on each stride you can set the machine faster. In essence, you are jumping up and down while the belt goes faster. Don't spoil your form with excessive vertical lift. Push off with the calves to go forward, not upwards.

"A second problem is the position of the controls. If they are in front of you, they can hinder your arm carriage.

Running in a vacuum is no fun.

Blood donation

Giving blood will take about one tenth of your Red Blood Cells (RBCs), so you'd think it would decrease your performance by 10 percent: It only decreases it by 2 percent.

The other factors--amount of air taken in by the lungs, muscle power, number of mitochondria, inherent ability and background training are still intact. Even the blood _volume_ is replenished within a few hours. And it is less thick; it flows more easily.

This is not the day or week to increase your training, but you don't need to decrease it either. If your usual 400s take 100 seconds, you will be able to run 102s at the same effort level 6 hours after giving blood--provided you hydrate properly. If you usually run at 2 mile pace, you'll be running at 5 k pace, yet the heart and lungs will still be at 2 mile intensity. The cardiovascular system at 2 mile pace--your lucky legs will only be trashed at 5 K pace. A win-win situation.

Over 75 % of Carbon Dioxide waste is excreted via the plasma--the fluid portion of blood. Thankfully, most is in a buffered form...as bicarbonate. Therefore, donating a tenth of your RBCs has minimal effect on CO2 levels.

After the donation, RBCs production--just like at altitude--will increase. The extras will come on line at 2 weeks and get you back to normal levels in 4. (It's no coincidence that you are only allowed to give blood every 4 weeks.)

Giving blood twice a year is more worthwhile than giving cash. It will give you a reason to back off from racing for a few weeks, and help save a life.

Wind Chill.

How wet you are, the speed you are moving at, the temperature, and the wind, all play a factor in heat loss.
When the wind chill index is below -25 F, avoid biking.
On all cold days:
Warm up before stepping out the door;
Layer clothing;
Wear a HAT...25-40 percent of heat loss is from the head;
Exercise at the warmest time of day, or when wind is lowest;
Put dry clothes on immediately after exercising;
Don't hang around getting cold while talking afterwards.

				Wind speed (mph)					
		0	**5**	**10**	**15**	**20**	**25**	**30**	**35**	**40**
		50	48	40	36	32	30	28	27	26
T		40	37	28	22	18	16	13	11	10
e		*30*	*27*	*16*	*9*	*4*	*0*	*-2*	*-4*	*-6*
m		20	16	4	-5	-10	-15	-18	-20	-21
p		10	6	-9	-18	-25	-29	-33	-35	-37
		0	-5	-24	-32	-39	-44	-48	-51	-53
		-10	-15	-33	-45	-53	-59	-63	-67	-69
F		*-20*	*-26*	*-46*	*-58*	*-67*	*-74*	*-79*	*-82*	*-85*
		-30	-36	-58	-72	-82	-88	-94	-98	-100
		-40	-47	-70	-85	-96	-104	-109	-113	-115

Note the relatively large increase in the chill factor at modest wind speed. There is a much greater increase from 5 to 15 mph than there is from 25 to 35.

Gracilis and Sartorius

When considering problems from the hip to the knee, don't forget these two muscles. They stabilize the upper leg, and play crucial rolls in lateral movement.

Gracilis adducts the thigh and flexes the leg on the thigh.

Sartorius flexes and rotates the thigh.

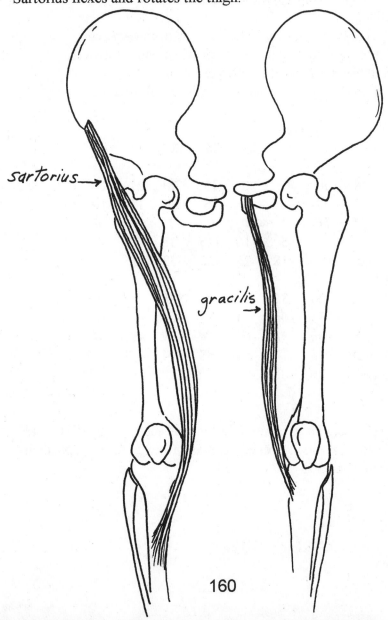

sartorius→

gracilis→

PART SEVEN

AVOIDING INJURY

Running doesn't seem complex; placing one foot in front of the other, leaving the ground on each stride is as simple as a sport gets--yet the repeated movement sets up a chain of events from your head to your toes, and vice versa. Be out of alignment at either end, and your entire body can be affected.

It's a fact--Physical therapists are guaranteed a steady flow of sports injury patients. In spring, baseball players come in with pulled shoulders from excessive bat swings or throwing; in the fall, footballers arrive with leg problems, not having kicked a ball for months. Runners are not immune--though training year round, they often move from endurance to speedwork or vice versa with no preparation.

"This part needs only six words," said the Guru.

Don't turn off the pain--pain warns you to slow down or stop.
Don't mask the pain with pills--you will lose the body's warning sign.
Ignore the pain at your peril--you'll get what you deserve...a long break from running.

161

CHAPTER SEVENTEEN

"FIND THE CAUSE...ACT ON IT."

"Or to be long winded--do something to correct the weakness or the problem which exacerbates an injury.

"Simple actions often prevent an injury, such as cutting the tabs off your shoes and other remedies suggested earlier.

"The skill is in locating the problem. Is your noggin at a bad angle; does your shoulder droop from a skiing crash; or, are your feet unable to move in those lovely shoes."

The Guru went on to say.

"To get faster, we've been pushing the body harder in terms of effort or mileage. Every runner has a training threshold at which each additional effort will give a decrease in performance--the law of diminishing returns has set in. For the lucky ones, it means frustration; for those who can't recognize it in time, it leads to injury.

"Train don't strain, is this planets old motto. Those three words, plus the six at the top of the page, are all this part needs. But you have a book to write, a destiny to fulfill, so listen closely."

That commenced our post-run fireside chats. A winter of advice to fill the next two parts. Here's what the Guru said.

"Six months of consistently running say 50 miles will allow steady progress. A few weeks at 60 miles may result in an injury. While recovering from the injury you lose training time; you lose a significant part of the fitness gained in prior months. You often go back to square one.

"Unfortunately...earthlings have different capacities before injuries occur. Each runner can handle a certain mileage without problems; increase the load beyond YOUR limit, and your body soon breaks down. You can only learn by experience how much your body can take before something gives.

"The prudent runner spots an impending problem early. When you recognize there is a problem, the simplest action, yet the action which runners resist most, is to...cut back on training."

Injury warning signs.

"Stress is often present--sometimes from the running itself, or from work, money, family or house moving etc. Signs to watch for include:-

1/ Feeling tired, perhaps not sleeping well.
2/ Illness, sore throat, colds or flu, skin conditions, mouth ulcers.
3/ Swollen lymph glands.
4/ Loss of weight.

Leg Length difference

A shorter leg alters the alignment of the spine, increasing injuries such as sciatica and I-T band syndrome. It decreases running efficiency.

Pelvis to foot x-rays are the most accurate way to measure leg lengths. However, most therapists can measure you adequately in their offices:

They'll have you lie down, place your hips in alignment, perhaps raise your legs to 'shake them out,' then check for the position of the heels.

You can self check while standing. In the mirror, see how level the top of the pelvis is. If one side is lower you have your first hint. Place a magazine under the foot of the short leg. Add more until the hips are level. See how it feels. Your spine may have curved over the years to help compensate for the difference.

If you've had unexplained problems with any of your leg joints or back, see a specialist. Otherwise, try a heel insert for all your shoes, and consider an orthotic.

The quarter inch or so pad may avoid future injuries, while shaving seconds off your running times.

"Stress or fatigue may express itself in your running speed--your pace may decrease for a given effort. You think you're running well at 7 min miles, but on checking the final time, it works out at over 7½ min miles."

"So I should reduce the stress level before an injury occurs?"

"Right," he said. "A reduction of mileage by 20 percent is a good start. Cut a mile or two off of most runs, and take an extra day off. Swap relaxed sessions of fartlek for track work or repetitions. The cause of the stress should be addressed. Do something about the stressors you have control over; live with, or completely run from those which you don't! If necessary, the running becomes something it frequently is not after you've reached a higher level--pure recreation.

"When moving house and or jobs, it's logical to have an easy four to six weeks of running. Do a weekly quality tempo, or session of reps--short or long--it doesn't matter which. Run moderately long also, and you can retain 90 percent of your fitness for months. When settled, you can return to your former intensity.

"Overtraining fatigue related to an increased non-running schedule, should be distinguished from **Delayed Onset Muscle Soreness (DOMS),** which is the muscle aches and pains you feel after a particularly hard workout or race. This may last several days, but walking at the end of the session and easy training for a few days should see you back to normal."

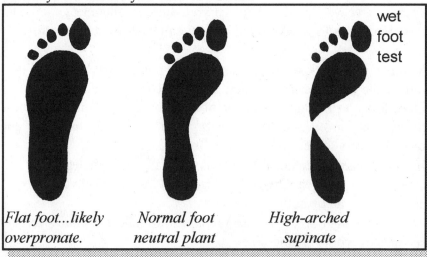

wet foot test

Flat foot...likely overpronate.   *Normal foot neutral plant*   *High-arched supinate*

"Runners with a low flexible arch or flat foot frequently over-pronate and will require a motion control shoe built with a straight shape on a board or combination last.

A high rigid arch person may under-pronate or supinate and need a cushioned shoe of a curved shape on a slip-lasted base to encourage normal movement. These shoes are soft and flexible.

"The medium arched citizen is likely to have something close to a neutral running gait. It still may need some correction from mild anti-pronation or supination shoes. Many only need a stable shoe of a semi-curved shape on a slip or combination construction...firm in the heel and flexible in the forefoot."

See also, Pronation and Supination in Part Eight.

I asked him about some specific injuries. "What about the strain resulting from a slight twist of the ankle or knee?"

"Usually the pain is immediate, though it may only last a few seconds in a minor twist. This makes a strain much easier to spot, though not necessarily easier to avoid, than stress. You may be able to continue the run in comfort, but the pain will return at the end of the run. Use the first aid actions at the end of the chapter.

The foot is simply a **bag of bones** kept together by ligaments and tendons. Keep it supple and free of cramps with stretching; place it in comfortable shoes with at least a quarter inch of space at the end of the toes; tie the laces for a firm, but not a tight fit; and there's a good chance they won't frustrate your running ambitions.

The foot absorbs shock on every stride; it adapts to the ground; it relaxes and rolls inwards (pronates) during midstance or the support phase as some call it; then becomes rigid again as its levers, and the muscles acting on them, propel you forward.

Got a pain on the top of your foot? Are your feet high arched? Do you have a tendency towards tight calves? These can cause your extensor tendons on the top of the foot to overwork. Pain can extend to the toe, especially at push-off.

Loosen those laces...use a good warmup with stretching...and the first time you make the mistake, use heat in the acute phase. The second time...change sports!

165

"Many runners fail to recognize the twist itself is the result of overtraining."

"How so?"

"When fresh, the awkward foot placement which sends you off balance can often be corrected over the next few strides. When you're tired from high mileage or excessive quality, you have less ability to make rapid adjustments in your stride--if you're less able to adjust...you're more likely to injure yourself.

"That said, old running shoes are a bigger contributor to injuries than overtraining. Restrict yourself to 500 miles per pair--do the last part of the mileage on very soft terrain--wear them for comfort and protection from sharps in the sand or grass, rather than cushioning.

"When injured, you should ease off or rest for a few days to allow the tear and associated muscle strain to heal. Don't train through the injury if it hurts--you will simply put more strain on the healthy muscles as your running style compensates for the unfit area. A two or three day calf strain can result in a hamstring injury lasting weeks."

Reducing the risk of a **twisting-type injury**:

* Don't hold the arms up too high. Run relaxed with a natural style. Push the arms straight back to decrease shoulder roll and twisting and strain on the back.

* Avoid fast running on sections of path with ruts or tree roots, for example, in fartlek sessions.

* Wear appropriate shoes for the surface...shoes with sufficient grip. Use studs or dimples, or whatever this year's term for a cross-country sole is. They should get you through most dirt. Spikes are a great aid if you like to do speedwork through mud or on wet grass. Unless you're going sub 16 for 5 k, or racing shorter stuff, don't use them on the track.

* Beware of excessive cambers and poor road surfaces.

* In particular, don't run across a hill if the slope is more than a couple of degrees. If a beach is minimally sloped at the low tide bar, or the flat area at high tide, running in both directions will equalize the wear and tear on the ankles, knees and hips."

"Then there's the pernicious overstriding problem."

"Is overstriding that wicked?" I asked.

"To get the best out of yourself, you aim to run fast for the entire race. To do this, you need to run with the longest stride compatible with your body type, height, joint ranges, muscle flexibility, footgear and running surface. Yet you must have control over unnecessary movements, and keep good leg speed for the duration of the event. To quote the 'Chariots of Fire' coach, you must avoid the slap in the face which occurs on overstriding.

"Your stride length should not put you at a stretch on each revolution of the legs or stride cycle. Adjust your stride length and leg speed according to the distance you're running. When commencing a ten mile or half marathon race, runners automatically (if after blowing up a few times), start at a slower speed than in a five mile race. They can't hope to run at the same speed for twice the distance--though some of your readers will run ten miles next year at a similar speed to which they ran five miles last year or the year before. This improvement only comes from the progressive training outlined in previous chapters.

"A long stride is inefficient. Even 400 and 800 meter runners aim to avoid overstriding, because it gives them an increased injury potential while slowing their race times.

Poor planning

"The warm up and warm down, including stretching and strides as explained in Parts One to Three, must be sufficient to prepare the body for its task, and to relax afterwards. They are of equal importance.

"The training schedule must progress in a logical fashion--just as this book does. While you could start with Part Two and build endurance with 20 or more striders each day...then add the steady runs of part one...it would be dangerous for most people.

"Most people commencing a running program do so from a poor fitness base--sprinting for a bus while out of shape is an invitation to the emergency room--so ease into things as Part One encourages.

"Never make a sudden increase in mileage or pace; a ten percent increase for two or three weeks may be alright--but consolidate for a few weeks at this level before moving on."

He gave this example:

"A runner has been doing five 4 mile runs per week for several months and feels ready for a new challenge. He does 5 miles twice the first week; three times the next week; then each day during the third week. He consolidates for two weeks, then adds another mile onto two of his runs each week. Mileage would be 22, 23, 25, 25, 25, 27. The increase from the original base was 10, 5 and 10 percent."

The Alien would like to see the runner doing a few striders and other Part Two sessions, leading to some gentle tempo running--but the main thing is the 33 percent mileage increase occurred over six weeks.

"What you're looking for is a manageable level of fatigue; three weeks after an increase you should have adapted to it...and returned to homeostasis. Then it may be time to increase the load again, going faster or further--or you can simply enjoy your new level of fitness."

For the more advanced runner he had this to say.

"Olympic medalists run at 3,000 to 5,000 race pace at least one session a week in winter. So should you. This will help you maintain good form, thus decreasing injury potential. Move gradually to track work in the spring, keeping at least a couple of steady runs to maintain strength in the summer and acting as a base for the mileage build up in the autumn.

"Running is more productive as it gets more efficient. Straight lines, rhythmic movement, proper alignments make you faster and less injury prone."

Self-inflicted injuries

"Plan your weekly schedule to put stress on a different aspect of running on consecutive days. You may be able to handle 10 efforts of 200 meters up a hill on a Monday, but you wouldn't want to repeat it on the next four days....and 'kill' your Achilles in the process. Don't run a hard six miles and repeat it each day either.

Spread the fast and steady running throughout the week and over future weeks.

"Certain sessions require an easy run or rest for the day or many days after. The body takes at least a week to get over a ten mile race, and three weeks to recover from a marathon. During this time, the body needs rest, easy runs and gentle stretching. As the muscle stiffness and fatigue reduces enough for you to feel comfortable when running fast, do so...but only as relaxed strides which put very little stress on the muscles. This type of running helps the body to recover. Any attempt at fast long repetitions, tempo runs or racing is likely to result in problems. Long repetitions done slower than you would normally do them may be beneficial....provided you don't push yourself hard. Three times a mile at half-marathon pace, half-way through a recovery week, can be a pleasant session if you'd been used to doing five reps at 15 k pace pre race.

"Assess out how much time you need to recover from a particular session. You may need four easy days a week--allowing you to do three quality sessions. Or, you may need three easy days after every quality session...which, of course, could mean those quality sessions are too harsh for you.

"Back to back moderate hard days (the second day gives your legs a feel which is close to the mid and late race fatigue), followed by two easy days may work for you. Or they may be your undoing."

"Soft or forgiving terrain is important for injury prevention. The treadmills half inch give on each stride is clearly an advantage over asphalt. There is no camber. Note those drawbacks though."

Remember...FIND THE CAUSE OF THE INJURY...CURE THE CAUSE AND TREAT THE INJURY.

"Runners should keep a first aid kit to maintain comfort and for immediate treatment of an injury--thus reducing the severity of it.

Comfort items include:

Vaseline or petroleum jelly to stop chafing on long runs and races--groin, armpits, nipples and under the breasts in particular.

Baby powder and tape or moleskin for the well known trouble spots of your feet.

Band-Aids can be used to avoid painful nipples due to vest friction.

Cool drinks in the summer, warm drinks in winter, sometimes both in spring and autumn as conditions can change.

Liniment or cream--massaged into the skin helps warm up the local area--useful for old strains and aches, but not to 'hide' an injury where rest would be more appropriate. The major benefit is self massage...the tendency to get this muscle well warmed up before commencing the run; you don't need expensive creams.

Immediate treatment items include:

* Ice packs.

* Bandage, a wide crepe bandage is better than a thin one. Apply in a series of figure of eight, work towards the heart, with each layer half over-lapping the previous layer; with practice, it can be a good compression bandage. Ace bandages require less skill. Don't let either type become a tourniquet.

* Use sterile dressings and antiseptic cream or liquid to cover blisters after you've popped them with a sterile, or sterilized needle to allow the fluid out. A stretched out safety pin held over a flame until red is sterile. Let it cool before using it--take the dressing well beyond the edge of the blister.

* Felt can be positioned to take pressure off an area. Remember though...the pressure will be going somewhere else!

* Scissors and safety pins.

* Pain killers--aspirin or other member of the non-steroid anti inflammatory drugs family (NSAIDs). They will decrease part of the body's inflammatory response...decreasing pain and the perception of pain.

But some inflammatory response is needed to bring in nutrients and take away damaged cells. Ice and pure painkillers may be better for some people. Your decision can come down to whether you'd like to risk your stomach (one to two hundred thousand hospitalizations a year are from use of NSAIDs--ten percent result in death--equal to the participants in a major marathon each year), or your liver.

Don't take pain pills for a chronic problem. Find out why you have the chronic problem.

Never take pain pills before an event.

Do not mask the pain so that you can run.

*   *   *

Like all first aid, first aid on running injuries involves:

A/ Removing any danger to the runner or first aider--a dog for instance if one was involved, or removal to the side of the road, particularly in the early stages of a road race.

B/ Treatment of anything life threatening--relevant in hypo and hyperthermia, and where severe bleeding is involved--stop it by direct pressure to the bleeding area and raising the limb above the heart if possible.

C/ Stop the problem getting worse--for you, this means stop running and RICE, which stands for

R...rest;

I....ice applied for ten minutes;

C....compression--the application of a pressure bandage
     (by experienced first aider);

E....elevation...raising the limb (to reduce inflammation and relax tense muscles).

Take NSAIDs if appropriate, but not on an empty stomach. Ice should be applied several times a day for ten to twenty minutes, and the limb should be elevated whenever possible for the first two days.

D/ If pain is severe, seek medical attention because a fracture or sprain may be present. When pain free at walking pace, you can re-commence running.

Before running again, the joint and muscles should be put through their normal range of movement. Gentle stretching helps the muscles regain their formal length.

171

* **Blisters**--due to skin being subjected to more rubbing than usual. Avoid by building mileage up slowly; break in new shoes with a walk; do a few short runs before using them for a long run. Throw out old socks...they cost less than a beer. Pad problem areas.

If your smaller foot is significantly so, a second thin sock that side may help.

Treat blisters as an injury because your running style may change to avoid putting pressure on the sensitive area.

Calluses can be a later stage and should be welcomed as they protect you. Don't let them become too thick. File them, or use moisturizers. The edges have a habit of blistering. Wear well-fitting shoes and thick socks.

Airway...Breathing...Circulation

Despite the fact that this writer is a CPR instructor, I've chosen not to get deeply involved in the ABCs of first aid. While making sure the injured runner has a functional airway; is breathing through it; and has a heart which still beats, is vital first aid...it's not appropriate to teach a 6-8 hour course in these pages.

The few runners who have cardiac arrests while exercising are given huge press coverage. The incidence of these cardiac arrests in the fit and sensibly trained runner is lower than the public's perception of an honest politician.

Please take a CPR class. You're unlikely to have an opportunity to save your running friends, but you may have a chance to save a child, or an inactive, overweight smoker who is too feeble-minded to live a sensible life style.

Ignore the way they do CPR on television shows. Perhaps due to budgets, they rarely do CPR properly. Stroking the chest does not compress the heart. Cutting an emergency tracheotomy is cute drama, but is not appropriate when they've already demonstrated a patent airway.

* Athlete's foot

A fungal infection which is itchy and painful. Avoid by drying your feet soon after running...like the male of your specie, the fungus loves warm, moist places. Use a fungicide several times a day. Or try a 1:1 apple cider vinegar and water soak three times a week. Treat for another 10-14 days after the symptoms clear.

* Bunions

Wear wide shoes. Use a spacer between the big and second toe. Doughnut pads can help. Don't eat them after using. Don't wear pointed narrow shoes.

* Hammertoes--claw like. The longer small toes may buckle under. Wear shoes which are long enough.

* Ingrown toenails--Pain, swelling and redness...use warm soaks.

Cut the toenail straight across; wear shoes which are wide in the forefoot.

* Black toenails. From shoes which lack room in the toebox (or forefoot); typically from downhill running. Use a sterile needle to drain the blood or let the body reabsorb it. Antibacterial creams will decrease the risk of infection. The nail will fall off in a month or two.

Your injury rehabilitation commences the minute you get hurt. Early use of cooling measures...a pond can reduce the swelling while waiting for transport...will save you much distress. Be aware of burnout and overtraining syndromes. Once you've chosen the right shoe type for you, rotate several pairs.

It may take several little injuries to find your training threshold this year, or to find an exercise which enables you to overcome it. By training a little below this injury threshold limit, and investing time to correct a weakness, improvement can be maintained.

A question from March '95s Runner's World

A serious runner had been training hard for a year, incurred a stress fracture, and is looking for ways to improve. The pace of this person's running had recently slowed by a minute per mile.

Training harder when you suffer a rapid decline in pace is rarely the solution. You should look at performance-damaging stresses in your life.

Take a thoughtful look at yourself and your environment, and ask yourself what, if anything, has changed for you in recent months. Daily routine--work hours, type of job, sleep pattern?

Physical changes--significant weight gain or loss? Eating habits changed? Any illness or health problems? Anything changed in your life--even unrelated to running--which could affect your performance?

It could be a medical problem; a physical may identify why you are run-down. Blood work should include a ferritin test, a good measure of a runner's iron stores.

Reason identified or not, take a month off running to allow overtraining to be corrected; allow the body a chance to adapt to its first year--then get back into it at a sensible tempo to avoid excessive fatigue next time. *Gently* crosstrain twice a week for health while resting.

John Babington...Olympic coach.

CHAPTER EIGHTEEN

STRETCHING

"If you have a choice between a 50 minute run or a forty minute run plus stretching...do the latter. Stretching is vital to avoid stiffness and injury. I'll sidestep the time to-hold-the-stretch debate. Ten seconds to 30 seconds, it's up to you. At the end of this,, period you may be able to stretch an extra bit if the muscle has relaxed--do so for a few seconds before moving onto the next exercise. Doing each one several times, and several times a day is what counts. In addition to the earlier exercises...try the following.

"**Calf Muscle**--two muscles. The gastrocnemius' origin is above the knee, and therefore best stretched when the knee is straight. The soleus' origin is below the knee and is best stretched with a bent knee.

a/ The lunge (as in a sword fight) is suitable for both muscles. The gastroc is stretched by keeping the heel of the back leg on the ground. The front leg goes well forward--keep your balance--stay tall...in this upright position, lean forward until the stretch is felt on the straight back leg.

"Placing the front foot flat on a chair, the soleus can be given an extra stretch. Push the bent knee forward with the hands until the muscle starts to feel a little tight.

b/ Stand with your toes on a step or stair with the heel flat and extended over the edge. Allow the heel to drop down slowly until resistance is felt in the muscle or tendon, hold for the usual length of time before pushing up (which is, of course, exercise).

Do some with straight knees, some with them bent.

"**Hamstrings**--the back of the legs--these work over two joints--they extend the thigh. To stretch them, the knee must be straight (or almost straight) and the hip bent. Thus the head goes toward the knees, and the hands toward the ankle. Movement should be around the hip; mere bending of the back is pleasant, but will not stretch these muscles.

a/ Barrier Stretch--Standing, put the foot of the leg to be stretched on a support between waist and knee height. The weight bearing leg can be straight or a little bent. Bend forward until tightness is felt at the back of the supported leg. Hold your hands or hand out toward or beyond your toes to measure the progress of the stretch.

Don't stretch with the arm or shoulder--keep them relaxed. Roll around the hip joint and measure your progress a knuckle at a time as you regain years of lost flexibility while reaching your limit. Don't expect to reach the limit of a gymnast or a drawing in a book--just the limit of your body. You may get a little further each week until you reach this limit. You're less likely to reach your usual limit in weeks of higher than typical mileage. More likely if you cycle!

b/ Lie on your back, keep the resting leg flat on the floor. With the knee of the leg to be stretched bent, bring it up towards the chest. Note...no tightness should be felt because the hamstring is relaxed. Keeping the knee in the same position, slowly pull the lower leg (by grasping the calf area) until tightness is felt in the hamstring. Hold this position and repeat. When you can straighten the leg with the knee a certain distance from the chest, bring the knee closer to the chest before straightening it.

Use any old piece of rope or a towel to help with your stretch-ing--especially the hamstrings. You <u>can</u> pay $20 for a <u>special</u> rope, and another $20 for a video showing you how to use it, but your imagination should be sufficient to ease your muscles through their motions.

c/ Lie supine on a soft surface. Keeping your hands by your side for balance, extend both legs up and over your head. Rest the toes on the ground above your head. Do it slowly--backs may object to this exercise. The only contact with the surface will be head, shoulders, arms and toes. If in doubt about this exercise, extend the legs into the air a few times, pointing towards the ceiling. When you feel ready--confident enough, allow the legs over your head. The knees can be bent at this stage, straighten until the stretch is felt. Feet can be together or apart. Yes I know it's old fashioned, but I like it.

d/ Eight-tenths of the way through half of your easy runs, do six 75 meter pick-ups at 5 k pace. The muscles are warm. Relax, use good form, and feel the hams loosen up as you stride.

"**Quadriceps**--the four main muscles at the front of the leg are frequently the first to ache if mileage is increased. One of them starts above the hip joint at the front and will require the body to be erect for it to be stretched. All four join to form the patella tendon inserting below the knee.

a/ On hands and knees like a dog, lift one leg back, then up, and pee...sorry, that was for a different book. Grasp the ankle and pull it towards your butt. Keep the knee bent (flexed) to stretch the front of the thigh.

b/ Kneeling on a soft surface, slowly lean backwards. To get the full benefit, keep the area from the knee to shoulders in a line until your buttocks are resting on or near the ankles. Using the arms for support, stop at the point of resistance.

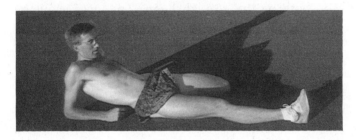

"Straight leg raises while laying on your back are useful to strengthen the quads. Raise the leg 12 to 18 inches and hold for 10 to 15 seconds. Do a third of them with your toes pointed in and a third with them pointed out to work the outside and inside quad respectively.

"**Gluteals**--if these are tight, they resist movement on each stride and can cause knee problems. Gluteus maximus extends the femur. Its family stabilizes the hip.
In an extended lunge position, the heel of the rear leg is allowed off the floor. Hands on the floor, knee bent at a right angle, the knee close to or touching the chest. Do the barrier stretch, too.

"**I-T Band...The Ileotibial Band** goes from the buttocks to the outside of the knee...bursa sacs at either end can become inflamed and painful. Keep the band loose--Stand close to and perpendicular to a support. Cross the outside leg behind the inner; keep both on the ground. Lean your inner shoulder toward the support and push your hip away from it.

"**Adductors**...inside the thigh. You should be able to split your legs to 90 degrees. If not, sit with your back to a support. With bent knees and the feet together, push down on the lower thighs until you feel resistance.

"**The trunk** doesn't move much in running, but it needs to be flexible. In addition to touching your toes each day..."

"Like a sprinter you mean."

"The opposite of a sprinter--they tend to do a ballistic stretch...not what you need. They do it for psychological reasons, not to stretch the hamstrings or the back. Do it slower than sprinters.

"Try the following:

a/ The lunge again--this time a relaxed position for the legs, then arch gently backwards to stretch each of those back and neck joints a bit.

b/ Lie on your stomach, go into a banana shape by raising the head and shoulders, plus the feet and legs off the surface. This stretches and exercises the back muscles. Push up with your hands if the emphasis is on the stretch.

"The back is best protected by keeping the abdominal muscles strong. Do crunches and sit-ups of course, plus seated knee raises. Sitting balanced on the edge of a seat, raise your knees to your chest, then push the legs out straight. Make the abdominals do some of the work.

"Do a quarter of your sit-ups right elbow to left knee and a quarter left elbow to right knee--this will work the oblique abdominal muscles--some of the seven or so muscle groups which pull the thorax forward to inflate your lungs. Strong abdominals help you run tall, decreasing injuries--you're only as strong as your weakest link--don't let the weak link be a supporting muscle group.

"Seated knee raises also work the under publicized Ilio-soas group (Iliacus and Psoas Major). This pair help to raise the thigh in fast running and hill work--that is, they flex the hip. See page 41-42. Use the quad stretches which extend the hip joint to keep them loose.

"Side stitch is a pain below the rib cage due to the diaphragm muscle cramping. It's usually due to improper warmup: contributing factors are drinking cold fluids just before you run, or gas or food in the stomach.

"Low oxygen to the diaphragm causes the stitch which comes on at fast or slow pace. Regular deep breathing exercises and avoiding the above three errors will decrease the frequency.

"Strengthen the diaphragm with the book on your belly exercise.

"Treat an acute case with various deep breathing techniques while either bending over at 90 degrees, or with your hands on your head. The simplest action, however, is to start again. Walk until you feel relaxed, do some slow deep breathing, then ease back into a run. If the diaphragm's blood supply is sufficient, it should not cramp."

Special tips from John Pagliano

* Improper biomechanics is probably the greatest cause of running injuries--learn the best way for your body to run.
* Fatigue causes inefficient gait profile.
* Use a tape measure from the Anterior Iliac Spine (hip) to the Medial Malleolus (inside ankle) to find the longest measure of your anatomical leg length.

* Muscle strain is usually due to disruption of the muscle tendon unit.
* Decrease muscle strains by flexibility. Use a warmup and pre-exercise stretching. This increases vasoelasticity through neural influence.
* Avoid ballistics. Hold the stretch for 10-20 seconds.
* Rest muscle injuries...otherwise, muscle is more susceptible to re-injury.
* Over 40 years since your birth? Take one day off of running each week.
* Feet type are split about 25, 25, 50 percent high, low and normal arches. This will help you to predict the most likely shoe for your foot type, but heavier athletes need a stiffer shoe than the prediction would suggest....A shoe to absorb the weight.
* High arch people may want to avoid the stair stretch--it may overstretch their Achilles complex.
* Pool exercise is especially good in the 1-2 weeks after a long distance race.
* A cap with bill will shade the face in summer. A visor will allow more heat out, but can be of less use on a windy day.

* High mileage runners have four times the upper respiratory infection than a non athlete. You do not get an infection from running on your own on a wet night--you get it from interaction with carriers, sick people who should have stayed home from work, etc., and from mingling with masses of people. Infections are especially common in the 1-2 weeks after a marathon race--which isn't surprising when you consider the number of hands you shake that day, plus the absence of hand washing options at porta-toilets, combined with the way most of us clear our noses while running.
* Delayed onset muscle fatigue--is usually due to microscopic damage of the contractile elements of the muscle. Pain peaks in 1-2 days; weakness and stiffness lasts a week. It is usually due to unaccustomed exercise.
Vasoelasticity...

John Pagliano, D.P.M. practices Podiatry in Longbeach, is a 2:28 marathon runner, and is a frequent contributor to the running press.

PART EIGHT...which is...CHAPTER NINETEEN

INJURY TREATMENT

Muscle and non-muscular injuries are frequently related to each other. Many problems can be treated successfully by the athlete. Should the problem persist, see your Doctor, or a Sports Injury Specialist--consider Physical or Massage Therapists, Chiropractors, Osteopaths, Rolfers, Podiatrists, or Acupuncture.

"I've given you a wide range of medical specialists to choose from," he said one day. "Numerous articles have been written about runners who've had remarkable results after seeking help from one of the above specialists....Coming after months of frustration with any one of the other specialists.

"Conspicuous by its absence is the Orthopedic person..."

"You mean an Orthopedic Surgeon."

"They are surgeons. But many of their treatments don't involve surgery. Like other specialties, many orthopod cures involve a manipulation of soft tissue, or the correction of an underlying cause as discussed in Part Seven.

"The best person to assess your biomechanical imbalances which caused the injury--and it's a given that poor biomechanics cause most injuries--is a sports specialist from any field who has an interest in and an understanding of the mechanics specific to running."

"Or to read the message between the lines...a fellow runner."

"Yes. At least a person who speaks the runner's language. Referrals from runners or track teams work best.

"If the front office questionnaire includes a section for your typical weeks training, and other hints suggesting an athlete or runner is given individual attention, you could be at the right office.

"Your mechanical problems are unique. You should be measured (leg length, muscle size or strength, flexibility) and watched (when running).

"The treatment should emphasize...Prevention, Stretching, Strengthening, Treatment and Rehabilitation. You should have input on those rehab decisions--maintain control, just like you do with your running.

"The expert should refer you to more appropriate specialists early on.

"He or she should be runner conscious enough to spot *long-term overtraining syndrome (LTOS)*....Don't forget to inform the specialist of other recent, even minor injuries which you have suffered. Give the person a chance to diagnose you properly...you're the one paying for it--financially, and in pain later if you don't get the problem resolved."

LTOS should be distinguished from the normal muscle soreness which we look for as a result of our training. Engross the slight soreness--the result of a sensible increase in training or effort level--but be careful to what degree you ache.

It's okay to feel slight soreness for days at a time...soreness heaped upon soreness from doing many types of session...each session offering the body a different challenge--taking the body toward overload, but not through it.

Then the rest days and the easy weeks will allow recovery, and you should be stronger the next time you work through the schedule; you'll have fewer aches.

MUSCLE PROBLEMS.

"Most muscle injuries should be treated with RICE."

He gave me a strange look..."And don't ask me if I mean white or brown, boiled or egg fried."

"That was the last thing on my mind. You meant: Rest, Ice, Compression and Elevation."

"Good man. Ice is your friend; it decreases inflammation, preventing many sore spots becoming injuries. Hosing your legs with cold water after a run has the same effect--it can ease significant fatigue; it'll also bring your body temperature down.

"Inflammation constricts blood flow, it can interfere with healing--combat the swelling with ice. Use each hour for two days. Use warmth--mild heat--only after all the swelling has subsided."

"As a rule, muscle strains at the back of the legs are from running too fast, or overstriding. You will need to rest."

"Does cutting out speedwork for a few days qualify as rest?"

"Yes, it would. Active rest, putting the muscles through a comfortable range of motion, will bring nutrients to the muscle and stimulate repair. You will also maintain fitness.

"A major muscle tear will require you to stop running; minor tears, if not hurting when you run, will heal with this active rest. But:

* Run 30 seconds per mile slower than usual;
* avoid long runs...do two sevens instead of a 14;
* avoid hills...you tend to go too fast down them.
* no speed running.
* don't overstride.

"The combination of easy running and RICE for the acute phase of about two days, then stretching and massage later, and an anti-inflammatory if appropriate, should help the muscle to recuperate.

187

"Consider your form when preparing for speedwork again. Wear appropriate shoes--if you're advanced enough to use lightweight racers for speed sessions, do copious stretching of the calf and achilles to prepare them for the lower heel. Ease into the fast running after drills and striders. Do fewer reps for the first couple of sessions back."

Now, without quotations, here's his advice on individual muscle groups.

CALF MUSCLES

Causes--see Achilles tendon. Include overload; too much track speedwork; or a series of very minor twists on rough trails.

Many problems are resolved by use of a heel lift in all shoes and regular stretching. Some people say avoid walking barefoot; others say walking barefoot will stretch the calf to its ideal length.

The gastrocnemius responds well to ice, strains more when running up hills; and you may recall, it requires a straight knee to stretch it.

Because the soleus is under the gastroc, it's less amenable to ice therapy.

Both are receptive to massage. Use fingers or finger shaped gismos or a roller to break up adhesions. Massage toward the heart.

Both heal well with active rest--keep to soft even surfaces.

Use mental preparation when on trails. Expect and look forward to adjusting your stride. Be ready to take several short strides or relax at the knee to make those adjustments. See sprained ankle.

HAMSTRINGS

No surprise that this is an injury of fast running--after all, how often do you hear of a sprinter who strained a quadricep. RICE and active rest is effective. Like the next muscle, you can sit on the ice--adjust it to hit the right spot. The tendon of origin at the buttock and insertion below the knee can develop an itis. Running fast or slow, be mindful of form.

Later, strengthen the hamstrings with leg curls. Do single leg curls...don't let the weak leg cheat. Don't let the buttocks do the work either. Also, try lying on the floor with your feet on the bed and thighs perpendicular to the floor. Lift your pelvis a few inches off the floor for a few seconds and repeat 10 times.

CHARLEY HORSE or SEVERE Muscle Cramp

An acute agonizing spasm caused by prolonged contraction at the muscle fiber level. The cramp can last minutes.

Causes include:

post exercise--often many hours post exercise--due to buildup of lactic acid...

or small areas of muscle damage;

after repetitive movement--such as five miles on a treadmill at constant speed and elevation without changing cadence or style;

exercising more than usual: Over fatigued muscles;

sitting or lying in an awkward position, which compromises circulation;

excessive sweating or exercising with a fever or in hot conditions;

Loss of sodium; insufficient intake of calcium; low potassium;

Treatment and avoidance

Many books say massage and stretching. If you massage a cramping muscle you will certainly strain it; if you try to stretch a cramping muscle you'll strain it some more.

Do this: Place the cramping muscle in its shortest anatomical position. For the calf, this means bringing the foot back to your butt--the position in which the calf is least likely to

Buttocks--GLUTEAL muscles

Renowned for aching after distance runners do sprints. "My butt hurts" means the runner did too many short efforts, too fast, without adequate preparation. Yes, there should be a degree of fatigue, but some runners ask these important speed muscles to strain by ignoring them most of the year. Twice weekly striders and sprint drills will help to keep these muscles in shape and avoid the bun burn when you do eight times 150 meters at the end of your summer track sessions. RICE and get someone who adores you to do the massage.

remain in spasm because you have "told" the stretch proprioceptors the muscle is in its absolute resting position.

As it relaxes, you can use gentle touch followed by gentler massage...a slow kneading to locate the sore spots. Then use ice alternating with low temperature moist heat to further relax the muscle and bring nutrients in...while flushing wastes out. Eat something with sodium and potassium; take a tum or glass of milk for calcium; add an anti-inflammatory for pain. Diazepam and diphenhydramine can help, too.

In 12 hours you may be able to take an easy run. If the cramp was due to a severe strain, you may need several rest or cross-training days.

Except in the case of a minor spasm while exercising, hold the stretching until after the acute phase. Avoid heat for the first 48 hours.

GROIN pull

The adductor/abductor group. A groin pain which comes on during or after sprinting is treated with RICE and stretching. Pain coming on over several weeks could be hernial, or a hip stress fracture.

Because these muscles have multiple functions in stabilizing the hip, there is great potential for misdiagnosis. The deep upper hamstring pain/strain which hurts when you sit down, could be one of the adductors. If the knee gives out when walking, or the pain moves toward the back and hip, seek an expert. It may even cause leg length problems...messing up your entire running form.

If you do lateral movement or kicking sports, consider the three main adductors (Brevis, Longus and Magnus); and the Sartorius (which flexes and rotates the thigh); Gracilis (adducts thigh; flexes leg on the thigh); Piriformis (outward rotation of the femur). Watch for Piriformis syndrome...a butt pain which can be confused with sciatica.

Muscle injuries to the **front of the leg** are due to overtraining--too many miles before your body has adapted to the load--or too much tempo style hard running.

Cut back on mileage by taking a couple of days off. Very gentle cross training may be okay. Resume with fewer, less intense miles. Give your athletic body a chance to change.

SHIN SPLINTS - painful shins

Symptoms - Tenderness in the lower third of the leg on the inside, and along the entire shin. Pain is felt on extending the toes and weight bearing. It hurts if you press the area with your finger. Physiologically, it's an inflammation of the tendons OR muscle in this area. Pain eases when you're well warmed up, but resumes at the end of exercise. A stress fracture pain would be continuous.

Causes - Running with the weight too far forward;
striking the ground with the first third of the foot;

over-striding;
shoes too tight around the toes;
inflexible shoes;
weak arches may be present;
tight calf muscles stress the shin structures;
running on hard surfaces;
overpronation;
overtraining is its trademark;
beginners are very susceptible.

Prevention--Flexible foreshoe--use a combination or slip lasted design. Use a heel lift to reduce jarring, along with arch supports or padding if necessary. Run fewer miles; do them on softer surfaces. Pool run. Bring back road mileage a mile or two at a time as you ease back to full training. Use orthotics or anti-pronation shoes.

The shin muscle works against the large calf muscles; it is the last muscle to warm up and the first to cool down. With this in mind, do an exercise to build it up--the paint pot of page 39, or hooking an elastic belt or similar item under the toes and pushing against it ten times each day should suffice. Wearing long thick socks will help to avoid the chill when not running, making it easier to warm up the muscle before you do run.

Treatment - Flexibility work: ice alternating with moist heat...then put the muscle through its full range of motion. Use NSAIDs.

Note - shin splint symptoms are similar to a stress fracture.

COMPARTMENT SYNDROME

This is a muscle pain due to the muscles growing faster than the sheath surrounding them. It includes one form of shin splints; it also affects the other smallish muscles of the lower leg. Ice and anti-inflammatories can help, but surgery may be required to allow the muscle more room to expand.

Some muscles grow so much that they constrict the blood flow into the sheath...resulting in necrosis (a medical emergency) of the muscle.

192

QUADRICEP STRAINS

The four cylinder engine of motion. The thigh muscle propels you while stabilizing the knee. Actually, the calf is the main muscle group for moving you forward. The quads cushion the body, set up the calf to do its job, then devour the ground through the balance of the stride cycle. This biggest of the muscles has multiple functions. If you are not using any other muscle group properly, the first sign can be aching quads. It is likely to ache after longer than usual runs, or running downhills. Quads are more likely to ache if you wear worn out shoes.

Prevention--Increase mileage in a steady manner;
incorporate hills regularly;
practice relaxed downhill running;
and run on grass downhill if possible;
land with a slightly bent knee;
run tall to bring in the iliosoas group.
Work other muscles appropriately so as not to over-stress this group. Do your half squats one leg at a time. Remember the iliosoas stretch; ili works in tandem with the quads, helping to lift the thigh.

*   *   *

Soft or connective tissue injuries are often caused by equipment problems, poor biomechanics or increasing mileage beyond the body's current abilities. They can be difficult to diagnose...there's a thin line between the knee pain from small sprains of the ligaments at the back of the knee, and a strain of the popliteal muscle which crosses the same area. Fortunately, both are treated with rest.

Tendon--sinew--can take huge amounts of abuse. Usually, it's stronger than muscle, but push it too far and it will fail. The weakest point will go first; training through the injury can lead to an "itis". Rehab--RICE--can be long and slow.

193

Most of the following injuries are insidious--they creep up on you week by week. Their stealth makes you change form in little ways...pushing you toward other injuries. It could be your big toe which is causing the knee pain or your hamstring to repeatedly strain.

HALLUX LIMITUS

Push-off in running is between the first and second toe. The big toe joint with the metatarsal should dorsiflex (move up) about 65 degrees. Less, and you could be liable to numerous injuries due to gait changes needed to compensate. Seek an expert if it hurts because Arthritis and Gout attack this joint.

PLANTAR FASCITIS

Symptoms - Pain at the base of the heel--may feel like a stone bruise. Pain is worse at the start of the day or run. A bone spur may develop where the fascia has partially torn off of the heel.

Caused by stretching or inflammation of the Plantar fascia--the structures making up the sole of the foot--at its attachment to the heel. Often due to:

stress and tension on fascia;
tight Achilles;
overpronation;
stiff or worn-out shoes;
running on hard surfaces;
a rigid high arched foot;
or a stiff big toe joint;
too small a heel on running shoes.

Prevention - Correct the above--wear shoes with a higher heel, or use sorbothane inserts; keep mileage in lightweight races to a minimum; run on softer surfaces most of the time; use arch supports or a strip of orthopedic felt under the joint between the toes and the end of the foot (the metatarsal phalangeal joint). Stretch the calf muscles.

Develop foot strength by flexing the toes. Alternate curling the toes as if to pick up a golf ball, with extending the toes up toward the shin.

With the feet flat on the floor, grab a towel and pull it in with the toes.

Walk in unsupported footwear for part of each day.

Treatment - RICE may help; massage the bottom of the foot; using ice made from a disposable cup mold, roll the foot over the ice. If this fails, seek specialist advice. Steroid injections help some people. If the injury is chronic, minor surgery to the toe, or to remove a spur on the heel may be useful, though the latter doesn't address the cause. Some recommend the fascia be cut on the basis it has minimal function.

OVERPRONATION

Not an injury, but let's raise a few eyebrows by calling it one.

Symptoms - Pain in the arch of the foot which can radiate toward the toes. Pain on the inside of the shin as the foot rolls over too far. You may notice the inside of your shoes are compressed more than the outside; the inside feels spongy when you put pressure on it. Look at your shoes on a table; if they tilt inwards, you probably overpronate.

Cause - Slapping the feet too much, weak ligaments of the feet and ankles.

Prevention - Recognizing you pronate too much is the first problem. Most runners land on the outside of the foot, which then rolls over as the foot passes through its support phase. Some runners feet roll too far, placing extra pressure on the inside of the leg. Four minute and nine minute milers overpronate. Check your stride length-- if it's too long, you may not be able to control the excessive movements. Improve muscle tone with rotation exercises of the ankle.

Treatment - You should benefit from one of the antipronation shoes. The basic design is for a harder substance on the inside of the shoe, either in the form of a wedge--thickening towards the medial side of the shoe, or a block. A negative heel counter or other stabilizing structure may also be used. Different pronators need different amounts of resistance on the inside to stop them rolling over. Just because your pronating friend swears by his 'newbok' 75s, doesn't mean they'll suit you. Have an experienced runner at the track watch your form, or get yourself video taped. An expert in a running shoe store is your best specialist. Show him or her some of your old running shoes; have them watch you test run a few pairs.

METATARSAL INJURIES

The five long bones which connect the ankle to the toes have their own arch; it's sometimes called the foot's second arch. Most problems occur at the distal end--at the metatarsal heads close to the toes. The most important prevention technique is to wear wide, well padded shoes to allow the foot its natural shape.

Morton's neuroma is an inflammation of the nerve which runs between the 3rd and 4th metatarsals. That is where your pain will be.

Dropped metatarsal head. Any of the five may drop out of the arch. Given time, it will find its own level, but if pain is severe you may have...

Stress fracture to the "neck of the metatarsal" (a sub-set of March fractures...due to over use and jarring), would require several weeks of non contact running or rest. The bone may find its best position for you to run, but it may not.

Signs include swelling, tingling, burning in the ball of foot; a stone like bruise. Expect the same problem with the other foot.

Use ICE, wide shoes with cushioning, good insoles, arch supports, orthotics; add metatarsal pads at the first sign of pain. Take NSAIDs.

The feet may roll at different rates--the wonkiest foot needs correcting. Stop that one from wobbling on each stride, and the better foot's workload will be lessened. Heed the store-person's advice; but give a nod to how each shoe feels to you. Arch supports or orthotics inside the shoe may also be needed.

Overpronation causes many other problems, including Tarsal Tunnel Syndrome--an irritation of the posterior tibial nerve behind the medial maleolus. Seek an expert if you can't find the cause.

SUPINATION--under pronation of the foot

Not *enough* inward roll of the foot. Shoes wear on the outside edge. On a flat surface the shoes tilt outward. Lightweight trainers of a slip lasted design may help. Supinators are prone to I-T band syndrome, Plantar Fascitis and Achilles problems. Do stretches for all the related muscles...and get yourself appropriate shoes.

Inflamed ACHILLES TENDON or ACHILLES TENDINITIS

The tendon connects the gastrocnemius and soleus muscles to the heel bone.

Symptoms - Dull or sharp pain and inflammation of the tendon cord or its sheath--from the back of the heel and ankle, up through the cord and could extend into the calf muscle. Pain may be gradual or come on suddenly; it's especially stiff in the morning. Tendon often thickens; a nodule may be felt; a cracking sound may be present.

Causes: The tendon tries to compensate for *tight muscles*. Stress at footstrike and push-off must be absorbed by the cord. Damage can be the result of a gradual increase in mileage that catches up with the tendon, or

a sudden introduction of hill work;
short, inflexible calf muscles...perhaps secondary to increased, slow mileage!

A lower heel on shoes (running or non-running);
increased running intensity;
sprinting--all can stretch the tendon too much.
Not warming up properly--calf stretches are vital.
Running with the weight too far back;
striking the heel;
worn-out shoes.

A history of weak feet or Morton's toe (long second toe) predisposes you to this problem.

The back of running shoes digging into the tendon on every stride is a major culprit. For some reason, manufacturers insist the tendon needs protecting, whereas all we need is sufficient support for the shoe to stay on. Shoes with an Achilles dip are also bad--the top of the "dip" is often higher than the level at which runners feel pain. Overpronators are prone to this injury, perhaps because after the tab has slammed into the tendon, it rubs the tendon as the foot rolls inwards; in addition, the tendon is given an extra twist on every stride.

Prevention - Well fitting shoes with heels in good condition: cut the tabs off if necessary; or, make two vertical slits where the tendon will go; this allows the now floppy tab to roll gently and almost innocently up and down the tendon.

Prepare your Achilles for speed and hill sessions with copious stretching of calves; stretch before and after running. Avoid sudden changes in training.

Loose, full length, warm calf muscles will ease the strain on the tendon during all running--not just the quality running. There are many Achilles stretch gismos on the market--visit your lumber store, a triangle of wood works just as well.

Treatment - Rest if painful to allow swelling to decrease. Apply ice for ten minutes several times a day and take two aspirin or other anti-inflammatory at the same time--both will help reduce the swelling. A strip of tape applied along the length of the tendon when in the relaxed position will act as a splint, discouraging you from using and stretching the tendon further.

Massage nodules away. Do toe raises.

If the pain stops on warming up and it does not put extra stress on the muscles, you may continue to run. Look for the cause in your case, if it was due to other factors, you may not need to mutilate all your footwear.

In the acute phase, use heel pads such as sorbothane or orthotics to raise the heel--high enough for walking to be pain free. Check your non running shoes--these can also rub the tendon. Using flat grass areas may help for the first few days back in training.

Avoid hills and track until you've stretched the calves for 10-20 sessions. Run some of your track miles counterclockwise.

Cortisone will not help--its use is likely to lead to rupture due to continued use of a damaged tendon. A few runners may resort to surgery--scare tissue removal--easing the tendon's movement within its sheath--but it often stimulates more scar tissue. If you don't address the short calves, foot control, low heels or inappropriate training, treatments will be pointless.

SPRAINED OR STRAINED ANKLE

Ankle ligaments are overstretched. There may be a popping sound. A true STRAIN will take a couple of months to recover from. Seek out an expert. Cross train until you can walk without pain.

A SPRAINED ankle has less ligament damage. The main calf muscles may be strained also, and require nursing back. The real problem is often the smaller stabilizing muscles such as the Peroneous Longus and Tibialis Posterior; the flexors and extensors...the everters and inverters, will need to be iced and rehabbed. For instance, if it hurts you to invert (inwardly turn) your foot after a strain, ice the area which hurts; later, stretch the ankle to its everted position to regain the ligament's mobility; stretch in the inverted position to regain the muscles' flexibility. Make a wobble board to build strength.

When walking is pain-free, ease into running with a support such as ace bandage or an air splint. Avoid rough surfaces for 6-8 weeks; then get gently back to the trails.

SHIN STRESS FRACTURE.

The fracture does not show up on x-ray until healing is well under way; it can be confirmed quite early by a bone scan. The dilemma--a fracture requires six to eight weeks non weight bearing exercise to heal. A compromise of three weeks reduced training on very soft terrain at modest pace, followed by an X-ray could be acceptable. Non running exercise to maintain muscle tone may be more appropriate. If you feel pain when you put pressure on the shin...rest.

CHONDROMALACIA...Runners Knee

Symptoms - pain or tenderness close to or under the patellar or knee cap at the front or side of the knee. Pain is gradual, increases over several weeks, usually in one leg.

The Patella's cartilage--under the kneecap--wears away; it becomes sandpaper like, often makes a grinding sound as it no longer rides smoothly over the knee.

Causes - Running on a camber--the slope at the side of the road, or if a large part of mileage is across the slope of a hill;

long runs;

not warming up properly;

tight, weak or fatigued quadriceps;

tight, overly strong hamstrings;

kneeling;

going up and down stairs or hills;

sitting still for long periods;

cycling;

overpronation.

And sorry people...running too hard, or too much, too early (in the training cycle). Rushed morning or lunch-time runs without a warmup can cause it.

Prevention - Stabilize the foot with well-fitting shoes; use foam, heel and or arch supports to improve fit. Avoid cambers; run on a variety of soft surfaces; try pointing the toe slightly to keep the kneecap in position. Avoid downhills. Reduce the cycling element of your training, or go higher cadence with lower resistance. Do a complete warmup including quadriceps strengthening exercises; don't allow the quads to get more than 50 percent stronger than the hamstrings. Stretch the hamstrings, quads and calves. Avoid deep knee bends.

Treatment - Run if you catch the problem early; experiment with the above to find the cause. High intake of vitamin C may help. Aspirin three time a day for three months can block cartilage breakdown, but don't risk your intestines unless you're also going to find the cause.

Seek medical advice. X-rays may be needed to check the wear of the joint surfaces. When swelling is down, strengthen the quads. Orthotics may help. Swim or pool run. A rubber sleeve with a hole for the kneecap helps many--don't use this device as an excuse to avoid quad exercises and stretching.

ILEOTIBIAL BAND SYNDROME or I-T SYNDROME.

Pain on the outer side of the knee

Symptoms - pain usually increases gradually on a run; it may cease afterwards.

Cause - This strong band goes from the muscle at the outside and front of the pelvis (tensor facia latae muscle), down the thigh to insert at the shin. Where it passes by the knee, cushioning small sacs of fluid stop it rubbing against the bone. The sacs or the band may become inflamed - typically by:

running down hills;
a change in surface or training;
excessive foot movements;
running on cambered surfaces;
bow legs;
overpronation;
worn out shoes;
worn out body--(overtraining)
tightness in the band;

unequal quad strength, or leg length differences predispose you to I-T.

Prevention - make changes in the type of training slowly. Avoid hill reps on a camber; avoid tight bends. Do the I-T stretches; and stretch the other major muscles. Strengthen the weak quad with straight leg raises and leg extensions. Podiatrist to check if a special insert for the shoes would help.

Treatment - Attack the cause, but back off the mileage and take anti-inflammatory drugs. ICE it often. Cortisone may help relieve the bursa; or the inflamed area can be removed.

To decrease both types of knee insult, don't do stair climbing in rehab.

Remember the top end of the band--It can cause problems, too.

Hip/Low back pain

Symptoms - Soreness, tension or pain in the back, which...
   may radiate down buttock and back of the leg;
   tingling or numbness in leg or foot;
   secondary muscle spasms in upper back or shoulders;
   hamstring tightness.

This is a common problem for the new runner, due to weakness after perhaps years of under use.

Cause - Leg length difference;
   back strains or vertebral disk problems, (the area of leg pain is dependent upon the origin of the spinal irritation)
   Weak abdominal muscles;
   failure to warmup properly;
   running with the weight too far back.
   Running up and down hills--you're likely to feel this after or towards the end of a hill session if you do them on an irregular basis--as such, it is an acute injury and will require active rest. Seven to ten days later do another hill session, but with fewer reps.

Prevention - Whether purely a muscle problem or the sciatic nerve, you need to strengthen the abdominal muscles to improve posture. Work on posture in all phases of your life. Do sit ups with the legs bent, and the feet tucked in close to the buttocks. Do hamstring stretching while easing the back through its range of motion. Buttocks, I-T band and calf need stretching. Lift properly.

Treatment - Exercise is better than rest for back problems. Stay flexible. Use cross training if running hurts. Otherwise, keep to soft surfaces and avoid hills. Use ice alternating with moist heat. Have massage or manipulation by an expert. Raising the feet should help to relax the initial strain--use pillows at night. Seek medical advice. Find the cause or it will come back.

If you get repeatedly injured, or you have chronic injuries of the knee, check to see if you need a full-length orthotic. Orthotics can prevent the feet collapsing inward on every stride, and enable you to push evenly off the ball of the foot.

Look at your injuries objectively; take them as a chance to reassess your training. During prolonged recoveries, do something non-running that you've been meaning to do.

If you're running poorly, but don't have an injury, consider medical attention to rule out the various anemias, yuppie pseudo fatigue syndromes such as Epstein Barr, or glands dysfunctioning...be it thyroid, heart or simply the brain.

There is a PRICE to be paid if you increase your training. The P is for protection, which we think is covered by the other elements of RICE. Use RICE early to help you cope with this reaction from the body. Most of the time, the reaction takes a while to show itself--but it will--either as improved performances, or aching limbs and injury, depending on how close to your optimum training you are. If injury occurred, you may need some days or weeks to get over it. Rebuild with a different combination of quality and quantity.

Remember--if it's worth doing--it's worth doing slowly. While more injuries occur from high mileage than from speedwork...do your speedwork sensibly, using good form at realistic speeds.

The Edge.

Speedwork can aid recovery

Human growth hormone is secreted by the pituitary gland. It helps muscles and bones recover quicker from exercise, and helps break down fat. On the track circuit, it is illegal. But you can increase your own supply.

Simply train faster than lactate threshold several times a week.

Check pages 1-6 to see how easy this training can be added. Six to ten strides in every other run is all you need.

SPEEDWORK CAN ALSO DELAY THE DECREASE IN YOUR PERFORMANCE AS YOU AGE.

Your VO2 Max will decrease each year past about 35, but prudent use of quality sessions will delay the loss.

PART NINE

THE YEARS AHEAD

The Guru geared my training to specific targets, some short term such as next months half-marathon, and some long term such as next years track season. Training sessions for most runners need only slight changes as the year proceeds--with further tweaking from year to year.

The Guru, of course, is simply a device I used to make this "how-to" book more fun to write, and I hope, entertaining to read. Giving myself two voices enabled me to avoid the frequent quotes (with a line or two of their qualifications), which interrupt the flow of many how-to books.

This part, and the essays which close out the book, will be in my voice only.

The well trained athlete derives minimal benefit from the energy in drinks--provided his glycogen stores are adequate before he commences the run. The undertrained athlete lacks endurance because his muscles have not been educated (trained) to exercise for long periods. If you are undertrained, 16 ounces of a sugared solution before the start, then 8 ounces of half strength sports drink taken every 15 minutes during, can increase the distance you're able to run at a set speed...by 12 percent. Half of the increase will occur with water alone, that is, by staying hydrated.

Beware the research on this and related subjects. Unless you see a group of international class runners--not bikers, they can consume all they wish--who have reached their limit from training...your training is the best way to get faster. If you have no interest in going beyond 40 miles a week, sugar drinks can help delay the wall.

Young runners

I've received comments about the lack of a **youth** chapter. I don't think they need one. Their training is exactly the same as for adults. Modest amounts of mileage and quality in the early months and years; remaining injury free always; increasing mileage later. Some youths are physically developed enough to train 80 miles a week at 16, but most should be doing less.

	miles	max race distance	max run
Ninth grade	30-40	10 k	10 miles
Tenth	45-50	12 k	12
Eleventh	55-60	10 miles	14
Twelfth	Less than 80	Half marathon	16

Max race distance is roughly based on the British rules. Allow the young bones and muscles to develop fully. Include anaerobic threshold, VO2 max and the long runs, but emphasize running form and allow sufficient time for them to do other sports.

There is no reason, and no excuse for allowing children to race longer than these distances. You don't have to attempt to fly across the U.S.A. to hurt your body!

CHAPTER TWENTY

TRAINING PHASES

There will be several phases to each year's training; autumn / early winter, the emphasis is on building mileage and strength; late winter / early spring, the strength is maintained but more speed is brought in; late spring, you get used to track sessions prior to the track season or a series of 3 to 6 road races.

Coaches of the past have had different ways of putting this into practice:-

Some have emphasized Long Slow Distance (L.S.D.)--As many miles as the body can handle at a modest speed to develop capillaries in the muscles; plus the oxygen uptake and the oxygen use system.

Strange we aren't born with a complete supply of blood vessels. Just like the brain, which grows new capillaries if part of its original system is blocked by a clot; active muscles improve their circulatory system. The most obvious improvement is of course the slower heartrate. This is because the heart gets stronger, pumping more blood on each contraction. Your needs at rest are no more than a non-exerciser, so this greater volume per beat means it takes fewer contractions per minute to supply those needs.

In addition, blood volume of exercisers increases...giving the muscles more fluid to use.

The body produces more hemoglobin than normal, further increasing the blood's ability to deliver oxygen. Due to your increased blood volume, however, your tested hemoglobin level is likely to appear on the low side of normal; indeed, many runners show near anemia due to their high blood volume.

Inside the muscle cells, more and bigger mitochondria result from the training--more energy can be synthesized.

L.S.D. is done at a steady pace, not super-slow pace; a pulse of 130 per minute, should ensure all the training is aerobic--at 60-70

L.S.D. is done at a steady pace, not super-slow pace; a pulse of 130 per minute, should ensure all the training is aerobic--at 60-70 percent of max heartrate. After a year or two, many runners do their L.S.D at 80 percent of max H.R.

After at least three months of steady running, the athlete does a part of the race distance at race pace each day; typically only a quarter to a half of that distance--most mileage stays at the aerobic pace. After six weeks, a final polish of speed runs is done, for example, three miles of fifty meters fast, fifty slow. This is done for a further six weeks before racing commences. The proportion of speedwork is kept to one mile in thirty-five. Though the first three months lacks variety, the risk of injury is reduced. Fitness is reached slowly; racing may not be appropriate in the early stages.

A second style advocates Fartlek and varied pace running over various terrain--variety is the name of the game. Strength is built up with fairly high mileage, a substantial amount through mud, sand and on hills. Strides, track sessions and time trials develop more speed in the second phase. Weight training is used as necessary to develop certain muscle groups. The development of the runner's mind is as important as the physical fitness.

Intervals or stress tolerance was practiced by many. To get the runner used to the stress of the race situation, the three or four important sessions are done mainly on a track throughout the year. Speed progresses from modest pace at the beginning of winter, to a little faster than race pace over the six months. Rest periods and distance of efforts vary--steady running and gentle fartlek is done on the days away from the track; mileage is usually less than the two types above.

I declined suggestions of a history lesson in this book--I recommend you read about Percy Cerutty, Arthur Lydiard, Bill Bowerman, Bill Dellinger and the Hungarian coach Mihaly Igloe: add in Weldermar Gerschler of Germany and the Finn, Pehhala from pre world two and you'll get a feel for our game--which is how you should consider our sport--you'll understand why we've come to recognize *balance* as a key to success.

All these systems aim to develop oxygen uptake and use pathways...runners develop speed from the early strength phase. If you want to adhere to one system to prepare yourself for 5 or 10 k races, you can do base training at anything from 60 (L.S.D. style) to 90 percent max heartrate (Stress tolerance)--you can train at minimum aerobic capacity, or at anaerobic threshold and close to VO2 max.

Most runners now use a combination of the above, as I've outlined in previous schedules. In October, even with types two and three, only 20 % of the mileage will take your heartrate much above 150; the bulk is moderate paced as you build up. Over the winter, another 10 percent a month is done faster, so that by May, 80 % is of good quality.

The fast sessions then, should not be flat-out in winter; the idea is to build strength. It worked for Roger Bannister four decades ago, steadily decreasing his 400s from 66 seconds in winter to 56 by spring. It can work for you. You can still run at 1500 meter, or mile race pace, but do it for short periods with short recovery. Relaxed strides of 100 meters with 15 seconds rest is ideal; it keeps the session mainly aerobic--and helped 1980 Olympic 800 meter gold medalist Steve Ovett maintain his natural leg speed during high mileage winters--so it should be fast enough for the rest of us.

In practice. These were the goals of one runner's winter training
a/ To increase mileage from 50 miles per week in August to average 60 miles per week for the whole winter.
b/ Run in several x-country races November-January.
c/ Speed development ready for relays and a five k race March or April and a ten mile road race before:
d/ Specific track work to cut 12 or more seconds off 5,000 meter time.

September - Week One
Sat - 40 mins gentle fartlek, then, 2 x one mile with two mins rest - 9 miles
Sun - long run at 1¾ mins slower than 5,000 m speed - 13
Mon - Hill reps, 8 x 300 meters with fairly fast jog down - 6
Tues- Longish run at 1½ mins slower than 5,000 pace - 10
Wed - Fartlek - not very hard as still not used to the mileage - 8
Thurs- Sustained or tempo run - with group if possible - 8
Friday or at the weekend, an easy relaxing run - 6

Week Two

Sat - 30 mins fartlek, then several short hill reps with high knee lift--followed by two miles at good speed - 9

Sun - as last week - 13

Mon - 20 mins steady running, 4 x 600 meters short recovery, 20 steady - 8

Tues - as last week - 10

Wed - 20 x 100 meter strides, 15 secs rest, then 30 mins steady - 8

Thurs - as last week - 8

Friday or weekend easy run. If he felt like an easy run eight hours after his long run Sunday, he did it. Sometimes he did this run on a Friday.

He wasn't a slave to the mileage, but by November he was consistently doing this extra run...completing 60 a week.

Most sessions then progressed over the winter. Some naturally as he got fitter (Sunday, Tuesday and Thursday, he allowed himself to speed up by 15 seconds a mile as he got stronger). But he did not push for the speed; he ran in control, and saved his legs for the speed sessions.

He changed the format of some sessions month by month.

His mile repetitions of Week One was always a nine mile session, but became--30 mins fartlek, 3 x one mile with 1½ mins rest in October; 20 mins gentle fartlek with 4 x one mile, 1 min rest in January and 5 x one mile after a normal warmup in February. In April, he took the session to the track. A 400 jog at first enabled him to run faster; he reduced it to 200 by the middle of the summer.

His hill reps increased to 16; he did sacrifice a little speed as the number increased. In spring, the speed came back. He then took a slower recovery jog down the hill, reduced the session to 12 and ran them three seconds faster than the previous summer--at what felt like mile pace intensity.

The Wednesday fartlek session remained relaxed, yet by November he had sped up the second half to about 5,000 meter race pace in mostly 200 to 400 meter efforts. By late January, the whole session was at this speed, though he still ran it on grass or trails. From March, he took it onto the track two out every three weeks as

16 x 400 meters at almost 2 mile pace; or as 20 x 300 meters faster than 3,000 pace--10 seconds per mile faster than his old 5 k best.

The short strides session increased over winter to fifty. The last two sessions pre-track, he did half of the strides down a gentle grass slope...working on good form at high cadence. In late February it was the first session to go back to the track--as four miles of bends and straights.

The 600 meter efforts had been a throw-back to the track season which had just ended. He'd wanted to maintain the feeling of speed, while coping with the bulk of his new training. As his legs tired over the winter, and despite mini rest-ups for races, this was the hardest session of each fortnight.

Running long at two mile pace is tough with fresh legs, so it was appropriate that as he increased the reps to 800 and then 1,000 meters with only a minute rest, speed did settle at close to 5 k pace. He used the road, the wind and the beach for this session. On cold days, he took 30 seconds rest, and ran more reps at 10 k pace. Often, he ran the session as long efforts on muddy trails or in the woods to stay out of the cooling wind. By spring, he was back to a full minute recovery--the session became 6 x 1,000 meters at five seconds per mile faster than target speed for 5,000 meters. This would have represented a personal record if maintained for 2 miles.

To help the transition back to the track, he did several sessions to develop pace judgment. It helped him to stay relaxed, rather than pushing for speed the first time he did 1,000s there.

He likes to run several distances. This year he did 5 x 600 meters, then 5 x 400 meters, then 5 x 200 meters. His legs got used to going reasonably fast in the first section and had to get faster as he moved to the shorter distances. He kept the stress low by taking a generous 200 meter rest, and running in control.

Next he did a session he hates...a pyramid. But he knows it's a useful session. He started his with a 1,000, then did 800, 600, 400, and 200...getting faster all the time while taking a 200 rest. Then he went back up--ending with the longest repetition. The key is the second half because he had to run each distance at the same pace as on the way down.

This is a harsh session, but very rewarding. It should total a similar amount to your planned sessions for the summer. His works out nicely at 6,000 meters.

His final transition session was to do a 600, 400 and 200, taking a 200 rest after each, and an extra lap between the five sets.

By May he was ready to do the track sessions which had developed from the winter work. Over each fortnight the main five sessions were repeated; his progress was easy to see. The steady runs were retained; hills were done once every three weeks--so the winter's strength was never lost.

Others might have made an easy six into a gentle fartlek session, so a few more miles are at race pace. He opted to do an occasional session at 800 to mile pace. Eight, very fast 300s, three fast 800s, and sets of 3 x 200 featured as substitutes for doing a mile race--but mostly he kept to VO2 max (2 mile pace).

You must set limits to your progress over an entire summer. If 16 x 400 at your 3,000 meter pace seems too easy, make it harder as outlined in Part Five. But don't go swimming off an ocean liner--the intention is to arrive on race day feeling fresh.

Many schedules I've seen recommend two or three weeks of training exclusively at mile pace, with minimal mileage to peak for a race. The peak tends to be very short--usually two races. Keep the long run and long reps at 10-15 k pace each week, and you can race real well for extended periods.

Try some of the techniques in part 6 for one or two races, but maintain strength throughout the racing season or your performance will decrease. Running within 12 seconds of that 5 k PR is still a good race. Don't be upset at not setting records all the time. Not getting a new PR can tell you how good your PR is!

Train consistently well, with a sensible combination of long and short, and your records will fall...until you reach your lifetime peak anyway...probably in your early thirties, or five years after you take up training for races.

CHAPTER TWENTY-ONE

THE MARATHON

A Marathon Runner's training may be the same as the previous chapter until February, then she will work on the endurance to complete 26.2 miles at close to half marathon speed. She would keep two of the speed type sessions a week, but increase the length of the long runs to 20 and 13 miles--simply add two miles to the Sunday run and one to the midweek run on alternate weeks--run at 1½ and ½ a minute slower than anticipated marathon pace. The Thursday run would remain a little faster than marathon pace.

The Sunday run might progress over the weeks as 15, 15, 10 mile race, 17, 17, half marathon race, 19, 19, 20 mile race, 17, 20, 17, 20, 15, *Marathon race*. Note the three races. Distance order is not important, but if the twenty mile race is early in the build up, it will need to be run slower than hoped-for marathon speed. A low key 10 k or 10 mile race two or three weeks before the marathon will help to break up the last six weeks.

Fuel is vital for the marathon--and your body is capable of increasing the size of the fuel lines.

At marathon pace, blood levels of epinephrine and norepinephrine--which make carbos more available to muscles--is increased.

Longish tempo runs at marathon target pace teach your muscles to process those carbos, and prepare the muscles for the marathons' demands.

Consume a carbo based meal a few hours pre-race, a diluted sports drink just before the off, plus a few ounces with sugar every 15 minutes, and you further delay the "have to resort to fat as the main energy source," syndrome...the wall.

Cut down the training load starting at least ten days before the marathon. See Part Six. Cut the mileage by half to allow the body to recover from the hard work of the build up. Do one gentle run in the final three days pre-race; resting gives the muscles an extra supply of energy to see them through the last few miles of the race.

At this level, two speed sessions a week is good. Ignore the three or four speed sessions which the 100 mile weekers do. They've had years to get used to doing 5 or 6 miles of speed on Sat, Mon and Wed; plus long runs Sun, Tues and Thursday. You can still do both types of speedwork each week.

By now you know what they.

* Anaerobic Threshold:

four to six miles of tempo,	*All*
2 mile reps,	*at*
2,000s,	*15 k*
mile repeats	*pace.*

Add 8 miles at 5 seconds slower than half marathon pace, and 8 x 800 at 10 k pace for variety

Repeat these six sessions once for a fourteen week build-up. The pre-marathon week, and post longest race week in the build-up, you'll do less...probably two times one mile at half marathon pace.

* VO2 Max--two mile...or for the faint-hearted 5k pace

Hills...thought you'd get away from these, did you?
 Do them at two mile intensity, not one mile.
400s...about 16
300s...20
200s...keep the rest short...don't go too fast
Fartlek...keep the efforts short
800s...not in the week you do them at 10 k pace
 six only at this pace. 8 x 600 would be fine.

Again, each session can be done twice. Rest up with five 400s four days pre-marathon; and probably eight 300s the week before the longest race.

Give VO2 max a miss the week after the long race...the two times a cruising mile will help your recovery.

214

The typical week will be:	miles
Day one...anaerobic threshold, with warmup etc.	10
Day two...longest run of week--marathon pace plus one to one and a half mins a mile	18
Day three...easy 3-7 miles	?
Day four...VO2 max	8
Day five...easy 6	6
Day six...second longest run--half a minute per mile slower than marathon pace. Every third week, include at least six miles at marathon pace.	12
Day seven...easy 0-7	?
Total	57-68

A one percent decrease in the energy cost of running saves 2 minutes off a 3 hour marathon. Efficiency is economy, so practice striders...semi-sprints after long aerobic runs...and:

Every three weeks during marathon training, instead of 20 miles, do 20-30 x 400 meters at 10 seconds per mile faster than marathon pace with 15 seconds rest. An area of grass allowing straight 400s works well. If the area is big enough, vary which section you use for each stride--an accurate 400 is not needed. One or two percent grades are fine too because they give still more variety--you can practice your form on very gentle slopes. If using a track, try 30 x 300 with a fast 100 rest round the curve. This will save you 3,000 meters of bend running. Or do 500s with the 100 rest to decrease the number of reps needed to make your five to seven or so miles at speed.

Do a few 100s with a few seconds coasting after every 8-10 reps to help break up the session.

This is high level aerobic training. Add the warmup and down, and you'll easily get 15 miles in.

If you slow in the last 8 miles of a marathon, your legspeed is likely to be unchanged, but your stride shortens. Running mile reps at half-marathon pace and the above session will give you a good chance of maintaining speed.

Both sessions teach you running economy, which equals running effi-ciency, which equals good marathon times.

Do at least a couple of miles the day after your long run, or ride a gentle 10-20 miles, or take a walk. How much mileage you do beyond the four basic sessions is up to you. Exercise physiologists tell us there are minimal gains to be made beyond 80 miles a week: The Kenyans don't appear to be listening.

I've not mentioned training twice a day. If you intend to progress beyond sixty miles, this becomes important. If all sessions were increased by a couple miles, mileage could easily go up to seventy-five, but it would place great strain on the body. The body recovers quicker from two seven mile runs at a given pace than from one fourteen mile run at the same pace.

It may have taken several years to build up to your sixty miles of good quality running on a consistent basis. Most of the sessions will at some stage feel hard, but to add another mile would make it intolerable. However, by adding a gentle 20 minute run say eight hours after the long Sunday run, many runners feel looser and more relaxed the day after.

After a few weeks it can be increased to 30 and then 40 minutes. Then you can practice lifting the knees up for fifty meters at a time. In a few months you'll be doing a fairly gentle fartlek session. Meanwhile, the other main sessions aren't feeling much harder--you manage to keep the same paces as before: you must be improving. Provided you rest up, this should show through in race times.

Why rest after a race.

If you rested up for a race, or you rested for a series of races, why would you need to rest for several weeks after those races?

The day after your last race is the first day of your winter or base build-up. You've probably done half your normal mileage for weeks; now is the time to enjoy your fitness and freshness as you cruise along at 70 percent max heartrate for whatever mileage you like. Don't lose fitness with inactivity.

If the last race was a 10 K, a fifteen miler will do you good. If the last or key race was the marathon, 5 miles on alternate days would be appropriate.

Some runners train 14 times a week. Most take a day or two of short and easy runs, but they're able to train intensely on the other five. The trick is to find your limit. Provided you still enjoy most of the training, and you remain fresh enough to run fast in your speedwork, go ahead.

Then you can add a five miler one day a week at pleasant pace; a few months later add another. For alternate additional short runs, include some strideouts--about 8 pickups of 100 meters to make sure the hamstrings and fast twitch fibers get some work. Otherwise:

* keep your feet close to the ground to minimize pounding;
* take short, fast strides to maintain legspeed;
* be efficient and economical....don't let these short runs become junk miles.
* watch for body changes and injuries.

Take care with the regular speedwork. If you're too tired to train at 15 k pace on your designated day--and quite frankly, you should always be able to cruise long intervals at 15 k pace--make adjustments to your mileage.

If you're planning a higher mileage phase, get the support and encouragement from training with others a few times each week. If the plan is 12 runs, get out 12 times. Often, we don't know how we will feel until a mile or two into a run. If life or training has worn you down, do those two miles. Hit the shower if you still decide on a rest day--often, the day you didn't feel like running at all, turns into a great run.

Clearly, those who intend to race the shorter distances should do fartlek, strides and weight training in these extra sessions. If the aim is towards the marathon, most extra miles should be steady pace runs, working on an economical shuffle.

However far you go, consider the possibility that rest might help you improve more than the extra training would. Some 1,500 meter runners do 100 miles a week, while some marathon runners compete at a good standard on only 50 miles--there are no definite rules on mileage. Enjoy your running and aim to reach a realistic target based on your ability.

Don't Run a Marathon Until You're Ready.

Be Macho--Save your body for another race-- Stay at home on the big marathon day. Instead of an injury from the big event, you can have a successful marathon later. It's not macho to run yourself into the ground.

* The side effects of running a marathon without sufficient training.

According to Dr. Sonny Cobble, of The Orthopedic Hospital of Los Angeles, who assists the hospital supported 'leggers' running group, "absolute devastating fatigue, can result when attempting a marathon with insufficient training." Problems include, "blisters, chafing, knee discomfort, hypothermia, dehydration, fatigue and in one case a fractured femur."
Chronic Fatigue Syndrome with anemia and other side effects is a long term problem. Normally associated with overtraining - which running a marathon achieves in just one run - this syndrome involves illness, stress and injury due to exhausting body reserves.
* Exercise physiologists tell us physiological adaptation relating to endurance and muscle strength, from training, takes at least 14 days. Therefore, the longest run must be at least 2 weeks before the marathon to give any benefit. According to most coaches, the longest training run for a marathon must be at least 18 miles. But it takes a good series of base runs to build up to the 18 miler.
Bone and connective tissue adaptation takes months rather than weeks. Assessment about marathon readiness should be based on the length of runners' longest run each week for at least the last 8 weeks; and, how well the body reacted to the longer runs.

* Race day pace should be based on the speed of the long runs done in training. Other factors are the number of runs over 15 miles, the length of the two longest runs, and the quality of speedwork. If you routinely do 5 miles at 15 k pace, your long runs can be a minute per mile slower than marathon pace; if you do negligible speedwork, half of your long runs should include a long section at marathon pace.

* Come to terms with not running the marathon. It's much better, healthier, and even acceptable to pass over the hyped-up event, in favor of a smaller event when your body is ready. Give your body the opportunity to perform to its potential, without the pain and medical bills of a serious injury. It's not heroic to run a marathon before the body is ready. Reduce the number of runners staggering across the finish line, and stop your fellow runners and TV viewers from thinking those who do so are brave, determined or courageous.

* For those with the wisdom to wait 2 months, build on your current fitness level. Repeat a 14 or 21 day schedule several times. Each time you go through the schedule, add two miles to the longest run, (until it reaches 20), and a mile to the two most important speed sessions, (until you're doing 5 miles worth). Go to the start line with an excellent chance of success.

The Beginner Marathon.

While I think it's better to get several years running background before you attempt a marathon, provided you've done the training up to Part Three, most people can complete 26.2 miles.

It only takes 20-25 miles a week to be able to run-walk a marathon. It won't be fast; but it doesn't have to be ugly; and, you can have fun. While I'm not keen on minimalist training, this section should help you run a marathon with modest injury risk.

You will do most of what 60 mile a week runners do--but do it every two weeks. Part three had you running short efforts and tempo pace each week. Two weeks in four, you will continue with this to maintain good form and leg speed.

The third ingredient is the long run at close to marathon pace.

Popular with the top guns.

Six to eight miles of long reps at anaerobic threshold or faster is a popular session for high mileage people. Many Kenyans do eight times one mile at 10 k pace on dirt trails; others do 10 to 12 times 1,000 with 400 or a one minute rest.

But what about the rest of us?

Don't do more than 10 percent of your mileage in one speed session, but try this four week rotation if you race once a month. Let's assume you run fifty miles a week--which entitles you to five miles of long reps.

* 4 x 2,000 meters at 15 k pace...true threshold pace.

* 5 x mile at 10 k pace...faster than threshold for most, but it will help your buffering system.

* 8 x 1,000 at 5 k pace...no pretense at threshold...this is close to VO2 max, and prepares you for

* resting up with...6 x 800 at 2 mile pace...true VO2 max.

The constant is the recovery. Take a 400 rest for all the sessions.

Don't repeat sessions more than every three weeks. If you elect to run them at 15 k pace, the 1,000s and 800s will need a 200 rest to ensure you give the muscles a chance to educate themselves.

Match each session with some kind of speed at short distances.

Multiply your 10 k race time by five (higher mileage people can use 4.6, but you'll be taking walk breaks.) and divide by 26.2 to get your run pace. A 50 minute 10 k (eight min miles) gives 250 minutes, or about nine and a half minute miles. Starting with your 40 minute run in week one, add five minutes, or half a mile on every odd numbered week in your build-up until you get to 10 miles or 100 minutes of continuous running.

* Odd numbered weeks

Day one...Run at marathon target pace. It will take 12 increases over 24 weeks to reach 100 minutes.

Day two...walk a mile, run two, walk a mile. In the early weeks, this can remain a thirty minute run, just like the end of part three. As your day one run increases, however, you will probably want to cut back.

Day three...rest

Day four...Alternate long reps and a tempo run. This is anaerobic threshold. Keep doing those two to three miles of fast running.

Day five...repeat day two

Day six...fartlek, or 100s, or 200s. Keep good form. This improves your oxygen uptake system.

Day seven...rest

Mileage is 20-25 for these weeks and sets you up nicely for the first day of each even numbered week.

* Even weeks

Day one...Run-walk starting with 60 minutes. Add ten minutes each time to give you three hours after the 24 weeks. The running should be a half to a minute per mile slower than marathon target pace. Run fifteen minutes at this pace, then walk at relaxed tempo for five. Practice taking in liquids with a little carbohydrate.

Days two-four...restive, but do 20 minutes of exercise two days, including a two mile run.

Day five....A--Once a month do hill repeats, but slowly. They are de-scribed in Part 4. If you prefer, do reps through mud. But do do this strength session. If you'd followed this book's format, you would have been doing them to make your 5 and 10 Ks faster. They are even more important for marathon running--you need all the

221

anatomical benefits which resistance training will give you. Six to eight long hill reps are better than short ones.

B--The even number weeks when you don't do hills, run intervals on the track. Sorry, did I say this was a minimalist schedule! Read Part Five. Try these sessions--six 400s; five 600s; eight 400s; four 800s; eight 400s; six 600s; at 5 k pace or 10-15 seconds per mile faster (VO2 max pace). Take the same distance as rest; jog it. This is clearly a vital day's training; you've had three rest days...so make the most of it, but don't run faster than two mile pace.
Day six...walk one, run two, walk one
Day seven...rest

* Resting up

The last walk-run pre-marathon should be an hour less than your longest.

Two times one mile at marathon pace should be the only speed session in the last seven days.

Everything is geared toward the long runs which build aerobic base to enable you to complete the marathon. Speed sessions give the benefits of every type of training which international class runners use.

You'll be able to run the marathon after six months. Hopefully, you'll do a few 10 Ks and a half-marathon in the build-up. You can also stay at week 25 level for some time. The longer you remain at week 24-25's level, by repeating it several times; the more you do on your easy days--the more likely you will be able to run most of the race at marathon target pace with minimal walks. Resting up may allow you to run for 30 minutes at a time with a five minute walk break. If you sense you're approaching poop-dom, settle back to 20 or 15 and five minutes walk.

Predicting marathon times

Earlier, the Alien and I discussed how much a 5 k runner will slow at 10 k. The conclusion was that a person in full training should only slow by 10 to 12 seconds per mile...compared to the 20-30 seconds a low mileage person would slow.

A similar thing happens to half marathon runners. Tables of actual performances show people slowing much more than you'd expect due to the high number of undertrained runners.

Run 60 to 70 minutes for the half, and you can double your personal record and add eight to ten minutes to predict your marathon time.

Many minimal mileage people come on-line beyond a 75 minute half, which stretches the amount added to their times. The 80 minute 'half' person needs an extra 20 minutes; the 90 minute halfers' need an extra half an hour. These numbers are out of all context to the percentage you would expect them to slow down.

Just because the average person slows this much, doesn't mean you need too. Gear your mileage up, so you only slow by one twelfth at the full distance.

For every minute per mile pace you run the half at, you should slow by five seconds per mile at the full distance. The 80 minute half marathon person runs 6:06 miles; he or she should slow by 5 secs x 6.1 mins--say 31 seconds per mile. Pace will be 6:37 per mile--a 2:51:45 marathon--or 8 minutes faster than the average.

Growing older is a delight--and perhaps a privilege. We have all the experience, plus we get to stay fit because we exercise. But we do tend to lose strength and speed.

Incorporate 20 minutes of weight work twice a week; a little cross-training and you can slow the natural decline in your racing times, while keeping most injuries at bay.

Remember to keep the speedwork after age 40--16 times 100 meters can be done anywhere--it really is not very demanding--provided you avoid sprinting it.

In the 1970s, many top runners had their VO2 max tested at the Aerobics Institute in Dallas. One of the highest values ever achieved was by Gary Tuttle, American record holder at 10 mile, one hour and 20 kilometers.

"High VO2 max by genetics or by training at 2 mile pace will not guarantee you success at a particular distance--You also need to train at speeds related to your best race distance.

"I never had the speed to be a good miler; but a prudent combination of hills and speedwork, which included long and short reps, helped me become the best I could be at the medium long distances. My dislike of runs longer than an hour, and my two percent body fat, were a hindrance at the longer races--I rarely educated my muscles to burn fat by going long, and there was little fat available anyway.

"Good coaching, Jim Hunt in College and Pete Peterson with the Southern California Striders, plus hard sessions at VO2 MAXIMUM AND Anaerobic threshold pace helped me to become a tough racer.

"The amount of quality work you do, is a better predictor of performance than the VO2 max value you achieve in a test. Train hard, and often....add appropriate rest phases, and you'll race as fast as your mind, and your body will let you.

"Do the distances well below your best every third race, for speed-work; race well above your best distance, for strength--then race your best distance, for place, for PRs, and for pleasure."

Gary Tuttle owns the Inside Track Running Store in Ventura, organizes or acts as consultant on about 20 races a year, and heads the Gary Tuttle running camp each year in Carpinteria (CA) Tel (805) 643-1104.

I ENTER THE DIET DEBATE

As a registered nurse, I witness the effects of poor diet on a daily basis: Most adult onset diabetics are overweight and inactive--that's why they are diabetic--the pancreas can't keep up with their abuse to the body. Like alcoholics, giving information to these people is fruitless...unless they are ready to act on the teaching.

You readers are ready, so I'll push a few buttons.

First, there's really no debate on diet: eat a sensible, balanced diet, and the person living in western society will get all the nutrients he or she requires.

Or as I'm sure my sidekick would say, "Eschew all fads...especially those which are at the heart of a book."

Fat Potions.

Don't take anti-fat absorption pills which will give you fecal leakage, plus other side effects.

Don't think you're doing the body a favor by eating fat products which cannot be absorbed--the bloating and diarrhea are unfair exchanges for cheating the intestines.

Don't take metabolism stimulation pills either.

None of these will make your heart stronger, your circulation better, or raise your self-esteem.

Exercise does all three, and more.

Exercise raises your metabolism, burns excess fat, cures bloating, and suppresses appetite.

Eating healthy foods has no side effects; and it requires no prescriptions.

You won't see a pharmaceutical company spending millions to promote healthy eating; for the same reason you'll never see a tobacco company encourage healthy breathing.

Make lifestyle changes for a healthy life...don't sell your self-esteem to a pill.

Avoid "Protein" or "Fat" diets which try to make carbohydrates the villain in weight gain.

The villains are on both sides of the absorbed versus used equation.

The only guaranteed ways to lose weight are to absorb fewer calories than you use, or, burn more calories than you absorb.

If you absorb more calories than you expend...you will gain weight.

HOW CAN YOU LOSE WEIGHT?

More exercise is an option for some--for those under the injury threshold. A mile of walking or running uses about 100 calories. Go from 14 to 21 miles a week, and this one hundred calories per day will take off a pound of fat every 35 days.

Keep your food intake unchanged, do the extra mileage, and every five weeks you will lose a pound--ten or eleven pounds per year until you reach your goal.

OR...decrease your calorie intake by 100 calories a day to lose another 10 or 11 pounds. Finding 100 calories is easy for most of you--check the calories per serving of your:

* Ice cream compared to iced milk, sherbet, or low fat yogurt.
* Current milk product versus non-fat milk.
* 8 ounces of orange juice versus a more filling orange.
* Cream of soups...please look at the label.
* Potato chips V pretzels.
* Regular beer over lite beer, or fewer beers--be aware that alcohol increases the affect of drugs like Ibuprofen...increasing the gastric irritation also. On the plus side, a drinker can use fewer pills for a desired analgesic affect.

Fast food eaters...look at:
* Jacket or baked potato (without butter) instead of fries.
* Soda...at least go fifty percent diet. The second glass or can, or the refill you always get. Or drink more water.
* The chicken sandwich usually has fewer calories; but
* Yank the Mayo and cheese from your hamburgers and it will be close. Request extra veggies on those sandwiches to make them more filling..

* Take fruit into the "restaurant" instead of eating two sandwiches. You'd think a fast food chain would be able to stock apples and oranges for a quarter each...as a gesture to their patrons' good health.
* Few foods are bad--consume the so-called unhealthy ones in modest amounts.
* Choco'holic--accept it, eat the stuff on a regular basis. It's the same as skipping meals if you don't. You're more likely to pig out.

Don't attempt to lose weight with diet alone. If you've decided exercise is good for you...why wait until you've lost weight. You don't have to start with running. If you lose weight by diet alone, 25 percent of the loss will be from your muscles. The human body is 50 percent muscle...retain most of it by exercising while losing weight--then you'll lose only 5 percent from your muscles--mostly the fat which was stored in them anyway.

The act of exercising can increase your muscle mass. It's the muscles which burn most of your calories.

The main benefits from consuming a vitamin or mineral is from the food you eat, not simply the vitamin. Taking a vitamin supplement to ward off cancer will not work, unless you also eat the fiber and healthy food which pushes the carcinogens out of your intestines.

We know women with less body fat have lowered risks from all types of cancer. It follows that exercisers, who have a low fat percentage, plus rapid bowel transit time compared to the sedentary, will have still lower cancer risk.

Eating 20 plus grams of fiber decreases cancer risk; fiber pills won't. The benefit is in the food combined with a healthy lifestyle in other aspects of your life.

Heavy (alcohol) drinking is bad for your health. Moderate drinking is only unhealthy if done in the company of smokers. How can alcohol increase your risk of mouth and throat cancer? Because you are more likely to be in a smoky place, socializing or dating smokers. And because after your two drink maximum, you're more likely to forget your intellect, you're more likely to smoke a cigar.

Your primary dietary goal...take your caloric consumption in the healthiest way you find palatable. Save all your arteries--the heart, brain and legs; kidneys and other vital organs--by taking 65 percent of your energy from carbohydrates. Match each fast absorbed fruit serving with a slower absorbed complex carbo such as rice, potato or pasta.

Protein should provide 15-20 percent of your calories; most of it has been provided in the pasta, bread, legumes (beans, peas and nuts) already. You'll only need a small amount at each meal to "meat" your needs--2 to 3 ounces.

The average diet contains 50-75 % above the protein RDA--You need few bovine products.

The low fat dairy product at breakfast will contribute to your calcium needs; two different sources containing iron should be eaten at lunch and dinner. A half cup of cooked lentils and kidney and many other beans contain 7 plus grams of protein, 20 percent of your iron and potassium needs, and huge amounts of Folate--crucial for production of red blood cells. A cup of pasta provides 7 grams of protein; those bagels you munch on, another six...that's before you add the cream cheese! Make use of low oil fish, and tofu; these, plus chicken, will provide over 20 grams of protein in just three ounces.

A heavy trainer only needs half a gram of protein per pound of body weight...75 grams for the typical 150 pound runner.

A mixture of protein sources (legumes + grains) will provide all the essential amino acids--the burrito with rice and beans is a good match--you don't need protein supplements; you don't need high priced amino acid pills.

A near vegetarian who eats one small hamburger a week for iron needs is kidding him or herself--it provides less than half of a single day's needs. The real problem for vegetarians is not lack of iron; it's the lack of vitamin B12...which enables the body to absorb iron.

A good source of vitamin C should be consumed with products high in iron--it increases the percentage of the iron absorbed--decreasing your potential for anemia. Avoid milk or caffeine at the same sitting as a main iron source--they decrease iron absorption. Ferritin levels below 25 ng/ml may be a warning sign of impending anemia; it's also a warning sign for overtraining...injuries increase by a factor of three.

The caffeine in twelve ounces of coffee or a 20 ounce soda increases the heartrate and the hearts irregularities, while increasing your body temperature. All three are bad for runners. It also gives a *net* dehydration affect. Sodas usually contain phosphorous, which because it competes for the same transportation site as calcium, results in less calcium being absorbed--watch out for those shin pains in the summer.

Fat will provide the remaining 15-20 percent of your calories, but you should never eat a food for its fat--you get plenty of fat elsewhere. Use mono' over polysaturated; use unsaturated in preference to saturated. Most meats contain more fat calories than protein calories. The dressings used on a typical healthy 400 calorie salad, often double the caloric intake. Use lean meats with the fat shaved off, low fat dressings, and please, if you must use them, keep the regular dressing at the side of the salad. Look at how viscous they are; imagine THAT trying to flow through your narrow and narrowing arteries. (I know physiology fiends, it doesn't reach the arteries in that form...but you get my point) Take it easy on those high fat veggies also--nuts, avocados and olives for a start.

Minimal fat consumption will give a feeling of fullness after eating; it slows the transit of food through the intestines, while meeting your requirement for the fat soluble Vitamins. Vitamin K is only stored for a few days; E is rarely a problem; but, A and D can rise to toxic levels...the liver holds up to a 6 month supply of both.

People exercising more than three hours a week should get most of their extra energy needs from complex carbs. The real problem is what you put on the carbs. Bacon bits and butter is a poor choice on potatoes; barbecue sauce or salsa is better. Two ounces of shrimp is better than eight of hamburger for the extra pasta--beware store bought pasta sauce--dilute its fat with a tin of tomatoes, or make from scratch. Lower fat (let's not kid ourselves and call it low fat) peanut butter and cheese spreads save calories; use small amounts of topping and enjoy the taste of the bread!

Each meal needs a mixture of protein and carbos; protein for muscle repair and to steady the foods absorption; carbos for re-fueling--fat will be present by default.

While there is no evidence of supplements improving athletic performance, most nutritionists recommend a daily multivitamin with iron. Use the cheapest available; there's no such thing as a super vitamin pill.

Trace elements such as Zinc and Copper, which enhance enzyme activity; and Chromium, which is needed to get glucose into the cells, can be missing from a diet if you're eating the same foods each day. Yet by including whole grains, dark meats, legumes, mushrooms and a little cheese...you've got them covered. How many servings? Try 12 of grain, 4 of Veg and 4 of fruit; add your protein sources and you should be in homeostasis, or balanced.

Runners only need so much energy from the body. Provided the diet is balanced, how fast they run is determined by training...and their parents. A 500 mg shot of vitamin C can help you bounce back from a tough workout--but so does appropriate background mileage. Vitamin C from natural sources (food) is a good antioxidant--deactivating free-radical molecules which harm all cells, including muscle cell membranes. Vitamin C from food will give you Folic acid also, pills won't.

"*The Zone*" fad does raise an important point. This fad recommends only 40 percent of calories from carbos--leaving 30 percent from protein to overburden the kidneys and liver which either excrete it or convert it to sugar; and 30 percent from the artery-clogging fat.

One of the arguments for the 40: 30: 30 diet is that we burn more fat calories sitting down than we burn carbos.

Of course we burn more fat while sitting--but we use very few calories.

It's only true, because we are able to take in sufficient oxygen to burn an inefficient fuel...fat. When we start exercising however, the efficient fuel, sugar, provides most of our energy needs.

Unless of course, you consume too few carbohydrates. The body will have no choice about what fuel to burn for energy. The body doesn't become more efficient at burning fat and protein--it simply has no choice because it is being carbo starved.

A second argument for 40:30:30 says carbohydrate makes the body respond by producing too much blood sugar. The body makes no sugar. What actually happens is the body absorbs the sugar from the consumed food, then efficiently stores it ready for use. If you consume most of your carbs as simple sugars, with negligible fat and protein at a meal, your blood sugar will peak a bit...then troughs as the pancreas (secreting insulin) tries to correct your *cruelty*. The sleepy feeling is not from low sugar--it will still be in the normal range--it is from the blood supply being diverted to your intestines, combined with the lassitude which occurs about an hour after returning to mundane tasks.

Eat complex carbs, a little protein and fat to slow the entire meals intestinal transit time--and food absorption, including sugar absorption, will be steady.

Carbohydrate loading used be associated with a depletion phase--you shunned carbos from day 7 to 4 days pre-race, then loaded up by eating all the carbs you could handle--which also meant low fat and low protein for the last three days. Problem--many people were lethargic during the first phase; the incentive was that you conned your muscle into storing extra glycogen pre-race.

The kinder way to load is to ignore the first phase.

If you are used to eating 55-60 percent of your calories from carbos, and you increase it to 70 percent for the last four days, your glycogen stores can go up 41 percent; the length of time you can exercise at 85 % VO2 max by 45 %...if you are male. Females get no increase in glycogen, though performance does increase by 5 percent as they use more lipids. (Tarnopolsky, MA et al Journal of Applied Physiology 1360-1368)

A high carbo diet does not make you fat. Consuming more calories than you use makes you fat; inactivity makes you fat.

Fat is a less efficient fuel source than carbohydrates. It takes 10 percent more oxygen to make you run each mile if the energy source is fat. You will have no choice but to run slower for a given effort. Claiming fat is the most efficient fuel is like saying crude oil is the best fuel to run your motor car.

This fad gives the essentially inactive 80 percent of the United States population, half of whom are overweight, another excuse for eating too much fat and protein. Unfortunately, several energy bars belong to the same camp.

Don't Take a Dump

Dumping is a physiological reaction to the consumption of too much simple or refined sugar. Symptoms include nausea and vomiting, sweating, faintness and palpitations, increased heartrate and hypotension. Simple sugars exiting the stomach too rapidly, attract fluid into the upper intestine--your blood fluid volume decreases as it attempts to absorb the sugar. Pre and post exercise, use complex carbs, plus protein and fat to ensure a slow emptying of the stomach. While exercising, take sugar in a five percent solution to avoid dumping syndrome. Avoid those super drinks or power drinks which flood the market--the sugar solution is too concentrated. Any drink with an action verb probably has too much sugar.

The worst offender is goos and goops--the quick fix of sugar for long runs. The 80 to 100 calories will only give you a mile of energy, yet you have several thousand in your fat stores. The goop will raise you heartrate by twenty per minute...which should be a big enough clue for you to realize it's bad for you.

Fluid _races_ from your blood vessels--you are less able to lose heat; the heart works harder due to the increased viscosity; you've given yourself an instant dehydration affect. But you get a buzz. A psychological boost. Unless you also consume several cups of water, the goop will have deleterious affects on performance.

Some of the better tasting energy bars on the market derive 30 percent of their calories from fat. So much, in fact, that you may as well eat chocolate, plus a multivitamin after a training run. However, its 30 percent calories from protein is useful to keep the blood osmolarity up, and to give a ready supply of amino acids for immediate repair work.

There's a simple way to correct the mere 40 percent carbos, and the overdose of protein and fat. We can dilute the protein and fat by eating two pieces of fruit. The complex carbos, fiber, plus the nutrients from the bar will then be a balanced recovery snack to set you up for a meal later.

If you exercise one-two hours a day, you'll need 4 grams of carbo per pound of your weight. Five hundred grams for a 125 pound person; a glorious 600 grams for a 150 pounder. You may need 5 grams per pound during the hardest month of a marathon build-up. This may sound like over-eating, but many runners regularly consume over 4,000 calories a day.

Don't be afraid of sugar; sugar **is** a carbohydrate. But you should keep your "ingestion" of the empty calories from added sugar, such as in soda, to a minimum. Carbohydrates are broken down into their constituent sugars by your body. We need simple and complex sugars.

* Just before or after exercise, there are advantages to consuming the monosaccharides--glucose (fruit and vegetables), galactose and fructose--they're absorbed quickly and can be utilized straight away. (Fructose is somewhat slower. It may slosh in your stomach if you drink it on the run, but it is a steadier energy source.)

* The snack an hour before exercise, or fifteen minutes after, should contain some disaccharides--two linked molecules which need dividing before they can be used--sucrose, lactose (milk) and maltose (cereal)--they are still absorbed fast, but not until the link has been disconnected.

* Moderate amounts of polysaccharides in the form of starch and cellulose can be taken two hours before exercise--too much and you will feel bloated. These cereals give you the steady supply of energy to fuel aerobic activity. Eat these starting fifteen minutes after

exercise to discourage you from consuming too many of the simple sugars, and to ensure a steady supply of glucose once the initial rush from the juice and fruit is over.

Our bodies store 1-5 percent of our weight as glycogen--human cellulose, waiting to be released into the bloodstream during exercise--enough to run a marathon. If you eat a low carbo diet, you'll have lower glycogen stores. If you run low mileage with no long runs, you'll have low glycogen stores.

After your next 10 k, drink a cup of water, do a mile warmdown, then try:

* 8 ounces of juice with at least two more cups of water
* a banana and orange for the carbo boost
* a bread or other wheat product (pasta, cereals)
* Then, within two hours, go eat a real meal.

The **glycemic index** is a tool used to describe how fast a source of sugar is absorbed into the bloodstream. The typical baseline uses white bread as 100. High numbers mean the sugar is absorbed faster. Post exercise, eat foods with triple digits first, add in foods with a lower index until you reach your real meal as described elsewhere. Note...different researchers use different bases: you may not be able to compare the index from book A with other foods covered by someone in book B. In a pleasant quirk of nature, overripe fruit has a higher glycemic index than under-ripe fruit...its sugar is absorbed faster. This is due to the starch changing into free sugars--the body won't need to do as much digesting.

Stick to the starches if you want slow absorption.

The general rules are:

A. The smaller the individual item of food, e.g. small shaped pasta Versus large spaghetti.

B. The longer you cook the food.

C. The riper the food is...

The *higher the glycemic index will be for that food.*

Thus, rice or spaghetti cooked for five minutes has a much lower index than if cooked for fifteen minutes.

Need more information...E-mail index@adds2u.com for an automatic response. Leave the subject and letter body empty.

What you eat the day of a race is not going to help if you've been eating badly for the weeks and months leading up to it. While easily digested pancakes or toast and jelly taken three hours before will help to charge up your muscles, they won't undo your two salads with minimal carbs and missed breakfast, or the eggs and bacon, hamburger and T-bone meals of the previous day.

Think **lactic acid** is bad for your running--then why do nearly all our body systems produce it.

According to George A. Brooks Ph.D. Director, Exercise Physiology Lab, at Berkley, "Lactic acid is not just a useless byproduct of exercise. It is an energy source involved in using glucose and glycogen. Oxidation of lactic acid is one of our most important energy sources. Don't let this important metabolite scare you. But do still:

"Train with a combination of long submaximal training and quality to minimize the lactic acid production and enhance its removal."

Losing too much weight can be detrimental to your running. Less than 5 percent body fat may hinder your performance at the marathon.

However, less than 10 percent body fat is where you are most likely to perform at your best...at all distances.

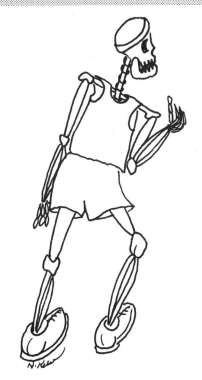

Want to cheat your body? Want to consume the same number of calories but lose weight? You can...in a healthy way.

1,000 calories consumed as fat require only 30 of your calories to digest it, to absorb it, to convert it to human body fat.

1,000 carbohydrate calories take a whopping 230 for the process.

If your current diet contains the U.S. average of 38 percent fat calories, and you consume 3,000 calories per day, you have 1,140 per day from fat.

Reduce your percentage to 25, a minimal target, and it will be 750 from fat. Every day, 390 fewer calories will be from fat. That's an amazing 142,350 fewer calories from fat each year. For each thousand of these calories from carbos, you use 200 more to convert it to fat storage compared to fat sources. You burn up to 28,470 calories a year just by changing the way you eat. Yet you're consuming the same number of calories.

At 3,500 calories per pound, the twenty-eight thousand calories equate to eight pounds from your girth. Eight pounds each year.

Of course, many of those extra carbohydrate calories are not converted to fat. Some are used for immediate energy; others are converted to glycogen for storage: Of the 142,350 calories changed, almost half are used by your body before being converted to human fat. The potential weight loss is therefore less than eight pounds. You make far greater *health* gains from the other factors of a low fat diet than you do from the four to five pound weight loss. Think of the weight loss as the bonus to your arteries clogging up slower; to your cholesterol being lower; to your energy level rising.

The First Meeting.

"Hullo," I said, "I'm Holt the Bolt."

"Heard about you," said my new running companion, "I'm Steve."

"What's your best 5,000 meter time?" I asked, getting straight to the important things in life.

"Slower than yours' if that nickname means anything."

"Bolt doesn't refer to lightning speed, it's just a memorizing technique a friend uses, but this one stuck."

Steve considered my statement, then answered, "I've done 15:45 for 5,000 and a 32:30 10 K."

I gave him my happy smile...he had real potential as a training partner, so I inquired, "How fast do you run your half mile repeats?"

"Usually 2:10 with a five minute recovery. What about you?"

Perhaps my smile had turned into gloating because I thought knew a 15:45 person *would* need five minutes to recover from a 2:10 half; but my voice seemed unchanged and modest as I said, "2:25."

He was as good at arithmetic as I, and came back immediately with, "So you must be a 17 minute 5,000 man, and about 36 for 10 K."

"No," somehow, still avoiding a boast, "I'm a 15:18 and 31:16 man."

"But how," he said, not showing any signs of feeling hurt, though perhaps a few brain cells were in the dis-believing stage.

"Because I don't run my legs into the ground," I started; "I take a one minute recovery when I do 800s." Then I had to tease the guy, "And because I race like lightning."

"The moral of the story, the moral is this"...as my favorite song ends...Use appropriate pace for your speedwork. Running at 100 percent of VO2 max (2 mile pace), or 110 percent (mile pace...as Steve did) has its place. Don't let those sessions swamp the 5 K pace sessions.

Lots of reps, with short rest.

Do anaerobic threshold. Note, Steve's problem could have been exacerbated by lack of mileage.

Note the Bolt was at 15:12 5 K pace in his 800s.

This essay owes its origins to discussions with Dr. Benjamin Levine of the University of Texas, Southwestern Medical Center, Dallas. (about his work with colleague Jim Stray-Gundursin of the Nordic Ski Team); John T. Reaves, an Exercise Physiologist in Denver; Andrew Young, Ph.D. studying Environmental Medicine with the Army Research Institute; George Brooks, Professor and Director of Exercise Physiology Dept. at U.C. Berkley.

LIVE OR TRAIN AT ALTITUDE

You can't train hard while living at altitude--Your legs just can't train because they outrun the lungs. Oxygen saturation is lower at altitude, about 94 percent at 6,000 feet, compared to 98 percent at sea level.

In 1990 three groups of 10 athletes either lived in Deer Valley at 8,200 feet and trained at altitude; lived there but trained in Salt Lake City; or lived and trained in Salt Lake.

* A lived at 8,200 ft and trained there (high-high)
* B "   "   "   trained at 4,200 ft (high-low)
* C "   4,200 and trained there (low-low)

Group B were able to train harder. They had all the advantages of living at altitude, but when they trained, they also had the higher oxygen availability from being closer to sea level. Perhaps because of the pace at which they trained, training and living at altitude appeared to be detrimental to performance.

A second factor effecting performance is nutritional status. In 1991, we had more women in our sample and the results were inconclusive. We believe the problem was an iron shortage. The women tend to be slightly anemic on arrival at altitude. The iron deficiency at the start results in them not reacting to altitude very well. They just can't produce the extra red blood cells because they lack the raw material (iron) to make them. Low Ferritin measures, below about 25 are suggestive of low iron stores. Even with good iron stores, it takes 6-12 months to see a meaningful increase in the number of RBCs. Living at altitude gives you some benefit racing against sea level runners. When you compete at sea level however, you'll have only a small edge: Mostly psychological.

Many people decrease food consumption due to suppression of appetite, and nausea.
The appetite change means lower glycogen stores.

Your VO2 max also falls. An 8 minute mile which was at 70 percent of max at sea level will be at 90 percent at 2,000 meters altitude, (6,300 ish feet). The result, of course, is you burn more glycogen; endurance is lowered because the low glycogen stores are depleted more rapidly.

Lactate levels at a set speed will of course be higher. Your threshold pace and VO2 max pace will be slower. Your heart and lungs get a full workout at these slower speeds, but your leg muscles produce less force, they de-train.

There is a hormonal response to correct the glycogen situation, Catecholamines, epinephrine especially, is secreted. This gives you a somewhat different high to sea level training, or perhaps it's just the scenery.

Out of necessity, your body will use fatty acids better, and blood glucose...thus sparing some glycogen.

Probably the main benefit is you can get a good cardiovascular workout at lower speeds...injury risk is lowered during your typical altitude visit--while you do higher than usual mileage.

Decrease the de-training aspect with a few quality sessions.

RACING AT ALTITUDE

Thinking of arriving in Boulder for two days of relaxation before the race? Think again. Most athletes compete at their worst 24 to 48 hours after arriving at altitude. If you can't train at altitude for at least two and preferably four to five weeks, your next best choice appears to be to compete immediately.

The evidence is subjective, but most athletes tell us they feel worst 24-48 hours after reaching altitude. Professional teams such as the Giants and Raiders reduce this low physical capacity by arriving as close to kick off as their governing body allows.

Runners don't have footballs' constraints--they can arrive as close to race time as flight time-tables allow.

The key reason to compete immediately is the instant reflex of the body to breath deeper and faster, resulting in more air passing into the lungs. All other body reflexes result in a temporary decrease in physical capability.

Red blood cell production does increase, but it takes about a week before the extra cells begin reaching the bloodstream.

However, within 12-24 hours, to create an immediate, artificially increased RBC concentration, there is a shift in plasma volume; plasma (the blood fluid) leaves the blood vessels, pushing the RBCs from their normal 45 % at sea level closer to 50 %. As a result, hemoglobin might rise from 16 to 17-18.

But this increase doesn't help the athlete. The blood volume is thicker. The body is dehydrated, resulting in reduced cardiac output--a key ingredient in the oxygen carrying equation.

There is an acid base change in the blood. You pee out bicarbonate, which is a buffer for lactate--you therefore fatigue earlier.

The OXYGEN that hemoglobin can carry =
cardiac output x hemoglobin x oxygen saturation x a constant
The body attempts to compensate for the decreased oxygen saturation by increasing the other two factors. But the body is stupid initially. Concentrating the blood to raise hemoglobin decreases cardiac output, AND creates heat dissipation problems and loss of muscle function (discussed at length elsewhere in the book).

RANTINGS OF AN OFT FRUSTRATED RACER

Race day--here's my wish list addressed to race directors everywhere.

Give us concrete whenever possible. Concrete is six times harder than asphalt, so it will give us shin splints more readily; ruin our knees earlier; and, give us back and hip pains so much sooner. Asphalt is far too soft for us--if you can't give us at least a mile of concrete we might actually set PRs because we're denied a chance to lose rhythm on the hard stuff. Make us run down the concrete sections; running up the concrete hill would negate the potential for damage.

Give us dirt, sand and mud whenever practicable; design the course specially to go through it. We didn't enter a road race to run on a smooth road surface. We have our light-weight, near soleless shoes on, so find us potholes, do; gravel and pebbles, please; and mud to make our shoes heavier.

Give us lots of turns--sharp turns preferably. We do 50 U-turns in a 10,000 meters on the track, so this should be your goal--surely you can find 50 turns...one block north, one east, one north, etc.

Make a special effort. Plot a winding route to connect the most acute corners in busy shopping areas. The more snaking your course the better.

Surely someone can fit more than two U-turns into a 5 k race (Carlsbad). Don't cheat though. No large keyholes allowed now. Multiple loops up deadends will give you ample opportunities. You can blame the course on police--but please give us those U-turns...we dream of them.

241

The ideal U-turn has a cone in the road, a chalk line 10 yards away, and a course marshal another ten yards away to watch us guess which one is the actual turn.

Course marshals need other specialized training. Instruct them to hide behind cars at turns--to jump out as the runner approaches. Remind them not to point the direction the race goes--don't take the guesswork out of the race course.

Ensure that most mile markers can be parked on. Marshals should cruise the course in case a marker is still visible...and rectify it.

Don't, whatever you do, start the race on time. We're always late signing up, and none of us did a three mile warm-up with strides. So start at least ten minutes late. Then, having already stripped off our sweats, we can do another 10 strides to stay warm; or watch lovingly as the temperature rises further into the nineties.

When you call us to the line, talk to us for at least five minutes.

Make sure you have a dud in the first chamber. This is a must. And do the unexpected. We all know distance races commence after two commands--take your marks...go (or a gun). Sprinters have a third command sandwiched between the real athletes' commands.

Saying, "get set," to distance runners will achieve three things. Reformed sprinters will instinctively go to the ground and prepare to place themselves in non-existent blocks. Experienced distance runners will instinctively start racing. The noise came from the starter, it must be his or her way of saying go.

The nuevo runner will look around in confusion. Many will sidle back to their cars, never to be seen again. Others will run a race, but if they make it back to the finish, won't know how far they ran, and will not return for another race either.

Keep other new runners away by holding several races on the same course. With good planning, the second and third races can be at least 25 and 40 minutes late. If possible, set courses so 10 and 5 k runners trail through hundreds of cups, orange rinds and banana peels from the half-marathon.

Water stops need to be placed carefully. The apex of corners or hills are perfect. If you have one--and surely you must have at least one--the sharp corner on top of a hill cries out for a water stop.

Don't rush the awards. Mid-afternoon would be fine for an 8 am race. Or we could re-convene the next morning before going to work.

Finally, the perfect race requires restrooms...but not too many. Estimate the number of portaloos required--get one quarter the amount. If half the race entrants are in line at any one time, you've been successful.

A secondary target is for a quarter of the entrants to still be in line when the gun goes off. A third goal is for 30 per cent of the toilets to be dysfunctional very early in the day--from the moment they arrived on site would be ideal. Naturally, the toilets should be placed on an uneven sur-face, surrounded by deep mud. And please...no spare toilet paper in sight.

As race organizers achieve many of the above without any planning, a well organized race should be able to incor-porate virtually all of them. Are you up to the challenge?

A version of this article appeared in the May 1995, Running Times.

VOLLEYBALL TO P.R.s.

Want to improve your 10 K time. Try volleyball. Jumping vertically to your maximum height will work your calves, hamstrings and quadriceps to their fullest. The result will be stronger muscles for running - enabling a longer stride and or later onset of fatigue - giving you faster race times.

According to Jim Mclaughlin, coach of the hugely successful USC team, volleyball playing ability depends on two main factors - conditioning and contacts.

Most runners are in reasonable physical condition, so they should not get tired during a game. But to improve your conditioning - jump. "Jumping is the most important preparation for volleyball," says Mclaughlin. "Just jump high and practice landing softly. Land on the forefoot with slightly bent knees; easily roll back onto the heels as you allow your quadriceps to take the strain while bending your knees further. Prepare to turn this coiled up energy into your next movement towards where you anticipate the ball will be.

"Weight training - squats, lunges and power cleans especially, will give you extra strength - enabling you to maintain an even higher standard of play. But don't try to build excessive muscle mass.

"The next phase is to run intervals - intervals specific to the game. 100s, 50s and 40s. When your body is used to these, include a series of 20 yard dashes." At the end of practice you could try the school's ten minute drill - designed by USCs track coach - 10 X 100 flat out, with the reps. starting every 60 seconds. The recovery is therefore only 40-45 seconds.

Contacts refer to the number of times you hit the volleyball. Like running intervals to educate the body to run faster, volleyball players practice a type of shot until they improve to their own or the coach's standard. "Repetition of shots will improve your accuracy and control," says McLaughlin.

An additional skill to practice is moving to the side while watching the ball. McLaughlin suggests practicing two and three step moves to each side until you feel confident about the physical movement - then doing it again while watching the ball. Hand-eye skills are dependent upon the amount of practice.

He also advocates injury avoidance by taping ankles and using a good flexibility routine. Stretch the hamstrings, quads. and calf muscles especially. Do sit-ups to ensure good balance with the strong back muscles, and stretch those back muscles out also.

"Above all," McLaughlin says, "stay under control."

"The aerobic benefit can be significant," says McLaughlin, "Games can last up to 3 hours, and individual rallies can be very long. The anaerobic benefit is from the jump - recover - jump aspect of the game."

Sand or boards? "Start anywhere," says McLaughlin, "The number of contacts is the key. The beach or sand in theory is harder work, but with practice, you can jump just as high from sand as you can from wood floors.

"With good endurance and practice, volleyball players are able to play as well at the end of a game as at the beginning."

Volleyball and the training for volleyball, can improve your 10 k times significantly. Just two inches per stride, without loss of cadence, will gain you a whopping 60 seconds.

OUR WORLD RECORD

The gun is fired. I'm with Kirui as we set off at world record pace: We all are. No matter which part of the pyramid of running ability you occupy, you're as much a part of his world record as he is. Eight or twenty-eight minutes behind him, we take pride in our performances. So here's the clean version of my thoughts.

As the mile marker approaches, I realize I'm having an out of skin experience with 5:10 showing on my watch - only 45 seconds behind the leaders - but I'm working just as hard. Maybe if I did more 400s in 62 seconds I'd be able to stay with them; maybe if I could run one 62 second 400 I'd at least be closer to them.

The second mile slows to a 5:15 suggesting I didn't start excessively fast, merely a little too fast. I'm surrounded by fellows who will run this pace for several more miles, and already catching those who went too hard in the first mile. The lead group is only another 42 seconds up on us, so in a way we're already closing the gap.

Ah, the third mile, we're really rolling now; same time as the last, but the leaders repeat also. The eight 5,000 meter races this year which resulted in a 16 second improvement, have taught my quads to expect discomfort early, but I don't feel anything yet...What a difference 15 seconds a mile makes.

I'm sat behind a group of five runners, if sitting is an appropriate expression at eleven miles per hour. The leaders are lounging at thirteen mph of course.

Five seventeen's not unexpected as I wait for my group to weaken. Twenty times 300 meters with a 100 jog ten days ago passes through my mind. That and many similar sessions free me of fear at four miles due to the speed endurance and aerobic capacity I've developed.

The five by 1500 and eight by 1,000 sessions which I alternate, naturally cross my mind as we head for half-way in 26:18. The 5:21 gives another 48 seconds to the leaders - but they're welcome to it. My skin, and the skin of many others running at 6, 7 and 8 minute miles continues fairly sloughing off as we run toward likely personal records.

Oh, the race is nearly over, the race is nearly over: get ready to sprint. Or I could if it was a ten kilometer instead of a ten mile race. But at least it's not ten k pace...anymore. It was very close to 10 k pace for a few miles but now we will pay the price. Five twenty six is not too high a price - three years ago it would have been unheard of for me to run so fast - yet now it represents a slowing.

I don't have a six mile session to help me through this mile, so I think of all the rest I've had this week. The leisurely, flat 12 instead of a hilly 14 at the weekend; three times a mile instead of the usual five midweek; and doing only two speed sessions has left the legs feeling fresh. It's good to reap the reward of the hardest type of training: rest.

I have to share the pace now as the "group" is down to two. We chase some dying runners whose positive splits will make our positive splits look positively negative. And the 5:30 mile is the most positive mile we will do today.

Each mile from here I'm thinking about my running form even more than before. First, extending the ankles and working the calves to their full contraction. Next, whipping the leg through a little closer to the buttock to decrease the pendulum drag and increase cadence. Then picking up the knees just a little more to devour the ground. And finally, leaning forward a micro percentage of one degree, to ensure the energy propels me forward, rather than upwards with more hang-time than Michael Jordan. Long hang-time is bad for distance running.

As we storm towards the eight mile mark, I know we're in the personal record make or break section of the race. The third 200 of the 800 meters is where records are lost; as is the forth thousand of the 5,000. I cheat: pretending it's only an eight mile race as the legs begin to scream at me to slow - but instead of surging at seven and a half, I merely extend the effort into the ninth. Chasing down fellow competitors also helped us to a 5:23; a mere 44 seconds slower than the winner.

Now it's the penultimate mile.

Don't gather yourself for a finishing flourish, I say to myself... give everything now. If you have a sprint at the end, you obviously didn't run the first nine and half miles hard enough. Picking off people as we reverse the slowing from earlier, these endorphin numbed legs carry me through a 5:21 mile--surely we're gaining on the leaders at this speed.

At some stage in the last mile, those who didn't run hard enough earlier come screaming by. No matter. I've run my...my...legs off. I know I'm slowing just a little, yet I'm still catching a few. With 600 meters to go I try an extended sprint for the finish. My increase in pace is so devastating, that two of the guys at my side take 10 meters out of me in a hundred...and will be 50 ahead by the finish. Did they run hard enough in the prior 15,490 meters?

Kirui got his world record, many went sub sixty and sub seventy minutes for the first time, and due in part to a superb 5:25 last mile, I slashed my PR to 53:23. Positive splits yes; but still a very positive race.

ADVANTAGES OF SNORKEL USE FOR POOL TRAINING

Some run, and some swim, but why not combine them in one session such as, 15 minute swim for warm up with swim goggles, 20-30 minutes with a snorkel (100-200 meters swim alternating with 50-100 running). Finish with 10 minutes swimming. If you are not used to swimming, do mostly running at first. If you have a good swimming background, gradually introduce running. The key is to adjust the run/swim ratio to your needs and level of fitness.

A snorkel enables you to practice the forward lean of speed work, but without the pounding the body takes from sprinting. Injuries are less likely.

The face mask of a snorkel set gives relief from the pressure of swimming goggles--it puts pressure on a different part of the face.

A snorkel avoids having to buy a specialized piece of equipment (running vest) - and you can use the snorkel for snorkeling. And many runners own a snorkel already.

In addition, there's an easy transition from swim to run and back to swim. Taking a break from swimming, also makes a pool session more interesting. It's boring enough to run the same route twice in a week, variety in the pool is even more important to avoid the monotony of just swimming or only using a flotation vest.

There are drawbacks to snorkel use. While snorkel running, you can't talk to training friends. If your pool session is group based, you may wish to retain the social aspects.

Don't swim the backstroke with a snorkel. Reserve your backstroke for the warmup and warmdown while wearing goggles.

Forward progress is not the main aim while pool running. Avoid the fast swimming lane, unless you are sharing a lane on the one side each basis, instead of the circle swimming routine used with three or more swimmers.

Why run in water: Flexibility is improved--you can do an exaggerated knee lift. Going through a larger range of motion will help your stride length, and therefore your potential speed. Use it for injury prevention, as a recovery session between hard days, or as a second session.

Dehydration problems are reduced. There is nothing like a fifty minute run to make you dehydrated. Yet, a similar workout in a pool will not require the same level of fluid replacement. Instead of the body being heated from the sun, it is cooled by the water. Although you do still sweat, you will not sweat as much.

Finally, don't expect to do a speed session of running as your second workout of the day. The pool session will work your quadricep muscles, leaving you "heavy legged" if you attempt to run fast.

Here is some more wet stuff. See resistance training page 76.

DREAMS

"Dreamers never achieve anything...unless they act on those dreams."

Dreams have to be worked on. Dreaming, or positive thinking is not new. Billy Mills' commitment to staying with the pace in 1964 owes its source to his own prediction or dream resulting in a 28:24.4, 10,000 meters gold medal. Alberto Salazar came through with his predicted time at New York in 1980 and 1981; running the fastest debut 2:09:41 then a world best of 2:08:13 which was later lost due to course inaccuracy.

Can we mere mortals dream our way to world class accomplishments.

Alas, no. But we can still dream to greater achievements?

Just placing 21:41 in your diary, then racing 5 kilometers isn't going to get you below your dream seven minute miles if you currently race in the mid 24s. Try taking less dreamier steps at 5 or 10 second per mile "barriers." Five seconds per mile has a great ring to it; after all, it represents a full 15 second improvement. If Bob Kennedy had done that in 1995 he would have smashed the world record by 9 seconds (12:48). Oops, Gebreselassie beat him to it with a 12:44:39.

After writing the 15 second improvement in the diary, how will you run it?

The last thing you will do, is run the opening mile of each race within 5 seconds of your predicted average pace - probably a few seconds faster rather than slower, but close to even pace is the key.

No, the paragraph is not out of order. To run the first mile at your dream pace, you will have to practice it: In order to maintain your pace in the second and third miles you will have the fun of practicing more than the first mile in "training".

It's this second part, the training, training inspired by the dream, which will enable you to achieve your predicted time. Mills had the strength from the '64 marathon trials and speed from 200 repeats;

251

Salazar the confidence and endurance from his infamous mile repeats on woodchip trails.

But how can you cross dreamy pseudo-barriers with your training?

Just follow the advice from previous chapters--run speedwork slower, the same as, and faster than race pace.

Long reps, usually a mile or more at 25 seconds per mile slower than 5 k race pace; medium reps, usually 800 to 1200 meters at race pace; short reps of 200 to 600 meters at slightly faster than race pace will improve your lactate threshold, aerobic capacity and running efficiency respectively.

Rotate the above three with resistance training on hills, sand or mud - plus your steady state runs, and you will be well on the way towards your dream.

Then persevere. For every 10 times you don't PR, there are 10 more places and races - where you can get that all important first mile right.

SAVE YOUR LUNGS

DECREASE SMOG EXPOSURE

Few serious bikers smoke cigarettes, yet thousands smoke car exhaust fumes almost every day. Cyclists are destroying their lungs by training on or near busy roads, or in areas high in invisible ozone.

According to a report on smog prepared by the United States Embassy in Mexico City, riding on major boulevards subjects the body to at least three times more pollution than the rest of the city--that is, three times the highest pollution in the Americas.

Train or bike hard for your health and racing performances, but train sensibly to avoid damaging vital organs. Preserve your heart and lungs for the future, by being aware of the hazards: hazards which are in surprising places.

Libby, Montana (pop. 2,748) for instance, is the second highest polluted area in the U.S. for particles. Particulate matter (PM10) from tire wear and dust are forced deep into the lungs as bikers breath forcefully. Inside the respiratory systems defenses, these small particles, and the sulfur compounds which stick to them, reduce oxygen diffusion at the alveoli, and constrict the bronchioles. The result: less oxygen to the muscles. Thus, you will ride slower, or if you try to maintain the same speed, you will be using a higher percentage of VO2 max and therefore reach exhaustion quicker.

Nitrogen oxides or NOx, is the brown colored gas we see if looking across a smoggy city. The NOx stays close to the ground at night, so the concentration is quite high in the early morning. "The concentration further increases as morning traffic and activity rises," says Jerold Last, a professor and pollution expert at The University of California, Davis. "It irritates respiratory passages and the chest cavity lining, impairing breathing. NOx also reduces resistance to respiratory infections and cancer."

According to Richard Stedman, a senior Air Quality Engineer with the Santa Barbara Pollution Control District, treadmill tests at UCSB showed decreased performance in a high Nitrous Oxide environment. Problems included: shortness of breath, burning eyes and mucous membranes, and pulmonary edema (fluid in the lung)--which makes the heart work harder. "After exercise, an aching chest is the subjective results of the damage," said Stedman, "impaired future performance is the objective result--especially if you do future exercising in a high NOx area."

Carbon monoxide (CO) is a colorless gas which impairs oxygen transport by inactivating red blood cells (RBCs). The hemoglobin in the RBCs is 200 times more attracted to CO than oxygen. Every time you ride in traffic, 2-5 % of your RBCs are inactivated, resulting in a short-term loss of athletic performance.

However, the real problem is long-term. After RBCs give up the CO, they remain permanently weaker at transporting oxygen. The RBCs are significantly debilitated for the remainder of their 120 day cycle (RBCs are replaced about every 120 days). More RBCs are damaged every time you bike, or commute, or even walk in traffic; therefore, the effects of CO are cumulative over a 120 day period.

The damage to an athlete is subtle--the repeated exposures decrease his or her performance potential.

You can think of CO as altitude training in reverse. Cyclists train at altitude to increase the number of RBCs, thus improving performance at sea level. But don't use this as an excuse to ride in smoggy areas--you'd need to cease carbon monoxide damage to RBCs three to four months before a race to reduce the affects on your physical performance.

By avoiding the three main auto pollutants, you prolong the health of your vascular and respiratory systems: the main reason many recreational exercisers bike.

By avoiding the three main auto pollutants, you can improve your vascular and respiratory system: the main reason most serious bikers ride.

This is what you can do.

* First, call your local pollution board to find out where most of the smog in your area / region is, and where it comes from. Chart the hot spots, including a separate sketch for each wind direction. Choose the location of your rides--the area with the lowest smog level--based on your research.

* Ride out of town whenever possible; as a rule, ride on the windward side of town where pollution levels are usually lowest.

* On busy roads, if space or bike paths permit you to, use the windward side also; otherwise, find a quieter road.

* For in town riding, ask your local parks and recreation department about trails and bike paths, and check for yourself to see if they are rideable.

* Consider a mountain bike for part of your base training and strength work. Trail riding will allow you to get further away from the smog, and it gives the senses a break too--no noise pollution to deal with, allowing for a more relaxing ride. You also get closer to nature.

* Don't train on roads at peak times, usually 6-9 a.m. and 4-7 p.m..

* Avoid heavily used roads, especially if the traffic is slow. Due to the inefficient burning of fuel at low speeds, and the higher number of vehicles per mile, boulevards are even more polluted than freeways.

* Don't bike round the edge of parks or athletic fields if a road is alongside. Use the sides of the park well away from roads, or ride the interior bike-paths. Always stay at least 200 feet from the road.

* Avoid parking lots before and after workouts because the pollution given off in warming up a car engine is equal to 45 miles worth of freeway driving. The amount given off after switching an engine off would get you 10 miles. Do your pre-ride stretching well away from where you park.

* When visibility is low, PM10 is frequently high; but you don't have to wait for an obvious dust storm before wearing a dust mask. Use one whenever air particulate matter is high--it's easier than you might think. If the California Highway Patrol riders are man and woman enough to wear them, so can you be.

* Take advantage of rainy days for a ride, but do take appropriate safety precautions. Avoid the first few hours of rain--in cleansing the air, the rain contains the same acid which kills our trees. Consider increasing your workouts in wet spells; then rest up a little when the smog returns.

* Make full use of vacations if you're away from the city--many cyclists neglect to train, despite being in a no or low smog environment. Getting away from your partner for a couple of afternoons may actually enhance your vacation experience.

* Windless days are a special problem, particularly in high sided valleys and bowls. The only options in many cities are to destroy your body by training, or spend hours traveling to a lower smog area. Do get out of town for at least your long rides.

* If you can't travel to a smog-free area, exercise indoors. Put the bike on a trainer, or use an exercise bike to enable you to stay fit until you can get out of town. But the indoor area must be pollution and smoke free. Don't open windows or doors before or during exercise. Try to do your full-house air exchange late at night or early in the morning when the air is freshest.

* Nose breath. "The nasal passages are a great scrubbing device," says Last. Make use of this scrubbing device when your training intensity allows you to.

* Never race in smoggy cities--choose cities with lower pollution levels. There are plenty of races in smaller communities. Encourage race organizers to put their events on in low smog areas.

Be careful about apparently pollution free biking areas. Ozone, the result of sunlight acting on pollutants, makes things tricky. Its concentration is highest in the city from noon to 3 p.m.. But according to Ron Robekar of the Air Resources Board in Sacramento, "The ozone peak downwind is later in the day and the peak is higher." For instance, the popular Big Bear ski and biking area (about 80 miles downwind from Los Angeles) exceeds the federal ozone limit 3-4 times more often than Los Angeles does.

The invisible ozone permanently damages the lungs: just like brain cells, lung cells cannot be replaced. Once an individual lung cell has been destroyed, it's gone forever.

Last says, "ozone damages all the epithelial cells lining the tubes of the respiratory tree...from the trachea down to, and especially the smaller bronchioles. Recurrent inflammations result in fibrotic changes. Collagen, a connective substance, is laid down. Cross-links stiffen the lung tissue--breathing becomes more difficult, and gas exchange is impaired. For the most part, damage is permanent." Every time you ride in smog, more non-replaceable lung cells are destroyed.

If you are unable to get out from the smog consider this: Exercising in moderate smog for 30-40 minutes, several times a week, is better than not exercising at all. But smog is a major factor in the health equation--make an effort to avoid it and you'll reap the rewards.

The Runners' version of this article sold to Runner's World in 1991.

Often, the coast is a low smog area; the surface is good for you too.

The Hood to Coast Relay.

Mount Hood to Seaside on the Oregon coast--one hundred and ninety-five, or two or six miles (depending on which year you race) broken into 36 legs--which happens to be the approximate number of pieces you think your legs have been chopped into after racing 4 to 7 miles three times--though smaller teams are entered by those feeling particularly suicidal, most use twelve people.

On Friday, August 25, five of us flew to Portland to join the rest of the team. We then donned red/yellow tie-dye running vests before lunching and shopping for supplies--including 48 bottles of sports drink, (to help us develop diarrhea), 12 gallons of water, 60 energy bars, 48 bananas, 36 bagels, sundry cookies, peaches and three jars of baby food.

We checked out the 13th leg - a central Portland section where our guy got lost last year. Rest and reading followed, then a 70 mile drive to half-way up Mount Hood at about 6,000 feet. We each took note of the terrain for our first leg...except we were driving them from finish to start as we headed up the mountain - and we would be running them at night.

The excitement level was so high...we were cheering each other and saying "good run" at each change-over point while merely driving the course. We signed in two hours before our start time of 7:30 p.m.. Each 15 minutes as we waited, a group of thirty, first leg runners would line up to commence their race. This had been going on since about 10 am. Each team racing those which it started with; gradually chasing down the teams which started before them; and trying to run fast enough to stay ahead of the (on average) faster teams coming on later.

We started with the Elite men--so our lead man saw certain of our non-opposition do 4-01 miles for five point six miles. Non-opposition because the sponsored sub 29 minute 10 k runners of Nike and Adidas are in a different league to a team averaging an incoming 34 minutes. Although one of our team so psyched out

258

Adidas, that he ran virtually the same time for his leg...for the most part, we were appropriately trounced.

Then again, we didn't just run. We drove; we massaged; we recorded; we team managed.

My job was to record the changeover times for our team--well, the first four of the six runners in our van; while the fifth runner was racing I'd be warming up. As time keeper I also worked out each runner's individual times and perhaps most importantly, kept the runner waiting to race appraised of the expected minutes before the arrival of the current racer. This simply required me to time the current runner with my own watch and compare the ongoing time to our team captain's computerized predictions.

Thus it typically went like this. Runner three (Cliff) roles in at 5-04 pace and hands off to four (Peter). I eyeball one of our master stopwatches and note the time. I stop my watch and make a mental note of the approximate split for Cliff; reset to zero and commence timing Peter. As Cliff is collected by five (John) to warm-down I calculate the actual split...using my approx. time to assist for those annoying math challenges. For some, any math is annoying at 4 a.m. on no sleep with a race only 5 hours ago and the second of three races just one hour hence. I return to the van, tell the guys Cliff was 65 seconds ahead of prediction, and we congratulate him as he slivers his sweaty body into the seat of honor...front passenger...placing his feet on the dashboard. All of us seat belted, we cruise off to the next exchange point.

I'm asked for the first of about twenty times how long to the next changeover. We've only used four minutes so it's still 28...but we have 6 miles to drive and John needs to complete his warm-up. We drive to the next change-over point, trying to spot Peter at about the one and a quarter mile point as we go. He's running smoothly, and we reach the next parking area with 18 minutes to his predicted finish. John exits first to continue his warm-up. Cliff slides his one thousand feet elevation loosed and stiffening quads out and walks (if that's what we can describe his motion as) off towards the exchange area.

With 8 minutes to prediction, John puts his racing shoes on and I (with my running shoes on to do minimal jogging at this stage) leave the van to set one of our guys 100 yards up the road to an-nounce the arrival of Peter. (No real need at most exchange zones, because the volunteers were calling out our numbers--thank-you people, you did an excellent job). A second guy waits to take John's last T-shirt at the exchange area, about two minutes before prediction, and he will help warm-down Peter...Actually, the way we are running, he will merely guide and hold Peter up as he directs him to the van.

Our fourth exchange is good, I have the time, the split and we are a total of 4 minutes ahead of pace. Into the van and I take up the second most honored position--next to the door at the back--I can be first out when we park. I pass the clipboard to Tyler (our second runner who finished an hour ago) and we feed Peter his choice of cold, warm, plain or sugared fluid. Cliff has dug into a bagel and banana, and Tyler finishes an energy bar. Having watched the other's excitement, and listened to the post race banter, I'm pretty high already. Yet here I am warming up my shin muscles to prepare for my race, which is actually one thirty-sixth of OUR race.

I've never heard 'how you feeling' and similar questions so often. I close my eyes and picture the course for my leg. I ignore the food being consumed as best I can, but take a sip of water. We park. My watch tells me the expected changeover time, and I slip out to run an easy mile. Moving away from the exchange area, I realize this is the closest I've come to quiet for a dozen hours. At the end of the mile, I repeat an activity which confirms I'm very well hydrated and return to the van.

Stretches are complete, I put my legs through the full range of motion by doing some butt-kicks and high knee raises at fast ca-dence. Sweats are off, flashlight in hand, I'm ready for my first ever road race in the dark, and at 10 pm, my latest race of any kind. I stop my watch, clear the time, and I'm ready.

John comes in, hands over the exchange wrap, and about five seconds into my run I start the watch. The wrap is a malleable piece of plastic which conforms to any wrist size; I've attached it securely above my watch to show my distrust of it, but it stays there, hot and sweaty from its previous five carriers, and disgustingly heavy for its mere three and a half ounces.

7.1 miles...the equal longest and second hardest leg of the race and I'm running exactly to my plan. First, no pre-race strides. This ensures I don't start off too fast. Cruise the first minimally uphill 2 miles as if it is a half-marathon. Then open it up for the remaining 5.1, attacking the ups very slightly, and stretching out on the downslopes, yet only aiming at 10 mile race pace overall. The road surface is mostly good, but like on a trail run, I'm mentally prepared to adjust stride if there's a sudden change.

The darkness poses several problems. My unwillingness to run fast fits in with the original plan...but I don't get any mile markers. Each leg in the relay has its own set of mile markers, so I could potentially see seven. I don't expect to see any though; alas my expectations are not exceeded. I check my time with the form effecting flashlight. The fatigue is minimal at 12 minutes; appropriate at 22 and I still feel fine at 33 minutes. A sustained stride down to the finish takes me through the exchange a significant 48 seconds ahead of prediction. After jogging a few hundred yards I return to wish the second van load good-luck.

We share opinions about a unique phenomenon as we drive into Portland for a shower and nap before meeting van two in three hours. Every runner gets a chance to catch and overtake 20-30 teams who set out before us. The night legs mean we see a moving flashlight...then the reflective vest, so you know what is coming up...but then, all of a sudden, you see the runner just yards ahead. They'll be going from 15 seconds to several minutes per mile slower than you. We each used the incentive of closing on the next runner as a bonus to keep us racing at good pace. Each time we passed someone we gave a few words of encouragement. Uphill passing might have received "good job." Passing on the flat, "keep it going," or if the person had good form, "looking good." Downhill comments might have left us with enough breath to combine a couple of the above, or a little humor such as, "not far to Seaside," or "is this the way to Seaside?"

The cellular phone rings. Anthony, the seventh runner answers. Sleepy, his last comment is a British expression which I translate to our van as "go away." We take over a few minutes later for legs 13-18. Antonio nearly gets lost on the tricky 13th. Anchoring our van, I have a 410 feet elevation gain in a 4.4 mile leg. I've studied the book of the course well, but still I nearly miss a turn. At the awards ceremony we hear about the many who took a wrong turn, so I get a belated bonus shot of smudginess to my veins. The first half a mile gave me cause for concern--my legs felt--well...as if I'd done a tough 7.1 mile hilly race just hours before...strange how the mind works on you at 4.20 am...another first for earliest race ever. Had a great run though, arriving to exchange English expletives a surprising 34 seconds ahead of prediction.

My third leg was 5 miles. Up a mere, yet grueling 80 feet before descending 605. This leg was made more interesting by the elite women's team. We spotted them a half hour lead at the start, but we'd closed within striking distance of Adidas (8 minutes) and Nike (2 minutes or so) with 12 sections, or over six hours of racing to go. We overtook Nike, but ran out of luck on leg 28--a wrong turn costing us five minutes--and Nike were ahead of us again. John found himself matched against a superb runner; despite going 48 seconds faster than projected on this very hardest leg of the race, we remained 20 seconds behind their team.

One thing about being a good club runner at a local level is I know there are few woman at the elite level who can beat me...by much. Easing into the flat first mile I adapted my tired legs to running fast yet relaxed; I could give all I had left on this one...no more races today. I pulled in the slower runners but stayed focused somewhat on the superb form of the Nike girl. The gap narrowed encouragingly fast, and I caught her before the serious part of the 80 feet upgrade. She was carrying the wrist wrap in her hand like a straight relay baton. I suggested she wrap it round her wrist like mine, and showed the snugly fitting item to her. Unusually for a woman, she did as I advised. Then she promptly tucked in behind me to draft her way up the hill.

"Ha," I said, "I don't mind giving you advice, but I didn't say you could sit in behind me."

This seemed to have the desired effect as she lost a step on me, and naturally I chose this point to increase my pace...though by precious little. I knew we had a mile of hill (with the steepest part near its end) before free-falling to the changeover. It was great to

see the road and the size of the hill instead of just a shadow loom-
ing ahead of me. Cheryl must be a great downhill runner because
despite almost running the soles of my feet bare (philosophically
that is) while fairly motoring down the other side of the hill, she
was still within 20 seconds of me at the end. Still, we'd overtaken
Nike for the very last time with a 68 seconds faster than prediction
run; due I'm sure to my pacing or holding back on my first leg.

Alas, they retook us for the last time on the next leg and finished
five minutes ahead. We ended the race one minute faster than
predicted; one guy had serious problems on his last section.

We had another race within the race. The van of runners closest
to predicted time (us) being bought dinner by the other van. Being
charitable fellows, we ordered the most expensive items on the
menu. They treated us with the same respect at Sunday lunch.

Track Night

The track session is not the important part, it's what comes before and after that REALLY matters.

First the warmup.

I know you old fashioned runners think the warmup is to get the muscles...well...warmed up--relaxed, and ready for some significantly speedy running.

The real purpose of those 20 minutes or more of easy running however is the peer review. You ask what training your friends have been doing the last week; how their weekend race went. Add in the sleeping routine of the new baby; the double shift worked; and the boss is away this week syndrome so I'm lucky to be here at all factor... and you come up with tonight's session--which is (of course) part of an overall plan.

"I want to work on anaerobic threshold," says Harold. "Aerobic capacity is my weakness," says Mike. "I'd rather do lactate threshold," says Terry.

Fortunately, the two thresholds mean the same thing, so setting the pace at 15 kilometer or ten mile race pace they opt for 1200s with a minute recovery.

As this writer has control over who's in the essay, it happens the aerobic capacity increase aspiring individual's 10 kilometer PR is about two minutes slower than most of the others. He can run just two laps with the group and take a longer rest while they do a third lap. He has his session nicely set at about 5 k pace--the speed which will improve his aerobic capacity. A slower runner might do the first and last lap of the 1200 at faster than 5,000 pace to work on his form.

The 5 hours sleep a night new parent, double shift and 70 hour weekers might do 1,000s to give themselves a physical or mental break, yet they are also likely to be inspired to do the whole session.

With endorphins at full flow, the second fun part commences...the cooldown.

Ostensibly to allow the muscles to cool off (they stay virtually the same temperature), the blood flow during these couple of miles does decrease muscle aches and get rid of wastes.

But the real purpose is to discuss the next run. Teaming up for the weekend long one, perhaps a run in the mountains--and maybe a discussion about next week's track session.

16 x 400 is a definite possibility, says Mike, with short recoveries. The 1500 specialists are happy, anything under 600 makes them smile; they will do fast 200s on Monday with long recoveries.

The 10 k guys eyes glint because they will keep the short recovery honest by putting it on a beeper; they will do three minute hill repeats or bounding in deep sand on Monday.

The half-marathon specialist will complement the 400s with 2,000 meter efforts or a 25 minute tempo run depending on whether his long, long run partner or his medium long run partner is available at the weekend.

Next week, if history repeats, half the group will do the entire 16 reps. One will do 8 x 400 a few seconds slower than the group, then 300s (he'll miss the first bend) with the group. One or two will end up doing extra reps faster than the average of the 16. If we're feeling generous, we'll wait those extra minutes to let them join us for the warm-down.

All in all, a fairly typical bunch of 32-35 minute 10 k runners who are able to train together once or twice a week, usually at the same pace, but frequently for different distances and always working disparate energy systems, while helping each other through the bad patches.

P.S. I suggested the warm-down was the second fun part, implying the session itself is not enjoyable. While most of us go through some degree of discomfort because we're running further at a certain speed than the body is able to do comfortably, we enjoy the session too.

The first few reps won't be overly challenging or uncomfortable. Even the last few will only be hard from about half way. In order to get to the difficult--and the satisfying ones--towards the end, we must toil through the middle reps. Pace judgment, running at your pace is the key to getting through the session with a smile in your quads. Hanging with a group which is faster than you, then running the second lap five seconds slower is a recipe for unhappy muscles.

The Secret Society

What runners know that others don't

By Scott Douglas

As if my life isn't miserable enough, I recently reread H. Richard Niebuhr's Christ and Culture. While I plugged away on the subway one evening, a fellow rider interrupted, showed me a flyer for a choral presentation and asked whether I knew how to get to the church at which it was being held. Still knowing little about Boston's geography beyond the city's bagel shops, I meekly demurred. Fortunately, the hordes of presumed pagans that he had burrowed past to get to me were willing and able to direct this lost soul.

Happy to have a reason to stop reading about Augustinian dualism, I pondered the events that had just occurred. Why had the would-be music man singled me out? It had to be because he had seen the title of my book and figured that, amid the potentially hostile, he had found a kindred spirit, someone who shares the esoteric commitment that shapes his life.

Well, silly him--just goes to show that you can't judge a person by his book covers. I must admit, however, that I often make the same presumption of fraternity when out in the would. My guilt comes when the accumulation of evidence--hollowed eyes, black plastic watch, unseemly chiseled calves--suggests that I've found a fellow runner. I imagine us traveling through the world incognito, the masses neither knowing nor caring what we do, but in an instant, I know that we know the same things that they never will. The pleasant lope of a well-earned cooldown; an acute grasp of how quickly an hour can pass, or how long 30 seconds can be; that the weather is never as bad as it appears from the office window; that the park that the hotel clerk says is "miles and miles from here" is usually but a 10-minute run away--we know all this and more, we know that it will remain forever hidden from the uninitiated.

My presumptuousness posits, too, that this apparent kindred soul has the virtue of quiet endurance, a trait that is, to say the least, rarely evinced among the hoi polloi. Years of running builds a certain noble tolerance, a willingness to persevere without much complaint, and to do so for no other reason than that it is what we require of ourselves. This constancy of spirit finds expression in that tenacity that sees you through the last five miles of a 20-miler or the last set of an interval workout, when you're not exactly dead, but your legs long ago got the point.

This virtue is put to the test in a lifetime of enduring well meant--but inane questions. I was reminded of this while on vacation recently. I returned to my hotel room after a 20-miler at 6:15 pace to find the maid cleaning my bedroom. When she came out to the living room, where I was slumped on the couch , coughing, grimacing and drenched, she asked, "Been joggin?" I nodded wanly, thinking, "If only you knew."

There's a satisfaction that comes only through association with other members of this secret society. The incognito aspect of our lives helps explain the easy familiarity that often exists among new running acquaintances. Without even asking, you're aware that your lives are ordered by like concerns. What can I run nest Thursday when I have that business dinner right after work? How can I get away with running more, not less, on a family trip? How can I discreetly bring my running stuff for the next day over to my new girlfriends place in case things work out really well? And so on. Within an hour of shared effort, you're likely to be discussing bowel movements with significant others. Had you met under ordinary guises, you'd still be running the superficial conversational gambit of job and family. Perhaps real estate prices.

Within a week of moving to Boston, I found someone to run with a few mornings a week. Although happy to have a training partner, I was forlorn because the usual quick association was missing. He said little as we ran, as if I had yet to earn my membership.

Then one morning, I awoke to a cold rain. I figured I'd be running alone, but headed out to the usual meeting spot just in case. He was there, and as we slogged through puddles and dodged fogged-over motorists, we talked more than in all of our other runs combined. By virtue of being there on a day that only a runner could love, I was in.

At the end of the run, I asked, "Same time tomorrow?' "Yup," he replied. "Same crappy weather, too."

I hadn't looked forward to a run so much in months.

Used with permission from Running Times.

Scott Douglas gave up the Editor-in-Chief roll at "Running Times" this year. He's still a senior writer for them and writes the "Scott Speaks" column. He has written numerous books about running.

PEER REVIEW

Peer review helps business people perfect their business plans by groups meeting monthly to offer honest - and critical - opinions. Which no doubt is why Running Times comes out monthly... Well almost. We get a chance to review top runner's training or come across a training concept that's new to you.

But you don't have to wait to have your peer review. You already have the opportunity for the review every time you run with someone.

Step one.

Most of us discuss our training with running partners, perhaps bragging about our own achievements. Yet isn't it more important to listen to THEIR training - then analyze it for anything useful to us?

If your friend did 8 x 800 in three minutes, find out why. Is three minutes 5,000 meter pace for him - faster, slower? What is the purpose of this specific session? Or is it just that he gets a thrill out of running 2 laps moderately, ungodly or only fairly fast (choose according to your own ability).

Is his intent to develop speed, aerobic capacity or increase his anaerobic threshold? Or does he merely want to persuade you he'll continue to beat you by half a minute in races?

Step two.

After the self-help review, consider one or more of your local standout runners. If *you* don't know the different types of training in the last paragraph and sidebar, most of the people finishing in the front 5 percent of races do. Ask one of these people to look at your training diary - assuming you keep one of course.

He or she may rapidly spot the absence of hills or long efforts at 15 k race pace or 30-40 second strideouts which you'd never even considered. He'll probably be able to tell you why a particular session is a good one to do every three weeks or so. He may spot you are always training too fast, rarely run long or that you always do 400s.

Step three.

Ask a coach to review your past training, to look at how you run and discuss your goals and time availability. Remember, the four minute mile was achieved on lunch-time running, you don't have to train hours every day.

NOTES

ONE. Anaerobic or lactate threshold is the pace at which lactic acid begins to build up in the muscles, and oddly enough, it corresponds to the pace at which we perceive significant shortness of breath: in other words, we fail the talk test. Your heart-rate monitor should be set to 87-92 percent of your maximum if you want it to tell you what pace to run at, or you can go at 15 kilometer race pace.

15 k pace should be about 25-30 seconds per mile SLOWER than 5,000 race pace or 15-20 seconds slower than 10 k pace.

The threshold is best increased by doing long repeats of 1,000 meters and up with very short recoveries - one minute. The track is okay, roads are fine, but grassy parks are kinder on the legs. It doesn't matter how far around it is, just plot a loop avoiding tight corners and do it.

TWO. Aerobic capacity or VO2 max. is the maximum amount of oxygen the body can process. It is best increased by running at 5,000 meter race pace. The rest interval is usually half the distance of the fast part, i.e. 800s with a 400 rest.

THREE. Speed is developed by running faster than 5,000 pace. This type of training is frequently over used. Bombing fast repeats at the track every week is likely to lead to bombing in races if the speed is not supported by regular aerobic capacity AND anaerobic threshold sessions.

FOUR. Four hundreds (meters) every week are not necessarily a bad thing, it depends on how you do them. A four week rotation as follows can develop most energy systems.
* 16 x 400 at 10 k pace...faster than the usual 15 k pace for anaerobic work due to the shortness of the reps.
* 12 x 400 at 5 k pace...fast 200 jog for aerobic capacity
* 8 x.400 at 3 k pace...slow 200 jog to develop speed endurance
6   x   400   at   1500m   pace...400   jog   for   pure   speed.

PISMO

The exuberance from exercising on a perfect spring afternoon.

Rain, wind and deep sand combined to give me a perfect 40 minute run. This run had almost everything:

Strength running--working full-out into a 30 mph plus wind; leaning so far forward--I would have fallen if the wind had suddenly stopped.

Strength running--the deep but even sand, blown flat by hours of wind.

Speed running--striding effortlessly at sub 3,000 meter pace with the same wind at my back--the rain driving into my hamstrings and all but tensing them up--yet they continue to float me down the beach.

Speed running--my calves are seemingly stretched out as never before due my ankles finding ever new degrees of extension. For once, my toes seem to be in a perfect straight line from my shins.

Yet instead of the sometimes harsh foot-falls of speedwork on a track, I land softly. Today, in these odd conditions, I may have finally found my ideal stride length.

Then, it's back into the driving rain again. My face grimaces with the discomfort of near hailstone moisture. The stuff must be 45 degrees Fahrenheit, yet the force of contact makes it feel like ice. I put almost as much effort into relaxing my grimace, as I do into my short stride and arm pumping--I maintain leg speed at negligible running form cost.

Then the sun comes out behind me on my right. Instantly I see the most beautiful sight.

The dozens of majestic deer and the lone wolf in 1991 were great. The slouching bobcat I followed at a walk for a hundred yards...and coyote's scampering away in '92 were special. The mountain lion who observed my steady passage, and the bison's steamy breath as we debated right of way, gave adrenaline surges....But non of them matched this day's spectacle.

271

On my left stretched a two mile wide double rainbow. The inner rainbow was perhaps one and half miles wide at the base and individually it was so pure and bright...it must have been the most perfect rainbow ever produced. The outer one was 2¼ miles wide, about half as bright and incomplete at its apex.

This phenomenon was wondrous enough for me to interrupt the run to show *my* rainbow to a girlfriend. A non-runner, she's at a loss as to why I run 60 miles a week; why I spend 1½ hours most Wednesdays at a track; why--despite little hope of winning a race, let alone going to an Olympics; why I and others continue to test the limits of our bodies against each other, a watch, and over time.

Oblivious to the spectacle behind her, she reads a book. I quietly ask her to get out of the car to look at something. Not a writer herself, she manages to ask all the Ws, though thankfully she knows how. Trust me, I say, giving her the pleading puppy look, and she gets out of the car.

On seeing the rainbow, she utters a thesaurus page-full of complements.

This is why we run I tell her. We never know when we'll come across a special surprise. It could be an animal just off of a trail or some dolphins close to the beach; it could be a mile of perfect mud, sand or hills for strengthening the legs; it could be a group of horse riders or bikers sharing a joke and the trail; or, it could be nature at its best.

I'll be back in 7 glorious minutes I tell her--unless of course, I find a good reason not to be; unless I find something else worth investigating during that time.

VO2 Max training pace based on 2 mile and 5 K times.

MILE TIME	Time for 2 mile	2 mile VO2 pace 400 reps	5 K (VO2) 800s	5 K Time 3.1m	5K 1200s	10 k 6.21m
4:20	9:19	69.8	2:23.6	14:57	3:35	30:54
4:30	9:40	72.5	2:29.0	15:31	3:44	32:02
4:40	10:02	75.2	2:34.4	16:05	3:52	33:10
4:50	10:23	77.9	2:39.8	16:39	4:00	34:20
5:00	10:44	80.5	2:45.0	17:11	4:08	35:27
5:10	11:06	83.2	2:50.4	17:45	4:16	36:37
5:20	11:28	86	2:56.0	18:20	4:24	37:50
5:30	11:50	88.7	3:01.4	18:54	4:32	39:00
5:40	12:11	91.4	3:06.8	19:27	4:40	40:09
5:50	12:32	94	3.12.0	20:00	4:48	41:15
6:00	12:54	96.7	3:17.4	20:34	4:56	42:23
6:10	13:15	99.4	3:22.8	21:07	5:04	43:29
6:20	13:37	102.1	3:28.2	21:41	5:12	44:40
6:30	14:00	105	3:34.0	22:18	5:20	45:56
6:45	14:31	108.9	3:41.8	23:06	5:33	47:35
7:00	15:03	112.9	3:49.8	23:56	5:45	49:18
7:15	15:35	116.9	3:57.8	24:46	5:57	50:41
7:30	16:07	120.9	4:05.8	25:36	6:09	52:44
7:45	16:40	125	4:15.0	26:33	6:22	54:41
8:00	17:12	129	4:23.0	27:24	6:34	56:26
8:30	18:16	137	4:39.0	29:10	7:00	60:06
9:00	19:01	142.6	4:54.0	30:25	7:21	62:42
10:00	21:30	161.2	5:23.0	33:36	8:03	69:16

If the 400s feel easy, but you have difficulty maintaining pace on the 800 and 1200s, you lack background base endurance. Look to those steady miles you do at 70 percent VO2 max, which build base aerobic ability.

If the 400s feel hard, incorporate 100s etc. to work on form at good speed. Do some 200s and 300s. Relaxed running at 2 mile pace only comes with practice.

Don't let 400s dominate; you can do 800s at 2 mile pace too.

The 1200s may be the most under utilized session.

Anaerobic Threshold paces at 10 K, 15 K and half marathon speeds.

MILE TIME	10 k 6.21m	10k pace miles	15 K time	mile reps	half marathon pace
4:20	30:54	4:59	48:19	5:11	add 12
4:30	32:02	5:10	50:02	5:22	to 15
4:40	33:10	5:20	51:34	5:32	seconds
4:50	34:20	5:32	53:27	5:44	
5:00	35:27	5:43	55:09	5:55	mile
5:10	36:37	5:54	56:51	6:06	
5:20	37:50	6:06	58:44	6:18	
5:30	39:00	6:17	60:26	6:29	from here
5:40	40:09	6:28	62:09	6:40	down
5:50	41:15	6:39	63:51	6:51	20 secs
6:00	42:23	6:49	65:24	7:01	
6:10	43:29	7:01	67:34	7:15	
6:20	44:40	7:12	69:17	7:26	
6:30	45:56	7:24	71:09	7:38	
6:45	47:35	7:40	73:38	7:54	from here
7:00	49:18	7:56	76:07	8:10	25 to
7:15	50:41	8:10	78:56	8:26	30 secs
7:30	52:44	8:30	81:43	8:46	
7:45	54:41	8:48	84:30	9:04	
8:00	56:26	9:05	86:50	9:19	40-45
8:30	60:06	9:41	93:12	10:00	secs
9:00	62:42	10:08	97:33	10:28	
10:00	69:16	11:09	107:12	11:30	

Anaerobic threshold is best improved with the 15 k pace sessions. Those on very low mileage or resting for a few months, may benefit from fewer reps at their 10 K pace.

Lactate Threshold Velocity incorporates elements of threshold and VO2 max and running economy. It is the highest rate of using oxygen without the buildup of lactic acid. It also equals *half marathon* pace.

Mix and match to meet your needs and the freshness of your legs on a particular day.

SPEED CHART FOR EVEN PACED PRs

MILE TIME	2 mile	3 mile	5 k 3.1m	5 m	10 k 6.21m	12 k 7.46m	15 k 9.32m	10 m	20 K 12.43	13.1 miles	Full Marathon
4:50	9:40	14:30	15:01	24:10	30:02	36:03	45:03	48:20	1:00:04	1:03:22	2:06:44
5:00	10:00	15:00	15:32	25:00	31:04	37:17	46:36	50:00	1:02:08	1:05:33	2:11:06
5:10	10:20	15:30	16:03	25:50	32:06	38:31	48:09	51:40	1:04:12	1:07:44	2:15:28
5:20	10:40	16:00	16:34	26:40	33:08	39:46	49:42	53:20	1:06:16	1:09:55	2:19:50
5:30	**11:00**	**16:30**	**17:05**	**27:30**	**34:10**	**41:01**	**51:15**	**55:00**	**1:08:20**	**1:12:06**	**2:24:12**
5:40	11:20	17:00	17:36	28:20	35:12	42:16	52:48	56:40	1:10:24	1:14:17	2:28:34
5:50	11:40	17:30	18:07	29:10	36:14	43:30	54:21	58:20	1:12:28	1:16:28	2:32:56
6:00	**12:00**	**18:00**	**18:39**	**30:00**	**37:17**	**44:44**	**55:56**	**60:00**	**1:14:33**	**1:18:39**	**2:37:19**
6:10	12:20	18:30	19:10	30:50	38:19	45:59	57:29	1:01:40	1:16:38	1:20:50	2:41:41
6:20	12:40	19:00	19:41	31:40	39:22	47:14	59:03	1:03:20	1:18:43	1:23:01	2:46:03
6:26			20:00		40:00		60:00		1:20:00		
6:30	13:00	19:30	20:12	32:30	40:24	48:28	1:00:36	1:05:00	1:20:47	1:25:13	2:50:25
6:45	13:30	20:15	20:58	33:45	41:57	50:20	1:02:55	1:07:30	1:23:53	1:28:29	2:56:59
7:00	**14:00**	**21:00**	**21:45**	**35:00**	**43:30**	**52:12**	**1:05:15**	**1:10:00**	**1:27:00**	**1:31:46**	**3:03:32**
7:15	14:30	21:45	22:31	36:15	45:03	54:04	1:07:34	1:12:30	1:30:06	1:35:03	3:10:05
7:30	15:00	22:30	23:18	37:30	46:36	55:55	1:09:54	1:15:00	1:33:12	1:38:19	3:16:38
7:45	15:30	23:15	24:05	38:45	48:09	57:47	1:12:14	1:17:30	1:36:19	1:41:36	3:23:12
8:00	**16:00**	**24:00**	**24:51**	**40:00**	**49:43**	**59:39**	**1:14:34**	**1:20:00**	**1:39:25**	**1:44:53**	**3:29:45**
8:15	16:30	24:45	25:38	41:15	51:16	61:31	1:16:54	1:22:30	1:42:32	1:48:09	3:36:18
8:30	17:00	25:30	26:24	42:30	52:49	63:23	1:19:13	1:25:00	1:45:38	1:51:26	3:42:52
8:45	17:30	26:15	27:11	43:45	54:22	65:15	1:21:33	1:27:30	1:48:44	1:54:42	3:49:25
9:00	**18:00**	**27:00**	**27:58**	**45:00**	**55:55**	**67:06**	**1:23:53**	**1:30:00**	**1:51:51**	**1:57:59**	**3:55:58**
9:15	18:30	27:45	28:44	46:15	57:29	68:58	1:26:13	1:32:30	1:54:57	2:01:16	4:02:31
9:30	19:00	28:30	29:31	47:30	59:02	70:50	1:28:33	1:35:00	1:58:04	2:04:32	4:09:05
9:45	19:30	29:15	30:18	48:45	60:35	72:42	1:30:53	1:37:30	2:01:10	2:07:49	4:15:38
10:00	20:00	30:00	31:04	50:00	62:08	74:34	1:33:12	1:40:00	2:04:16	2:11:06	4:22:11

FURTHER READING

Anything by Don Kardong, John. L. Parker, Scott Douglas or Hal Higdon...plus:

Power Foods by Liz Applegate Ph.D...Nutrition Columnist, Runner's World.

Sports Nutrition Guidebook by Nancy Clark R.D.

Galloway's Book on Running by Olympic marathoner Jeff Galloway

Running Injury Free by Joe Ellis D.P.M. Rodale Press.

Run Fast by Hal Higdon...training for 5 and 10 k.

The Runner's Coach by Roy Benson

The Olympian by Brian Glanville

Training Distance Running by David Martin and Peter Coe...Leisure Press

Competitive Runner's Training Book. Bill Dillenger and Bill Freeman...Macmillan.

Many are available from Cedarwinds Publishing
1-(800)-548-2388

Magazines
Running times...1-(800) 816-4735

Runner's World...1-(800) 666-2828

THE AUTHOR

David Holt, Registered Nurse, Diploma in Orthopedics, trained with English Cross-country champion and top ten in the World at Cross-country, Gerry North.
The English club system helped David to 31:16 for 10,000 meters (5:02 miles). Other PRs are 15:18 for 5 K, 67:52 for 20 K, 1:46:36 for 30 K, and a 71:12 half marathon.
At age 37, seven years after his peak, though still good for a 75 minute half, he did a 2:37 marathon. He runs 3,000 miles a year--the most he can do while remaining injury free--which he did for 11 consecutive years. He has done 300 plus races on track, road and cross-country.
He brings you 275 pages of experts, entertainment and information, from Kenyan, American and European training ideas. He has sold to Runner's World and Running Times.

Order Form

Post to David Holt
      PO Box 543
      Goleta, CA 93116

Online E-mail   holtrun@sprynet.com

Payment by check or Visa, Mastercard, Discover
Card Number
Name on card   Expires on
Or check number

Send books to me at Name
                      Address

                      Telephone

Running Dialogue $17:95 per copy
        shipping $3:05   Total $21:00

Add 7.75 % (of book price) if to California address $1:39

Also by David Holt...Retribution, The novel.
A runner corrects the injustices wrought upon him during
his divorce. One of the policemen is a cyclist. But it is
not a story about their sports; it's a story about justice.
$14:95 plus $2:05 shipping--Available November 1997.
At the stores use ISBN number 0-9658897-2-6